OXFORD MODERN LANGUAGES
AND LITERATURE MONOGRAPHS

THE POET AND THE
NATURAL WORLD
IN THE
AGE OF GÓNGORA

M. J. WOODS

1978

OXFORD UNIVERSITY PRESS

Oxford University Press, Walton Street, Oxford OX2 6DP

OXFORD LONDON GLASGOW
NEW YORK TORONTO MELBOURNE WELLINGTON
IBADAN NAIROBI DAR ES SALAAM LUSAKA CAPE TOWN
KUALA LUMPUR SINGAPORE JAKARTA HONG KONG TOKYO
DELHI BOMBAY CALCUTTA MADRAS KARACHI

© *M. J. Woods 1978*

British Library Cataloguing in Publication Data

Woods, M. J.
    The poet and the natural world in the age of Gongora.–(Oxford modern
languages and literature monographs).
    1. Spanish poetry–Classical period, 1500–1700–History and criticism
    2. Nature in literature
    I. Title   II. Series
    861'.3'0936   PQ6066   77-30352

ISBN 0-19-815533-6

*Set by Hope Services, Wantage
and printed in Great Britain by
Billing & Son Ltd., Guildford,
Worcester and London*

to

MY MOTHER AND FATHER

PREFACE

This study examines the description of nature in Spanish poetry in the period between the end of the sixteenth century and the beginning of the eighteenth. In so far as I use the adjective 'baroque' to refer to this poetry, I do so for the purely practical reason that this is a succinct way of referring to this period, and not because I give credence to any theories of 'The Baroque' as an ideology linking all literary genres and all the arts. But this is not to say that I seek to confine myself entirely to issues which are narrowly poetic or narrowly Spanish, or that I find the descriptive poetry of the period lacking in the coherence one would expect of a literary movement. Indeed, I hope the reader will be persuaded by the end of the book that we have here a unique and clearly recognizable poetic age, and that Góngora's role within that age is so central that he justly earns the tribute of having it named after him.

Except where there is any indication to the contrary, the translations of the illustrative extracts are my own.

During the preparation of this book, and of the doctoral thesis on which it is based, I have received valuable help from a number of people whose kindness I would like to acknowledge here. I am indebted to Professor P.E. Russell for his painstaking and honest criticisms; to Professor R.O. Jones, now sadly missed by his colleagues, for bibliographical advice; to Professor Nigel Glendinning and Dr. R.W. Truman for their detailed comments and constructive suggestions; to my wife, Shirley, for all her hard work in checking through the script; and to the Central Research Fund of the University of London for a grant enabling me to visit Madrid.

M.J. WOODS

LONDON,
June 1977

CONTENTS

ABBREVIATIONS

BAE	Biblioteca de Autores Espanoles
BHS	Bulletin of Hispanic Studies
MLN	Modern Language Notes
RFE	Revista de Filología Española

I

POETRY AND THE

FEELING FOR NATURE

There exist hundreds of studies devoted to various aspects of the treatment of nature in literature, but very few of these works give Spanish baroque poetry so much as a glance. However, my intention in the present study is not to attempt to fill this gap in the existing tradition as I understand it, for the traditional approach seems to me to be based on a number of assumptions which prevent a fair assessment of baroque poetry, and which in general discourage the investigation of the poetic function of imagery. The following brief survey of the main works concerned with the treatment of nature in Spanish literature will serve to explain my own approach which, by contrast, is primarily concerned with the rhetorical function of poetic imagery.

The most thorough over-all study of nature in Spanish poetry is probably R.M. MacAndrew's *Naturalism in Spanish Poetry from the Origins to 1900* (Aberdeen, 1931), but baroque nature poetry is not accorded a very important place in his scheme, except in a negative sense, and his judgement of Góngora as one who was responsible for breaking the progress of Spanish poetry now seems rather quaint.[1]

In Spanish, there is J. Lillo Rodelgo's *El sentimiento de la naturaleza en la pintura y en la literatura española* (Toledo, 1929), covering the period up to the end of the sixteenth century, although it does begin to look beyond by including a brief reference to Góngora's *Soledades*. The author draws on a wide range of examples, but as he himself admits, there is no analysis in depth. B. Isaza Calderón's *El retorno a la naturaleza* (Madrid, 1954) is another study which, like Lillo's, does not extend its inquiry beyond the sixteenth century. The author states that it was sparked off by an interest in Guevara.

José-María Sánchez de Muniain's *Estética del paisaje natural* (Madrid, 1945) does include a historical survey of the development of man's feeling for nature, but it makes no reference to seventeenth-century attitudes at all. The author seems to regard this as a period of literary decline.

---

[1] MacAndrew speaks of poetry being 'martyred' by Góngora (op.cit. 44), and adds, 'What might have been, had not Góngora made poetry bankrupt, must always remain an interesting inquiry' (op.cit. 75).

With the exception of the works already mentioned, the course seems to be charted by only sporadic essays and articles.[2] But there is one important collection of articles by Emilio Orozco Díaz, published under the title *Paisaje y sentimiento de la naturaleza en la poesía española* (Madrid, 1968), which avoids the twin dangers of theorizing without producing sufficient textual examples, and producing texts with insufficient commentary and analysis. This is one of the rare examples of a study of nature in Spanish literature which takes the seventeenth century seriously. I shall therefore have cause to refer fairly frequently to Orozco's approach in the course of the first two chapters, particularly since his views represent very well the two traditions of criticism which these chapters set out to examine. In so far as I am critical of his views, my remarks are intended as a comment on a whole tradition and should not be taken as indicating the relative merit of his contributions to scholarship which are far more valuable than most in the field.

The works so far mentioned in this chapter when taken together may not seem to represent a very substantial body of criticism. Nevertheless, seen in a European context, they may be regarded as part of a vast movement. The compilation of a full bibliography would be a daunting task, but the few following sample titles will indicate the range of studies I have in mind:

H.R. Fairclough, *Love of Nature amongst the Greeks and Romans* (New York, 1930).

J. Veitch, *The Feeling for Nature in Scottish Poetry* (Edinburgh and London, 1887).

A. Dauzat, *Le Sentiment de la nature et son expression artistique* (Paris, 1914).

D. Mornet, *Le Sentiment de la nature en France de J.J. Rousseau à Bernardin de Saint Pierre* (Paris, 1907).

A. Biese, *Die Entwicklung des Naturgefühls im Mittelalter und in der Neuzeit* (Leipzig, 1888).

O. Jansen, *Naturempfindung und Naturgefühl bei B.H. Brockes* (Bonn, 1907).

etc.[3]

---

[2] See J. Casalduero, 'El sentimiento de la Naturaleza en la Edad Media española', *Clavileño* (1953), No. 22, 17–23; Azorín, *El paisaje de España visto por los españoles* (Madrid, 1964); Miguel de Unamuno, *El sentimiento de la naturaleza* in *Por tierras de Portugal y de España* (Madrid, 1964).

[3] A useful foothold for the would-be bibliographer is provided by P. Van Tieghem's *Le Sentiment de la nature dans le préromantisme européen* (Paris, 1970), whose footnotes reveal how remarkably popular the study of the treatment of nature was as a subject for dissertations, particularly at the turn of the last century. Also useful for the range of works they mention are Orozco Díaz, op. cit. Fairclough, op.cit., and M.H. Nicolson, *Mountain Gloom and Mountain Glory* (Ithaca, N.Y., 1959).

Generally speaking, the point of departure of such studies as these is, as their titles suggest, a lively interest in the modern 'feeling for nature', and a desire to see how this feeling has developed from or contrasts with the attitudes of earlier ages or of different civilizations. One disadvantage of this kind of an approach is that it tends to assume, however unconsciously, the inferiority of most nature poetry prior to the Romantic era. For if the modern period is seen as the goal towards which all previous ages were moving, these earlier epochs are likely to seem more primitive. The result can easily be a rather patronizing assessment of pre-Romantic poetry.

Another feature of the traditional school of criticism is that it seeks first and foremost to analyse men's feelings rather than to analyse poetry.[4] The two activities may, of course, coincide, but one is not entitled to assume that they always do, or that one can always tell whether they do, or that where they do not, literary criticism is a waste of time. And yet these assumptions are deeply ingrained in the traditional criticism, whose tenets I shall examine in some detail now in order to explain why they are incompatible with my own approach, and why they have led to the neglect of baroque poetry. I begin by considering certain remarks about poetry made by John Ruskin in his essay on the 'poetic fallacy', for Ruskin is a man who was deeply concerned with men's feelings for nature, and one who gives unambiguous expression to the literary theories which seem to me to be implicit in much modern criticism.

Ruskin establishes a hierarchy of types of poet at the head of which comes the man of feeling. 'A poet is great', he declares, 'first in proportion to the strength of his passion.'[5] However, Ruskin is not in favour of undisciplined passion, and he distinguishes between poets on the basis of the degree to which they have a distorted or morbid vision of the world. Thus there are those poets who feel strongly, but manage for the most part to control their passion except on occasions of intense emotion, when the vision of nature in their poetry will become momentarily distorted. There are others who feel strongly, but whose reason is constantly producing distorted images of the world. Their feeling leads them to perceive wrongly, and this is a weakness. But, 'so long as we see that the feeling is true, we pardon, or are even pleased by, the confessed fallacy of sight which it induces.'[6] Coming further down the scale, there is a third class of poet who

[4] Lillo Rodelgo, for example, cherishes the ideal that one day the definitive work will be written telling the story of the Spaniards' feeling for nature through the ages, and sees his own discussion of poetry and painting as a step in this direction (op.cit. 19).

[5] *Modern Painters*, part 4, ch. 12, in *The Works of John Ruskin*, ed. E.T. Cook and A. Wedderburn (London, 1903–12), Vol. 3, p. 215.

[6] Ibid. 210.

'perceives rightly because he does not feel.' He is seen as far less praise-worthy: 'It is no credit to a man that he is not morbid or inaccurate in his perceptions, when he has no strength of feeling to warp them.' Finally, we have Ruskin's vision of the fourth and most despicable kind of poet who attempts to simulate what he does not genuinely feel. Ruskin condemns 'fanciful expressions,' distortions which passion normally produces, when they are used by:

Some master, skilful in handling, yet insincere, deliberately wrought out with chill and studied fancy; as if we should try to make an old lava-stream look red-hot again, by covering it with dead leaves, or white-hot, with hoar-frost.[7]

Ruskin's theory has a number of obvious shortcomings. For example, a poet of infinite passion yet infinite self-control would presumably be indistinguishable from the poet who has no passion and hence nothing to cause him to lose control. Similarly, the most despicable poet may be indistinguishable from the most noble. There is always the danger that some dastardly rhetorician may be skilful enough to deceive us with his hoar-frost. Perhaps he has read his Ruskin and knows that the most desirable effect is achieved by introducing just the occasional distortion. The 'insincere' poet may in fact be Protean enough to take on the features of any of the other three, which means that, given a particular poem, one has no means of telling, without outside in-formation, just what the thoughts of the poet as a man are, as opposed to his thoughts *qua* poet. The conclusion to be drawn from this is that 'sincerity' cannot be used as a criterion for excellent poetry. Yet even in recent times we see it all too often used as a touchstone, and I believe this criterion to be implicit in many of the attempts to trace through the arts the history of man's feelings for nature.

One can find illustrations of the attitude I have mentioned in Spanish criticism. For example, it will be noted that Ruskin contrasts the writing of passionate poetry with the deliberate use of certain tech-niques in nature poetry to achieve a specific effect by a 'master skilful in handling'. Azorín expresses similar disapproval when, rapidly brushing aside the importance of nature in Spanish pre-Romantic poetry, he says of Berceo: 'He only turns to the countryside in order to remind us of another brighter, loftier region. His love of nature is not direct and disinterested.'[8] Clearly he shares Ruskin's distaste for rhetoric, the implication being that to 'use' nature in a poem for a particular rhetorical effect is somehow an imperfection.

More recently, the rigid separation between rhetoric and true feeling has come under attack. Emilio Orozco, for example, has observed, quite rightly, that there is no real incompatibility between the two:

---

[7]   Ibid. 216.
[8]   Azorín, op. cit. 14.

That a feeling happens to be expressed by means of an expression which has been handed down does not entail insincerity or a lack of feeling. The deepest and most vivid feeling can be expressed by thoughts so often repeated that they are commonplaces.[9]

Similarly he writes:

Once more I repeat that there is no incompatibility between allegorical meaning and the direct vision of and feeling for nature. Nor between the use of a literary model, re-shaped, or re-lived, and the direct, concrete vision of reality.[10]

But the effect of such observations is only to reaffirm the Romantic view that 'sincerity' is one of the main criteria by which we should judge the treatment of nature in poetry. We are invited to view medieval poets as men who had a deep feeling for nature in spite of their deliberate adherence to rhetorical traditions.[11] But some of the emotions attributed to these poets are too vague to be convincing. For example, in the *Poema del Cid* a high proportion of the relatively few references to natural phenomena give information about the time of day.[12] No example is longer than two lines, and only one of the passages gives any hint of an emotional reaction to nature.[13] In Orozco's account of the poem this fact becomes thus transmogrified: 'The poet shows a deep feeling for Nature, albeit a basic and fundamental one, in the form of a feeling of vital continuity: the echo of the vital rhythms of the universe.'[14]

Similarly, the fact that Santillana's *serranillas* are set in specific places in Spain, the whereabouts of which are described in rudimentary fashion, leads Orozco to attribute to him a 'lively emotion of reality', though what kind of an emotion this might be is not at all obvious.

This kind of approach to medieval poetry is very much akin to a good deal of modern criticism of Garcilaso's poetry. In many judgements of his work there is an implicit acceptance of the same criteria. Critics have consistently protested his sincerity, doubtless because they believe that in this way they are meeting the possible accusation that Garcilaso's constant imitation of other poets and his acceptance of commonplace poetical traditions betray a lack of true feeling.[15]

[9] Orozco, op.cit. 27.
[10] Ibid. 53.
[11] Compare MacAndrew's view of Fr. Luis de León: 'In spite of León's occupation with form...he reached a personal attitude to Nature, the depth of which, compared with that of his contemporaries, seems explicable only on Nuñez de Arce's theory, that León, in spite of his absorptions in classical form, was saved from classical conventions by his sheer sincerity.' (Op.cit. 43).
[12] These are listed by Orozco, op.cit. 78–9.
[13] 'Ya crieban los albores e vinie la mañana/ ixie el sol. Dios, que fermoso apuntaba!' (lines 456–7). (Now dawn was breaking and the morning coming./ The sun was rising. God, how beautifully it dawned!)
[14] Orozco, op.cit. 38.
[15] For further discussion of this tradition of criticism of Garcilaso, see M.J. Woods, 'Rhetoric in Garcilaso's first eclogue,' *MLN*, 74 (1969), 146–8.

I believe that the attitudes I have outlined which place so much stress on feeling, and which implicitly or explicitly are unsympathetic to rhetorical traditions, are to a large extent responsible for the neglect of baroque poetry by those investigating the treatment of nature in Spanish literature. True, part of the neglect must be due to the kind of prejudice which led even so serious a student of Góngora as Lucien-Paul Thomas to suggest that the *Soledades* show signs of mental derangement caused by a fever affecting the poet's brain.[16] And one could hardly expect critics of the old school who regarded Góngora's major poems as the height of bad taste to accord him a significant place in the evolution of man's attitude towards nature. But on the other hand, the reputation which the rehabilitated Góngora enjoyed, and still enjoys today, as an essentially impassive poet is equally unlikely to have endeared him to critics who place so much stress on feeling. As Dámaso Alonso puts it:

Nobody, I suppose, is going to expect from Góngora a view of nature in the Romantic manner. . .One cannot even find in him those glimpses of human emotional reaction to nature seen sporadically in a few great poets of the sixteenth century, such as Garcilaso and Fray Luis de León.[17]

Yet it is precisely for evidence of some kind of emotional, Romantic response to nature that so many of the cultural historians are looking. Small wonder, then, that they find themselves more attracted to Fray Luis de León over whose 'unalloyed Romanticism' MacAndrew enthuses.[18]

But seventeenth-century poetry is far too important to be simply brushed aside and is something of an embarrassment to those critics like Azorín, for whom the emergence of nature in poetry as a subject in its own right is seen as a key step in the development of man's feeling for nature. For it was precisely at this time that a new genre of descriptive poetry appeared, of which Góngora's *Soledades* was one of the first examples, having as its subject the world of nature, or so it seems. Present-day critics have not hesitated in seeing nature as the real subject of Góngora's major poems,[19] and I know of no earlier Spanish poet of whom one could confidently take such a view. Thus Góngora's reputation as a poet of nature makes his works very relevant to the tradition,

---

[16] L.–P. Thomas, *Le Lyrisme et préciosité cultistes en Espagne* (Halle and Paris, 1909), p. 84.

[17] 'Claridad y belleza de las *Soledades*' in *Estudios y ensayos gongorinos* (Madrid, 1960), p. 71.

[18] Op.cit. 46.

[19] 'Thus the real basis of the *Soledades* is nature', Dámaso Alonso, op.cit. 71; 'The plot is the story of the shipwrecked, lovesick youth; he himself, however, is merely one element in the theme, which is the richness of nature,' R.O. Jones, 'The poetic unity of the *Soledades*,' *BHS*, 31 (1954), 190; 'The *Polifemo*. . .has a large and serious theme: the world of Nature and man's place in it,' C.C. Smith, 'An approach to Góngora's *Polifemo*,' *BHS*, 42 (1965), 220.

whilst his reputation as an impassive poet makes him one of the writers least likely to fit comfortably into the over-all scheme.

Orozco's solution to this particular dilemma is to combine old and new by accepting that baroque descriptive poetry has a sensuous, pictorial appeal, a view made popular by those reviving an interest in Góngora in the 1920s, whilst at the same time attributing emotions to him. But, as in the case of the medieval poets, the emotions attributed to Góngora are of a rather nebulous kind. Orozco echoes Dámaso Alonso's view that in the *Soledades* 'Everywhere. . .there flows an awed spirit of exaltation in natural forces: beneath the most precise lines, beneath the most splendid words, there lies the vital flame of creative and regenerative nature, like a passionate ebullience.'[20] But little is done to demonstrate why this exuberance should be regarded as emotional, though there may well be a good point here.

On the evidence adduced one wonders whether anything more is really meant than that Góngora depicts the most dynamic aspects of nature. Perhaps to have probed deeper would have revealed more blatantly the fundamental contradiction in Alonso's portrayal of Góngora both as an emotional and as an impassive poet.

There are many difficulties, then, in trying to fit baroque poetry into the history of the development of man's feeling for nature. On the other hand, as I shall argue in the following chapter, there are no fewer difficulties in attempting to place it in the development of man's objective, aesthetic appreciation of nature. If this is the case, no attempt to find a compromise between these two ways of looking at nature poetry is likely to prove satisfactory. What is required is a fresh approach based on more readily verifiable criteria than the presence or absence of sincerity in a poet. It makes more sense to place a greater stress on observable traditions in poetry rather than on the inferred feelings of individual poets. This is not to deny that it would be very interesting to know what an individual writer's attitude to nature might be, but the most reliable information about this is liable to come from sources other than the arts. It is all too easy even in seemingly straightforward cases to jump to completely wrong conclusions about an author's likes and dislikes from studying his writings. Pereda's novels offer a salutary warning on this score. Anybody noting his obsession with mountain scenery might innocently imagine that this was the result of some personal enthusiasm for the landscape he depicts. But Unamuno, who knew him personally, tells a rather different story: 'Pereda, our mountain novelist, so skilful and felicitous in describing the countryside, hardly had any feeling for it. He himself confessed to me that he took

---

[20] Alonso, op.cit. 71. Compare Orozco, op.cit. 63.

very little pleasure in the countryside.'[21] A simple remark like this may reveal more than a whole novel if it is the writer's attitude as a man rather than his novels which interests us. Indeed one could argue that the study of literature can never be of much benefit in an inquiry of this kind, as one can only know how far a work reflects its author's true feelings where there is corroborating evidence, such as personal correspondence. But even here, the study of the work itself would seem to be unnecessary since the following fork presents itself: where the work diverges from the extra-literary evidence it is unreliable; where it is the same it is redundant.

If we now turn to consider Spanish poetry from the rhetorical point of view, considering it, that is, as an exercise in public communication rather than as an expression of private feeling, it is surprising how rapidly and simply we can learn about the Spaniards' attitude to nature. For unreliable as poetic imagery may be as a guide to a poet's personal attitudes, it may give us some very revealing information about the audience for which he was writing. A consideration of a commonplace classical theme will serve to illustrate this point.

Ernst Robert Curtius has drawn attention to the existence of the commonplace theme in European literature, handed down from classical times, of the description of the pleasant spot, the *locus amoenus*.[22] There are numerous examples in Spanish literature before the seventeenth century of the traditional description of the cool, green, grassy meadow, with its clear stream, its shady trees, and its sweet-smelling flowers. One of the most famous examples, from Garcilaso's Third Eclogue, is examined a little later in this chapter. A much earlier example is to be found in the introduction to Berceo's *Milagros de Nuestra Señora*, as Orozco has noted.[23] Neither of these poets takes as the main theme of his poem the enjoyment of nature. Nevertheless, unless their descriptions seem pleasant to the reader they become rhetorically pointless. We may assume, therefore, that whatever the personal tastes of either poet, both were attempting to depict something which they thought their readers would find extremely pleasant. To have done otherwise would have been to risk writing nonsense. We may infer, then, that already well before the seventeenth century the reading public were attracted to the natural scenery described by the poets.

However, one should bear in mind that the examples to which I have referred do not necessarily demonstrate that most people had an immediate practical enjoyment of the pleasures of nature. We may have here merely an example of the pleasures of the imagination. For

---

[21] Unamuno, op.cit. 145–6.
[22] *European Literature and the Latin Middle Ages*, trans. by W.R. Trask (London, 1953), pp. 115–200.
[23] Orozco, op.cit. 41.

example, an inhabitant of an infertile region exposed to extremes of temperature may write a poem describing lush natural scenery and a docile climate. In practice, he and his readers may find the countryside as they know it rather distasteful, and his verses may offer a welcome escape into some imagined paradise. It is only in a limited sense that such people could be said to have a love of nature. We may therefore be on firmer ground if we select an illustration where there is no hint of escapism, and no exaggeration in the picture of nature. Such an example is Juan Boscán's *Epístola a Mendoza*, a poem in an intimate style, expounding the simple philosophy of the Golden Mean. The whole point of the poem is the shunning of the extraordinary. Boscán argues the delights of practical, everyday pursuits, and his poem is interesting in that it shows human reactions to nature. He goes further than simply describing scenery, and he writes in a way which suggests that enjoying the countryside is a simple, everyday pleasure:

> Passaremos assí nuestra jornada,
> agora en la ciudad ora en l'aldea,
> porque la vida esté más descansada.
>
> Quando pesada la ciudad nos sea,
> iremos al lugar con la compaña,
> adonde el importuno no nos vea.
>
> . . . .
>
> Los ojos holgarán con las verduras
> de los montes y prados que veremos,
> y con las sombras de las espessuras.
>
> El correr de las aguas oyremos,
> y de su blando venir por las montañas,
> que a su passo vernán donde staremos.
>
> El ayre moverá las verdes cañas,
> y bolverán entonces los ganados
> balando por llegar a sus cabañas.
>
> En esto ya que'l sol por los collados
> sus largas sombras andará encumbrando,
> embiando reposo a los cansados,
>
> nosotros iremos passeando
> hazia'l lugar do stá nuestra morada,
> en cosas que veremos platicando.[24]

[24] Lines 220–5 and 295–309. *Obras poéticas*, ed. by Martín de Riquer, Antonio Comas, and Joaquín Molas (Barcelona, 1957), pp. 359, 362.

(Thus will we spend our day,
now in the city, now in the village,
so that life can be more relaxed.

Whenever we are weary of the city
we shall go to the village with our friends
where pesterers cannot reach us.

. . . .

Our eyes will delight in the greenery
of the mountains and meadows we see
and in the shade of the woods.

We shall hear the streams running
as they glide through the mountains
towards where we stand.

The breeze will move the green rushes,
and then the flocks will return,
bleating to reach their fold.

And then, since the sun will be sending
its long shadows up to the hilltops,
bringing rest to the weary,

we shall stroll back
to where our abode is,
chatting about the things we see.)

Boscán was obviously writing here for an audience who would have found
it plausible that a normal person could take pleasure in the things he
describes, and who would have regarded them as unexceptional. Unless
the reader takes this attitude the poem loses all its power as an exercise in
moral persuasion. So here we have clear evidence of a positive practical
enthusiasm for nature amongst the sixteenth-century reading public.

One would have thought, then, that the Spaniards' love of nature
would have been sufficient to have inspired the writing of descriptive
poems taking nature as their theme by the middle of the sixteenth
century. The lack of any such poetry suggests that there was some
restraining factor at work. The most likely explanation is probably
that traditional preconceptions about genre and about the function of
description in poetry acted as a barrier. The following paragraphs set
out to examine the Renaissance attitude.

The growth of pastoral literature in the sixteenth century meant
that the world of nature was far more in evidence in poetry than
before. There is a marked contrast here with poetry in the fifteenth-
century *cancionero* tradition where it is often rare to find a concrete

noun in a poem, let alone a description of the physical world. Boscán's ode, 'Quiero hablar un poco', though written in Italian metre, illustrates well this rather austere Castilian tradition. Its 450 lines are devoted entirely to abstract psychological analysis. The only concrete nouns it contains refer to the lover (*coraçon, seso, sangre*), with the exception of the nouns *figura* and *camino* (lines 388, 128), which in any case are used metaphorically. One passage is particularly revealing:

Todas las cosas tienen
sus puntos naturales y mudanças,
y su curso alcançaron ya medido;
sus ratos de bonanças
hallan con que sus fuerças sostienen.
Mas yo. . .²⁵

(All things have
their natural ups and downs,
and all have followed their set course.
At times they find a lull,
and can rebuild their strength.
But I. . .)

Here Boscán is beginning to relate the lover's experience to the outside world. But whereas a poet wholly absorbed in the Petrarchan tradition would have taken the opportunity here to illustrate and amplify his point with examples drawn from nature, Boscán leaves the whole thing on a general, abstract level.

Although the importance of the physical world in Renaissance pastoral poetry sets it apart from earlier Castilian poetry, this Renaissance exuberance is only relative. On closer inspection the function of nature in Renaissance poetry appears to be fairly restricted. For example, introductory descriptions of the kind one finds in Virgil's Eclogues were a more or less obligatory feature of all poetry with a narrative content. It was the author's duty to inform his reader of the time and place of the events recounted.²⁶ That such passages were recognized as set pieces is clear from the fact that technical rhetorical terms were assigned to them. Description of the time of day was known as *cronographia*, and description of place as *topographia* if the scene described was fictitious, and as *topothesia* if it was real.²⁷ The fact that such

---

²⁵ Boscán, op.cit. 121, lines 406–11.

²⁶ Lope de Vega excuses a rather prolix description in his *Arcadia* on these grounds: 'Ya saueis que es obligacion del q[ue] comiença alguna [historia], la descripcion del lugar do[n]de sucede'. *Obras Completas*, ed. J. de Entrambasaguas (Madrid, 1965), I, 10.

²⁷ See Rosemond Tuve, *Elizabethan and Metaphysical Imagery* (Chicago, 1961), pp. 80–1, and Herrera's notes, A. Gallego Morell, *Garcilaso y sus comentaristas* (Granada, 1967), p. 553, n.781; p. 554, n.784.

descriptions had an introductory function, preparing the reader for
what was to follow, meant that they could not be too lengthy without
spoiling the structure of the poem. In terms of this classical tradition, a
poem consisting solely of a description of nature would have been
meaningless—a preparation for nothing, leaving the reader in suspense.

One of the more extensive introductory descriptions is to be found
in a well-known passage from Garcilaso's Third Eclogue, yet despite
its relative length it is a model of classical control and illustrates perfectly the subordination of detail to a single theme:

Cerca del Tajo, en soledad amena,
de verdes sauzes ay una espessura
toda de yedra revestida y llena,
que por el tronco va hasta el altura
y assí la texe arriba y encadena
que'l sol no halla passo a la verdura;
el agua baña el prado con sonido,
alegrando la yerva y el oýdo.

Con tanta mansedumbre el cristalino
Tajo en aquella parte caminava
que pudieron los ojos el camino
determinar apenas que llevava.
Peynando sus cabellos d'oro fino,
una nympha del agua do morava
la cabeça sacó, y el prado ameno
vido de flores y de sombras lleno.

Movióla el sitio umbroso, el manso viento,
el suave olor d'aquel florido suelo;
las aves en el fresco apartamiento
vio descansar del trabajoso buelo;
secava entonces el terreno aliento
el sol, subido en la mitad del cielo;
en el silencio solo se 'scuchava
un susurro de abejas que sonava.

Ya aviendo contemplado una gran pieça
atentamente aquel lugar sombrío,
somorgujó de nuevo su cabeça
y al fondo se dexó calar del río;
a sus hermanas a contar empieça
del verde sitio el agradable frío,
y que vayan, les ruega y amonesta,
allí con su lavor a estar la siesta.

(Beside the Tagus, pleasantly secluded,
there stands a thicket of green willows

all decked throughout with ivy
which climbs from trunk to treetop
and there so weaves and binds the leaves
that no way can the sun reach the green grass.
The water washes the meadow tunefully,
gladdening the grass and the ear.

So gently did the crystal Tagus
wend its way just there
one scarce could see
which way it flowed.
Combing her pure golden hair,
a nymph raised forth her head
from the water where she dwelt
and saw the pleasant meadow
full of flowers and shadows.

The shady spot, the gentle breeze impressed her,
and the sweet scent of the flower-strewn ground.
She saw the birds in their cool retreat
at rest from their laborious flight.
For at that time the sun, high in mid-heaven,
scorched all the air below bone dry.
In the silence the only sound
was the resonant buzz of bees.

Having contemplated a long while,
alertly, too, that shady spot,
she dipped her head below once more
and dived down to the river bed.
She starts to tell her sisters of
the pleasant cool of that green spot,
and begs and urges them to go
to spend their siesta weaving there.)

This passage prepares us for the emergence of the water-nymphs
from the river, and its central concern is with the suitability of the spot
described for a siesta. And so the poet makes it pleasantly restful for
all the senses. We have the pleasant scent of the flowers, the quiet
sound of flowing stream and buzzing bees, and the restful sight of
greenery. But these alone are not quite sufficient to make it plausible
that the nymphs would wish to leave the cool water at the hottest
time of the day. Herrera pedantically opines that in any case Garcilaso
has committed a technical blunder in thinking that naiads were capable
of leaving their native element.[28] Be that as it may, Garcilaso is

---

[28] Gallego Morell, op.cit. 554, n. 788.

remarkably adept at persuading the reader of the naturalness of their action. He offers them the necessary seclusion, for it was essential for the nymphs to avoid mortal gaze, and it is the approach of two shepherds which eventually makes them take to the water again. But above all he tempts them with the coolness of the spot. Time and time again it is to this feature which Garcilaso returns.

At first sight, the initial image of the ivy intertwining the branches of the willow trees might seem a whimsical detail showing Garcilaso's freedom from classical restraints and a love of detail for its own sake, and possibly his powers of observation. But in fact Garcilaso uses it to establish at the start the central theme of the coolness of the spot. By picking on the unusual circumstance of the thickly matted branches Garcilaso is able to emphasize the quite exceptional shadiness of the thicket. The sun simply has no chance of penetrating the foliage. Having then described the river—another cooling feature of the landscape—Garcilaso tells us what the nymph sees and how she reacts to it. Again the theme of shadiness is subtly stressed by an unusual combination of words, 'de flores y de sombras lleno'. After the reference to the tangible flowers one does not expect anything as insubstantial as shadows, and the effect is to throw the word 'sombras' into relief. We may regard this as an example of the figure syllepsis, made all the stronger by being placed at the end of a stanza, and having a close parallel in the concluding line of the first stanza of our passage. The nymph's first reaction to what she sees is again significant, as she is attracted to the shade and the breeze. She notes that the birds in the trees are enjoying the cool respite from the heat. Another little detail here adds to the persuasiveness of the passage, for the fact that everything is silent but for the hum of the bees indicates that the birds are not singing. They are taking their siesta and hence offer an example to the nymphs. It thus comes as no surprise when the nymphs eventually emerge, having been persuaded of the 'agradable frío' of 'aquel lugar sombrío'. In this poem, then, we have a remarkable example of the importance of thematic relevance in Renaissance poetry.

So far we have examined only the introductory function of description, but we do also find natural imagery integrated into the main body of some sixteenth-century poems. In love poetry, such imagery usually has the specific function of amplifying the expression of love and of suffering, so that again one can say that the theme of nature is not a rival attraction diverting our attention from the main purpose of the poetry, but a means of intensifying the main theme. In Garcilaso's First Eclogue, for example, none of the nature imagery is irrelevant to or independent of the human theme of the love of the two shepherds.[29] Again, in didactic, as opposed to love poetry, although nature sometimes has an important function, it is not a theme which one can isolate from the central moral issues involved. Praise of the country life is carefully linked to moral criticism of urban or court life. There is a continuance here of the classical tradition as seen in Horace and Seneca.[30]

To write poetry which sought first and foremost to describe nature, as our look at the sixteenth-century tradition shows, meant in effect creating a new genre of poetry in which description had a rather different role. At first sight, it might not seem such a large step to progress from Garcilaso's Eclogues, in which there is no shortage of images from the natural world, to poetry which has nature as its central interest. But when one notes the careful control and the relevance of every detail to the primary rhetorical objectives in his poetry it becomes clear that there was quite a barrier to be overcome by the would-be nature poet. One has to look at the function of natural images in Renaissance poetry as well as their frequency in order to appreciate this.

How formidable the pressure of the Renaissance tradition was can, I think, be seen in a number of baroque poems in the new genres which fail to break completely free from the old patterns of thought although they have obviously outgrown them. For example, in 1652 there appeared a fascinating poem by Francisco de Trillo y Figueroa, a self-confessed Gongorist, which is couched in the form of a Petrarchan topos very familiar to Renaissance poets. The theme is that of nature pursuing her habitual course as day and night succeed each other, whilst the unrequited lover finds that the natural rhythm of waking and sleeping has deserted him as he leads a life of constant weeping. We see this theme in Petrarch's *canzone*, 'Nella stagion che'l ciel rapido inchina', and it is echoed in Garcilaso's First Eclogue, part of which is clearly a direct imitation of Petrarch, in that Garcilaso has adopted not only his theme but also his unusual stanza form.[31] The interesting feature of Trillo's handling of the motif is that his is a poem of 336 lines, and the unrequited lover, alluded to briefly near the start of the poem, does not really make his apperance until the final sixteen lines, almost as an afterthought, it seems. The effect is almost of burlesque. But the author's title, as well as the general tone of the poem, shows us

[29] See my article, 'Rhetoric in Garcilaso's first eclogue', *MLN*, 84 (1969), 145–50, where I indicate that in Salicio's song the imagery is used as part of a subtle argument to persuade the elusive Galatea to return.

[30] For an example of the use of this theme in Seneca, see G.A. Davies, 'Luis de León and a passage from Seneca's *Hippolitus*', *BHS*, 41 (1964), 10–27.

[31] E. Segura Covarsi, in his *La canción petrarquista en la lírica española del siglo de oro* (Madrid, 1949), pp. 105–6, indicates that Garcilaso has slightly modified Petrarch's metric scheme, but a more accurate count of the syllables in the Italian poem reveals that this is not the case.

that he had a serious intention, and that this was to offer the reader a description of natural phenomena. He calls his poem a 'Pintura de la noche desde vn crepusculo a otro. Heroyco.' (A picture, in the heroic manner, of night, from twilight to twilight.) This shows that his primary intention was not to write a love poem, but to offer a description of nature.[32] In effect, a poem like this has two themes; nature and love. The grotesquely unbalanced combination of the two here indicates that although poets were fascinated by the prospect of presenting natural phenomena in their poetry, there was nevertheless some feeling amongst them that one could not use description in a poem unless it was given some manifest rhetorical function of the traditional kind.

Another very similar poem to that of Trillo, in which the tail again appears to wag the dog, is a *romance* by the court preacher, Paravicino, and addressed to Góngora, beginning 'Ya muere el día . . .'[33] Again this is a poem which may be accounted for in terms of the traditional rhetoric. It is a poem offering encouragement to a friend in distress, comforting him with the thought that although the sky may darken with the approach of night, a new dawn will always break. But, as in Trillo's poem, there is a marked imbalance, and it is quite clear that the poet's main interest lies in the description of the phenomena of nature. Nevertheless, one does not doubt that at the same time Paravicino genuinely wished to convey his good wishes to Góngora, and the very fact that he does dally over his description of nightfall is a kind of tribute to Góngora who pioneered the new poetry.

We see in this last poem a glimpse of one of the problems which confronts the critic of baroque poetry, namely, the ambiguity of its subject matter. The seventeenth century saw the emergence of a new genre of what might roughly be termed descriptive poetry about nature. But to say categorically that it is about nature is to over-simplify. Sometimes a poem may quite explicitly take nature as its theme. But at other times there may be an implicit theme which differs from the overt theme of the poem and which is balanced with it in such a way that we may be in doubt as to what the poet's true intentions are. The subject matter of Renaissance poetry is rarely as imprecise or enigmatic.

The relationship between the rival functions of nature imagery in baroque poetry is examined in Chapter Three, as is the precise sense in which the new poetry can be said to be descriptive. But enough has been said here to indicate that in order to write about nature, baroque

---

[32] Trillo, *Obras*, ed. A. Gallego Morell (Madrid, 1951), p. 225. It should be noted, however, that Trillo does not always take the classification of his poems very seriously. His *Romance IX*, for example, is described as *lírico*, when in fact it is quite clearly a *romance satírico*. (See op.cit. 72.)

[33] See *Obras Posthumas, divinas y humanas de DON FELIX DE ARTEAGA* (Madrid, 1641), fo. 13, verso.

poets had to overcome the traditional preconceptions about the rhetorical function of nature in poetry, and that in some instances the tension between old and new attitudes is reflected in the poetry.

The parallel here between developments in poetry and painting is significant. It is often assumed that the emergence of landscape painting and of nature poetry as new genres reflect common attitudes to nature.[34] But when we ask ourselves the question why, given man's early appreciation of the delights of nature, landscape painting did not develop sooner, we are led again to the conclusion that what artists thought about art was every bit as important as what they thought about nature. In painting too, preconceptions about genre and technical considerations were a strong restraining influence.

In the first place, medieval representation of landscape backgrounds was bound to be fairly rudimentary until the technical problems of representing the sky and the effects of light, and of creating an illusion of space by this means and by the conventions of perspective had been solved.[35] But the development of such techniques did not automatically lead to the development of landscape as a genre in its own right. For example, a painter like Leonardo was sufficiently gifted technically, and seems to have had the necessary interest in the physical world about him, to have been capable of producing pure landscape paintings, and yet he never did so. This is not so difficult to understand when one sees some of the attitudes towards landscape painting in the sixteenth and seventeenth centuries.

As a genre, landscape painting was still a relative novelty in the seventeenth century, as the theorist Edward Norgate, writing about 1650, indicates:

It does not appeare that the antients made any other Accompt or use of it [landscape] but as a servant to their other peeces, to illustrate or sett of their Historicall painting by filling up the empty Corners or void places of Figures and story, with some fragments of Landscape. . .but to reduce this part of painting to an absolute and intire Art, and to confine a man's industry for the tearme of Life to this onely, is as I conceave an Invencion of these later times, and though a Noveltie, yet a good one. . .[36]

[34] Lillo Rodelgo's study, for example, rests on the assumption that it is valid to compare the treatment of nature in poetry with that in painting at any given period.

[35] See Kenneth Clark, *Landscape into Art* (London, 1953), p. 26. A.R. Turner has also emphasized the importance of the solution of technical problems: 'Before a painting is an expression of a mood, or even a pictorial symbol, it is the solution to problems of pictorial structure.' *The Vision of Landscape in Renaissance Italy* (Princeton, 1966), p. 3.

[36] As quoted by E.H. Gombrich, 'Renaissance artistic theory and the development of landscape', *Gazette de Beaux Arts*, 6th ser., (1953), pp. 355–7, reprinted in Gombrich's *Norm and Form. Studies in the Art of the Renaissance* (London, 1966), p. 107.

But early reactions to the genre were not always enthusiastic. For example, Francisco da Holanda, the Portuguese theorist, puts some rather disparaging words into the mouth of Michelangelo in his dialogues on painting:

In Flanders really they paint to deceive the outward eye with things to cheer you, or things about which you cannot speak ill, such as saints and prophets. Their paintings are full of drapery, stonework, the greenery of meadows, the shade of trees, rivers and bridges. They call it landscape. And there are lots of figures dotted about here and there. And although all this may seem good to some eyes, in truth it is executed without reason or art, without symmetry or proportion, without substance or sinews.[37]

The Italians could identify landscape as a genre in which foreigners specialized. The fact that Dutch landscape tended to be compositionally unsound[38] does not mean that a new and better style of landscape is being advocated. Rather, the author's criticism reflects adversely on landscape as a genre. The whole attempt as he sees it to titillate the eye rather than the intellect means that the new genre cannot aspire to the greatness of figure painting, or the painting of historical scenes.

The strength of traditional views about genre is admirably illustrated in the case of the painter Girolamo Muziano, who regarded landscape as a suitable subject for drawing, a lesser branch of art, but who, in spite of the considerable promise he showed as a landscapist in his drawings, renounced the whole idea of landscape painting and was content to remain an indifferent figure painter.[39] And one can perhaps see in Giorgione a similar tension between old and new ideas about landscape producing the same kind of ambiguity of subject matter which one finds in baroque poetry, so that it is hard to say categorically whether his subject was nature or not. Giorgione's famous painting ·La Tempestà has this enigmatic quality. The subject of this small masterpiece has mystified and will doubtless continue to mystify art historians. The painting might be regarded simply as a landscape, but for the fact that there are two important figures in the foreground—a semi-nude woman suckling a child, and, some distance away, a man with a pike, standing in a relaxed manner. The subject of these figures is not obvious, but through the artist's use of colour they are so fused with the landscape that it is almost as if they form a part of nature. We may perhaps conclude that Giorgione was primarily concerned to paint

---

[37] *Da pintura antigua*, ed. Joaquín de Vasconcellos (Porto, 1918), p. 189. The dialogues first appeared in 1548.

[38] In this respect it is interesting to note remarks by Italian theorists about Paul Bril's change of style when, on visiting Italy, he moves towards more studied compositions in which there is some attempt to produce an illusion of atmosphere and distance. See Gombrich, op.cit. 355.

[39] See Turner, op.cit. 130.

a landscape, but that because of traditional prejudice against the genre he was wary of painting a picture in which human figures did not play a significant part. Citing Lionello Venturi's view that the subject of this painting is nature, and that the human figures are elements of nature, R. Turner comments, 'The Renaissance was not prone to such vagueness, and while our aesthetic sensibility remains with Venturi, our historical sense seeks a more precise explanation.'[40] But it is possible that in this instance the vagueness is there in the painting rather than merely in the minds of the critics, and that it is symptomatic of a conflict in ideas about genre, for there are other examples in the Italian Renaissance of a looseness of approach towards subject matter.[41]

If traditional prejudices about landscape restrained its emergence as a genre in its own right, there is no evidence that it was man's fascination with his environment which ultimately led to the emergence of pure landscape painting. Indeed, as Gombrich has shown, it may well be that the feeling for landscape was the result rather than the cause of landscape painting, and that painters turned to the new genre because they were influenced by classical theory. It was Vitruvius who had recommended that walls be decorated with 'images depicting the character of certain localities, painting ports, promontories, shores, rivers, fountains, straits, shrine, groves, mountains, cattle, shepherds.'[42]

In painting, then, as in poetry, developments were determined not simply by what men thought about nature, but also by what conception they had of their art. To this extent, the parallel development of the interest in nature in both painting and poetry is something of a coincidence. But in any case, it is a parallel which cannot be followed particularly convincingly in Spain, for there are many difficulties in arguing that Spanish baroque poetry and the new genre of landscape painting form a part of the same movement. Firstly, the timing is too vague. Landscape painting as an independent genre began to appear a century before Góngora's poetry. Secondly, the Italians and the Dutch do not seem to have produced any nature poetry comparable with that of Góngora, unless one excepts Marino, yet both nations produced excellent landscape painters. On the other hand, Spain seems to have shown no particular penchant for landscape painting, Mazo being the only landscapist of note. Jusepe Martínez, a seventeenth-century theorist who was very familiar with the taste of the Spanish court in painting, fails to give landscape so much as a mention in his *Discursos*

---

[40] Turner, op.cit. 91.
[41] See Creighton Gilbert, 'On subject and non-subject in Italian Renaissance pictures,' *The Art Bulletin*, 24, no. 3 (September 1952), 202–216.
[42] Gombrich, op.cit. 354–5.

practicables del nobilísimo arte de la pintura.[43] He mentions over sixty artists in his treatise, many of them Spaniards, but all of them are singled out for their qualities as painters of portraits or of historical scenes. Juan de Butrón seems to sum up the Spanish attitude to landscape painting when he disdainfully writes in his *Discursos apologeticos* (1626):

The only Painters worthy of the name are those who imitate human nature, painting the parts and the perfections of man, bringing life to a canvas or a board: not those who, having become Landscapists through an inability to reach the heights of Art, stoop to copying fields and meadows.[44]

One could hardly have a clearer illustration of the degree of contempt which landscape painting could arouse, and it is entertaining to note the distinction made between portrait painting, regarded as imitation, and landscape painting, regarded as copying.

I have tried to show in this chapter some of the advantages of examining the rhetorical traditions in the treatment of nature in poetry, and to point out how much prejudice there is against this kind of approach in modern criticism. The mistaken acceptance of the criterion of sincerity as a measure of excellence, and the search for predecessors of the Romantic movement in all poets who show an interest in nature, has not surprisingly resulted in the relative neglect of the baroque poets' treatment of nature.

The advantage of the approach I have suggested is that, in the first place, it broadens the range of poetry we can appreciate by not insisting that passion is the be-all and end-all of literature. On the other hand, it does not exclude emotional factors or attempt to de-humanize literature. As we have seen, rhetorical traditions may well indicate the emotional attitudes of the reading public in general. The study of poetic traditions also takes into account the fact that it is not simply the emotional make-up of a writer, or even his skill, which determines

---

[43] Ed. Julián Gallego (Barcelona, 1950).

[44] 'Aquellos son con justos titulos llamados Pintores, que imitan el natural del hombre, y le pintan sus partes, y perfecciones, dando vida a vn lienço, o vna tabla; no los que hechos Paisistas por no alcançar lo superior del Arte, se abaten a copiar los campos y sus prados.' *Discursos apologeticos, en que se defiende la ingenuidad del arte de la pintura* (Madrid, 1626), fo. 89 v. Compare Jáuregui:
   . . .El sumo honor
   Del escultor y pintor
   Es cuando imitar procura
   Al hombre, que es la criatura
   Mas semejante al Criador. . .
'Diálogo entre la naturaleza y las dos artes pintura y escultura,' in *Poetas líricos de los siglos XVI y XVII, BAE*, 42, p. 117.

absolutely the kind of poetry he will write. His conception of his art, which may be strongly influenced by previous traditions, is an important factor to take into consideration, as we have seen in the history of the development of both landscape painting and descriptive poetry.

II

POETRY AND THE SENSES

One man's meat is another man's poison. If the critics in the Romantic tradition described in the previous chapter ignore baroque poetry partly because of its alleged impassivity, those of the school with which we shall be concerned in this chapter take delight in it precisely for this reason. The revival of interest in Góngora in the 1920s was sparked off by those who saw him as a master of pure, objective, 'aesthetic' poetry, in which sight and sound are everything. And this is an approach which has by no means been abandoned today. Critics constantly refer to the strong sensuous appeal of baroque poetry as a whole. This is understandable since the poetry of this age was manifestly more concerned with the physical world and showed a new density of metaphor, placing special emphasis on images of brilliant colour, all of which encourages the assumption that one of the main aims of the poetry is to stimulate the visual imagination. And, of course, many readers of baroque poetry do in fact find that their imagination is stimulated by its brilliant imagery.

This concern with visual sensuousness, which we may for convenience refer to as the pictorialist tradition, is investigated here because it constitutes a challenge to the method I adopt of examining primarily the rhetorical function of baroque imagery. As I hope to illustrate, the more one regards poetic imagery as an objective stimulus to the senses, the less one will be concerned with its significance or point, and the less one will tend to see it as an example of human communication.

For the advocates of *poésie pure* it is not merely emotion, but apparently thought itself which is an impurity strictly to be avoided in truly aesthetic poetry. As Orozco puts it:

One is bound to admit, with Alfonso Reyes, that Góngora is not a poet of the spirit: he is a poet of the senses. Góngora at his most typical took little interest, of course, in depth of thought, or in emotional overtones, and even less in entertaining us with the narrative content. He was seeking a clearer, purer, aesthetic pleasure.[1]

The implications of this kind of view of the baroque poets' intentions are rather serious. In effect, we are invited to ignore certain aspects of their poetry, and perhaps even to regard them as artistic weaknesses. For example, Audrey Lumsden writes of Pedro Espinosa's *Fábula de Genil*:

---

[1] E. Orozco Díaz, *Góngora* (Barcelona, 1953), p. 92.

The narrative links may, and should, be ignored in any consideration of the artistic value of the *Fábula*. The real 'subject' of the poem is a synthesis of the host of vivid impressions of colour, light, perfume and sound which the poet has received from nature.[2]

The same critic regards what she sees as the occasional manifestations of emotion in Espinosa's poetry as a fault:

Since the process of exteriorisation has not gone as far in him as in Góngora, however, we may occasionally find a passage which reveals real emotion hidden beneath the elaborate superstructure of artistry. From time to time, such alien elements disturb the smoothly decorative harmony of his verses. Only when he ceases to stimulate feeling does he have moments of genuine vision and achieve effects of any subtlety.[3]

It is quite clear that for her the imagery has no rhetorical purpose.[4] Again, Walter Pabst in his study of Góngora acknowledges that not all of the poet's metaphors are purely sensuous, but boldly states that those which are not are of no great importance.[5] Even more dangerously, another critic, drawing what is nevertheless a legitimate conclusion from the premises implicit in the theory of *poésie pure*, concludes that where on occasions he has been unable to understand Góngora this is of little consequence for his appreciation of the poetry, since Góngora was primarily bent on producing visual and musical sensations with his poetry:

Some of these metaphors are, as metaphors, pretty feeble, whilst others are too involved to be made out, but since it was the conjunction of words and images of different sorts that the poet was principally aiming at, the occasional failure of the meaning is not a matter of much importance.[6]

When things reach this stage we are justified in questioning the soundness of the whole concept of sensuousness in poetry.

There have already been a number of criticisms of the tendency to place stress first and foremost on the sensuous content of poetic

---

[2] 'Sentiment and artistry in the work of three Golden-Age poets,' in *Spanish Golden-Age Poetry and Drama*, ed. E. Allison Peers (Liverpool, 1946), p. 44.

[3] Ibid. 41–2.

[4] 'His perception of reality is not passionate but contemplative and detached, and he apprehends purely sensuous qualities *without reference to their immediate dramatic and emotional value.*' (op.cit. 40–1); 'The essential aspect of his verse is thus aesthetic. He exemplifies exactly the qualities of display, sensuous exuberance, decoration, formalism, *exaggeration of means without reference to an end* which are found in those aspects of life and art known collectively as the Baroque,' (op.cit. 46–7). The italics are mine.

[5] 'Not all the metaphors are impressionist creations; often they consist, as we know, in a mental process. These latter ones are the least important.' *La creación gongorina en los poemas 'Polifemo y Soledades'*, Spanish trans. Nicolás Marín (Madrid, 1966), p. 115.

[6] Gerald Brenan, *The Literature of the Spanish People* (Harmondsworth, 1963), p. 224.

images. The most outstanding of these is Rosemond Tuve's *Elizabethan and Metaphysical Imagery*, mentioned above. She argues convincingly that at this time poets did not select images on the basis of their sensuous immediacy, but were almost exclusively concerned with their rhetorical efficacy. Others have sounded a warning that one should not give too much importance to the sensuous function of imagery.[8] And in practice, as the interest in the baroque conceit shows, critics have not been unaware of the intellectual qualities of Spanish poetry of this period. Nevertheless, there seems to have been no rigorous examination of the concept of sensuousness, and most critics still accord it a major place in baroque poetry. Even those who seem to harbour doubts about the applicability of the theory of *poésie pure* to this period still seem reluctant to abandon the old terminology. For example, Dámaso Alonso has drawn attention to the rhetorical qualities of Góngora's poetry, and sees it as fundamentally different from that of the symbolist movement, which in so far as it appreciated Góngora did so for the wrong reasons.[9] He stresses the logical aspect of Góngora's metaphors, as opposed to the intuitive imagery of Mallarmé.[10] Yet despite this, he still affirms elsewhere in the same book that no poetry is more sensual than Góngora's (p. 78), and he still sees Góngora's imagery as part of the 'eager, age-old struggle undertaken by men for the conquest of pure beauty' (p. 74). Similarly, C. Colin Smith, in a recent study of the *Polifemo*, doubts whether the idea of Góngora as a poet of the senses is likely to appeal to some of his more reluctant modern readers, and seeks some kind of philosophical purpose in Góngora's poem, but nevertheless acknowledges Góngora's 'total objectivism, and his replacement of the expected emotional content by a richly sensual one'.[11] A.A. Parker may perhaps be taken as representative of the modern approach when he says of the *Polifemo*, 'It is highly sensual art, but at the same time it could not be more intellectual.[12] But superficially elegant as the modern compromise view is, its soundness is soon thrown into doubt when we investigate the theory of sensuousness.

When critics say that baroque poetry 'appeals to the senses' they are, of course, speaking figuratively. The print on the page is presented to

---

[8] For example, A. Warren and R. Wellek who in their *Theory of Literature* (London, 1961), pp. 191–2, note I.A. Richards's views on the subject. See also Arthur Terry, 'Pedro Espinosa and the praise of creation,' *BHS*, 38 (1961), 130, who notes in connection with Osuna's praise of the creation that 'a superficial reading may exaggerate the sensuous appeal of such images.'

[9] 'Góngora y la literatura contemporánea', *Estudios y ensayos gongorinos*, pp. 547–57.

[10] Ibid. 556–7.

[11] 'An approach to Góngora's *Polifemo*,' *BHS*, 42 (1965), 217.

[12] See his introduction to Gilbert F. Cunningham's translation of Góngora's *Polifemo* (Alva, Scotland, 1965), p. 21.

the reader's eye, but the objects the poem describes are not. What is meant is that the poet's words stimulate the reader's imagination, and that this activity of the imagination is akin to that of the senses and is distinguishable from the abstract thought processes in that it has the simplicity and physical immediacy of sense perception. Many critics would also hold that the imaginative experience also has an aesthetic value, and may be enjoyed much as the sight of a painting or some beautiful object might be enjoyed.

We have here the idea that, sometimes at least, words function by a process of translation in to pictorial terms. This kind of translation was seen as a part of the normal function of language by some eighteenth-century theorists. For example, in 1721 Tamworth Raresby expounded the view that every articulated word is a picture of a thought which

must be immediately painted in the Imagination; because otherwise we could not with Words paint what we had conceiv'd. Our Thoughts then are follow'd by certain Traces in the Imagination; these Traces are followed by those of Speech, and those of Speech by others of Writing, when we have a mind to record our Conceptions . . . It is therefore manifest, that the exterior Representation of anything by the Mediation of Words, is the same as that first painted in the Brain.[13]

Of course, with a theory like this, one runs into the problem of how far universal terms are picturable, and in what way images could conceivably help one to understand a sentence like, say, this one. But the theory receives some measure of support from Locke's contention that language is totally dependent upon the senses, if not specifically on the sense of sight.[14]

There are obvious objections to these accounts of language, but they have the virtue of offering a consistent view of the whole process of language. By contrast, the theory of sensuous poetry implies that on some occasions language operates pictorially whilst on others it does not. Non-sensuous language engages us intellectually, and perhaps emotionally; sensuous language by-passes the understanding and simply presents pictures to the mind's eye. If this is the case, how is it that the mind recognizes sensuous language and responds to it in a different way? What kind of poetic language is in practice recognized as sensuous?

One might have imagined that poetry describing in a literal, detailed way aspects of the physical world would have been regarded by most advocates of the pleasures of the imagination as sensuous. But the

---

[13] *A Miscellany* (London, 1721), pp. 20, 21, as quoted by Ralph Cohen, *The Art of Discrimination* (London, 1964), p. 140.

[14] 'I doubt not but, if we could trace them to their sources, we should find, in all languages, the names which stand for things that fall not under our senses to have had their first rise from sensible ideas.' *An Essay Concerning Human Understanding*, ed. A. Pringle-Pattison (Oxford, 1960), p. 224.

attack against eighteenth-century descriptive nature poetry made by Lessing in his *Laocoon* (1766), and the continued attacks of later writers on the whole concept of descriptive poetry, on the grounds of its ineffectiveness as a stimulus to the imagination, raises some doubts on this score.

Lessing holds that since poetry organizes sounds in a temporal sequence, whereas painting organizes shapes and forms spatially, presenting them simultaneously to the eye, poetry is by its very nature doomed to failure if it attempts to describe by the lengthy enumeration of physical detail, which needs simultaneous presentation if it is to be at all effective. It is important to note that he is not criticizing the idea of sensuous poetry as such. Indeed, it is quite clear that he makes the visual imagination the touchstone of good poetry, declaring that 'the poet should always paint',[15] and seeing the poet's aim as the production of an almost physical illusion.[16] He is merely indicating that description tries to be sensuous but fails.[17]

If straightforward description cannot be regarded as an automatic stimulus for the imagination, perhaps metaphorical language may be regarded as sensuous. The use of the term 'imagery' to refer amongst other things to metaphor may encourage us to assume this. And the Imagist and Symbolist doctrines wholeheartedly adopt this point of view. T.E. Hulme speaks of metaphor as a kind of visual language which hands sensations over bodily rather than triggering abstract thought processes.[18] And Lorca's essay on Góngora puts much stress on the visual quality of metaphor: 'Metaphor is always governed by the sense of sight (sometimes sublimated sight), but it is sight which limits it and gives it its reality. Nobody blind from birth is capable of being a poet who moulds objective images.'[19]

But if the mind is to respond in a special visual way to metaphor it must first be able to distinguish between figurative and non-figurative language. And if the imaginative response is to be at all relevant to the poem, a prior intellectual grasp of the meaning of the words would seem to be required. For example, the Spanish word *oro* may mean the mineral gold; it may mean in a more general sense, 'wealth'; or it may, as in the case of so many Golden-Age love poems, signify a woman's

---

[15] *Laocoon*, translated by Sir Robert Philimore (London, 1874), p.141.

[16] 'We believe ourselves to be really conscious of his objects as if they were actually present to our senses.' (Ibid. 161).

[17] See Lessing's comment on a passage from Ariosto: 'What sort of image do these commonplaces suggest? ... In the poet I see nothing, and feel with disgust the failure of my best efforts to see something' (Ibid. 201).

[18] *Speculations*, ed. H. Read, (London, 1936), pp. 134–5.

[19] *Obras completas*, ed. A. del Hoyo (Madrid, 1964), p. 68.

hair. In the case of the two figurative uses of the word, the visualization of gold ingots would be a grotesque response to the metaphor *oro* equals hair, whilst the mere visualization of a patch of yellow would be an equally irrelevant response to the image *oro* equals wealth. The recognition of and the response to metaphor cannot but involve the understanding. Visualization is of necessity secondary to abstract thought, and the much vaunted aesthetic purity of sensuous poetry is already sullied at the very start.

However, once we do begin to visualize in response to poetry, having performed whatever preliminary mental tasks might be necessary, could we not then say that we are engaged in a quasi physical activity which has a greater immediacy than abstract thought? There seems no reason to think that visualization is physically more immediate than visual perception. Yet visual perception is itself a much more complex and abstract process than many writers imply. Complex, partly because it is dynamic, with the eyes constantly moving even when the scene which confronts them is static; abstract, because physically there are no pictures in the mind projected, as it were, by the lens of the eye. If there were such projected images they would need another eye to see them, whose projected images, in turn, would require yet another eye to see them, and so on *ad infinitum*.[20] Light entering the eye does not fall on the visual centre of the brain, but arrives translated into a form no less abstract than that of the electrical impulses involved in non-perceptual brain activity. When we look at a picture, there is no picture in our mind. It follows, *a fortiori*, that when we visualize something as we read a poem we are not contemplating a kind of picture.

If we consider the sense of sight in relation to the other senses, this again reveals the anomalies of the pictorial theory of the imagination. People report having auditory, olfactory, and motor 'imagery', but do not feel tempted to talk in terms of internal copies of previous experiences in these cases. For example, if I vividly remember the smell of an exotic perfume, nobody would claim that I have a kind of dummy perfume floating around in my mind which I am smelling with my mind's nose.[21] By analogy, it is just as absurd to talk about the visual imagination in terms of pictures seen by the mind's eye. If we feel tempted to talk in this way it is perhaps, as Ryle has suggested, because in practice we do associated visualizing with snapshots and pictures, since we do use portraits of people to help us to visualize them. Also, there is a temptation to explain vividness or lifelikeness in terms of similarity, as between an original and a copy. Just how persistent

[20] See R.L. Gregory, *Eye and Brain* (London, 1966), p. 7.
[21] See Gilbert Ryle, *The Concept of Mind* (London, 1949), pp. 252–4.

these inaccurate ways of thinking can be is illustrated by an article by one philosopher who, despite accepting the overwhelming arguments that we do not have pictures in our minds, still pleads for the retention of our confusing habits.[22]

When we are reading a 'sensuous' poem, then, we cannot be said to be engaged in a purer, more immediate, less abstract form of mental activity than when we are reading other kinds of poem. Indeed, we may well be thinking in a more complex way. But is our experience nevertheless aesthetically more intense? It remains for us to look at the aesthetic theory of the pictorialist tradition.

The pictorialist critics hold that the visualization of poetic images is an aesthetic experience because it is akin to the experience of looking at a painting, and is basically visual, as opposed to emotional or intellectual. We can already reject this account on general grounds since it is clearly based on the traditional misconception about the way our imagination works. Moreover it is remarkably naïve to think that neither our emotions nor our intellect are involved when we are looking at a painting. Nevertheless, it is worth looking at the theory in a little more detail and studying its operation in practice to see what its implications are for literary criticism.

What kind of beauty is it that the pictorialist critics invite us to admire? Even if we are thinking about the imagination in traditional terms, the analogy between reading poetry and looking at a painting is only valid in a very restricted sense. Presumably we could hardly be called on to admire the composition of the imaginary painting as one would that of a real painting, for no two readers would be contemplating exactly the same picture. Indeed, there is no guarantee that the same reader would have identical pictures on consecutive readings of the poem. Hence the composition could not be regarded as a criterion for the excellence of the poem, but rather for the creative power of the reader's imagination. In any case, to appreciate the 'picture' as a composition one would have to visualize it as being of a well defined surface area on a flat surface in front of one's nose, and it is rather doubtful whether people are in the habit of visualizing in this fashion. But what is it we are being called on to appreciate if it is not the artistic form of the painting? The pictorialist critics seems to have two things chiefly in mind: colour, and brilliance.

It is not uncommon to find detailed studies of the range of colour words used by particular poets.[23] The fact that the study of an author's

---

[22] 'It is far better to say that there are mental pictures, and at the same time issue a warning against asking questions about them that can sensibly be asked only of real pictures.' J.M. Shorter, 'Imagination', *Mind*, 61 (1952), 528–42.

[23] Examples include W. Pabst, op.cit. 90–9; E. Orozco Díaz, 'El sentido pictórico del color en la poesía barroca', in *Temas del barroco* (Granada, 1947), 71–109; D. Alonso, 'Claridad y belleza. . .', *Estudios y ensayos gongorinos*, pp. 78–9.

'palette'[24] is regarded as a viable exercise probably reflects a belief that all colour words have a similar function whatever their context, and that this is basically a sensuous one. Perhaps colour has been universally accepted as one of the touchstones of sensuous poetry because it is felt that colour in poetry is a decorative element which must be visualized if it is to mean anything to us at all. But by studying colour words in their contexts it does not take long to realize that the visual quality of a colour is by no means the only feature we need to consider, nor is it even the main one in some cases. For example, an account of a motorist passing a red traffic light is unlikely to be understood by a person whose first concern is to visualize the colour. Or, to take an example closer to poetry, if an author describes grass as being blue the vividness of the reader's imagination is no substitute for the realization that this is not the normal colour for grass. And so when Góngora at the start of the first *Soledad* describes Taurus, the celestial bull, grazing in fields of sapphire, the reader who is alive to the implied comparison between earth and heaven may well derive more aesthetic pleasure from the image than Pabst who seems to have been content merely to savour the beauty of the colour.[25] In fact, the special reading technique he advocates when he says, 'We ought not to "read", we ought to consider each line as a suggestion and drink its beauty',[26] can be an active hindrance to the appreciation of baroque poetry.

A good illustration of the possible dangers of indulging a fertile imagination when reading baroque poetry is to be found in a discussion of Rioja's poem in honour of the carnation by Audrey Lumsden. Miss Lumsden savours Rioja's colour gradations in the lines:

> Cuando a la excelsa cumbre de Moncayo
> rompe luciente sol las canas nieves
> con más caliente rayo,
> tiendes igual las hojas abrasadas.

> (When on Moncayo's lofty peak
> the shining sun melts the white snows
> with hotter beam,
> you too stretch forth your fiery leaves.)

She sees a steady gradation of tone from the pink flush of dawn ('rompe luciente sol'), to a more definite red colour ('más caliente rayo'), until finally we reach the deep crimson of 'las hojas abrasadas'.[27]

---

[24]   The very use of this term by the critics reminds us of the inadequacy of the analogy between poems and paintings.

[25]   Pabst, op. cit. 114.

[26]   Op. cit. 93.

[27]   Lumsden, op.cit. 35–6.

But in fact there are only two words in the passage which give any definite indication of colour (*canas* and *abrasadas*), and both of these may be regarded as metaphorical, since the adjective *cano* is usually reserved for the description of white hair. It might be claimed that it is relatively harmless for the reader to read between the lines and picture a progressively intense colour pattern. But in a passage of this nature it is difficult to see how one can do this and at the same time grasp the rhetorical point of the passage. Rioja is offering us a conceit, which like most conceits involves us in some process of logical abstraction rather than in a detailed visualization of a physical situation. In this particular case, the carnation and the sun are linked by means of the word *abrasadas*. Just as in springtime the sun becomes more fiery, so the carnation becomes more fiery in colour at this time of the year. The aesthetic value of the passage depends on one point of symmetry—the comparison between the sun and the carnation—and one subsidiary point of contrast, that between the snow and the sun. If one starts trying to visualize some contrast between the pink of a dawn which has not been mentioned by the poet and the crimson of the carnation, the whole point of the conceit, which is to equate one phenomenon with another (as the word *igual* indicates), will be lost.

Even when they are used in a perfectly simple non-metaphorical way, colour adjectives may have a special meaning which is not in the least pictorial. There is an interesting example in a passage from Lope de Vega's *Arcadia*, which is discussed by Orozco in the following terms:

Sometimes a simple adjective of colour, so rich in his poetry, is so effective, that without evoking the image of the object, it leaves us with an intense impression of colour which only a painter's technique can explain. One of his still-lifes is a good example of this, and shows us at the same time his love of colour combinations and contrasts:

> Las uvas verdes y azules
> blancas, rojas, tintas, negras,
> pendientes de los sarmientos
> los racimos y hojas secas.

> (The green and blue grapes,
> the white and red and black ones,
> hanging from the shoots
> and branches and dried leaves.)[28]

To read this description as a kind of verbal still-life painting seems to me to overlook its rhetorical function in the poem. When we read these lines in their context, it becomes clear that the colours selected by Lope are of no special importance. The poem is a love poem embodying

---

[28] Orozco, *Temas del Barroco*, p. 93.

a commonplace theme which we shall be meeting in a later chapter, and which may be conveniently termed *cornucopia*. The theme is that of the lover offering his beloved numerous gifts in return for her love, and the topos typically takes the form of a long list of birds, beasts, and flowers, and other natural products. The rhetorical purpose of all this is clearly to dazzle the lady with the prospect of untold wealth and variety. It is also, perhaps, a chance for the poet to display his encyclopedic knowledge by producing one or two obscure specimens. The grapes that we see here are just a part of the list, and the wealth of colour merely shows the poet's desire to include every known variety of grape on his list. If there were such things as orange and turquoise grapes, these would doubtless have been included too (metre permitting). For us to appreciate the passage it is merely necessary for us to grasp intellectually that here we have a great variety of colour, and that the whole gamut of grapes is represented. No matter how clear a picture we may have in our imagination of the grapes, unless we appreciate this we misread the passage.

From the specific examples we have examined of the pictorial approach to colour it does not seem that this is a very helpful method of reading baroque poetry. But there are also general reasons, associated with the poetry of this period in particular, why the method is likely to be a failure. Baroque poetry is rich in metaphor, yet, ironically enough, in view of the importance of metaphor in pictorialist theory, this is one aspect of poetic language which the pictorial method is least equipped to deal with. Metaphor is a device which is just not available to the painter. It is a poetic device which is incapable of translation into pictorial terms without becoming either enigmatic or grotesque. Baroque jewel imagery acts as a constant reminder of this fact. Usually these metaphors link two objects—rubies and lips, emeralds and grass, stars and eyes. If the painter paints (or the reader visualizes) the real term the result is banal and lacking the significance of the poetic image, since a plain, literal description would have achieved the same effect. If he paints the metaphorical term—the rubies or emeralds—the result is enigmatic, since we cannot be sure what these objects represent. Hence the enigmatic quality of emblems, and the fact that they usually require ✓ explanatory inscriptions. If he chooses to paint both, or rather to paint the metaphorical term in a 'real' context which will explain its meaning, the result is grotesque—a woman with a mouth full of pearls, or with diamonds where her eyes should be.

The satirical writer may exploit the absurdity of envisaging in meticulous detail ideas which people would usually visualize in a much more sketchy manner, as, for example, Quevedo does in his *Sueño del Juicio Final*, where he describes in a grotesque way the actual mechanics of people collecting their bodies on the Day of Judgement. But this is the stuff of satire, not of lyric poetry. And if in an allegorical work like Gracián's *Criticón* the visualization of some of the conceits seems appropriate, this is because in allegory the context of individual images is metaphorical, not real, hence there is no conflict between different levels of reality in the picture.[29]

Apparently, what the pictorialist critics choose to 'paint' in the case of baroque jewel imagery is the colour and luminosity. But when, for example, in Góngora's second *Soledad* the fisherman refers to an island as 'esta esmeralda bruta,/ en mármol engastada siempre undoso' ('This rough emerald, set in ever wavy marble'), the reader is not being referred to a kind of colour chart. One does not need to have actually seen an emerald to appreciate this passage, and if any one kind of reader is at a natural advantage here it is more likely to be an Irishman than a jeweller with a strong visual memory. Even to have a de luxe edition of Góngora with emeralds actually set into the page would not necessarily help. And to see an uncut stone, an 'esmeralda bruta', might even prove a positive disadvantage. To appreciate the passage the reader need do no more than understand intellectually that emeralds are precious, brilliant, and the epitome of greenness. He will also need to understand the basis of the continued metaphor and may call on his visual imagination to help him here. But to continue to explore the passage visually, as it were, will not enable him to extract an ounce more of meaning. On the other hand, a reader untrammelled by any pictorial fixation has the opportunity of examining more deeply the implications of the metaphor, such as, for example, the possibility that by this image the peasant is highlighting the value of natural beauty enjoyed by country folk by comparing it by implication with the kind of riches enjoyed by the courtier.

In view of the difficulty of coping with metaphor pictorially it is strange that Jean Hagstrum, who argues that there is a strong pictorial tradition in the poetry of all ages, should hold that 'It is on the side of imagery that poetry comes closest into relation with painting.'[30] Later she seems to concede that metaphor is not pictorial in the pure sense: Pictorial imagery is most effective when it is in some way or other metaphorical rather than purely descriptive or purely imitative of visual reality . . . the pictorial is most effective when it is more than merely pictorial and when it serves some larger aesthetic or intellectual purpose.[31] Already we are very close to an admission of the inadequacy of the whole analogy between poetry and painting.

[29] Compare R.D.F. Pring-Mill, who discusses incongruity in Quevedo, and the 'emblematic' approach in Gracián, in his 'Techniques of representation in the *Sueños* and the *Criticón*,' *BHS*, 46 (1969), 270–84.

[30] *The Sister Arts* (Chicago, 1958), p. xv.

[31] Ibid. xx.

Other critics who are prepared to make no such concessions keep the problem at bay by talking in only the vaguest terms about the images aroused by metaphor. One might have imagined that the pictorial approach to poetry would have been advocated by men with a strong visual imagination, and that a person with a weak imagination would find himself at a disadvantage in their company. But it is interesting to note, for example, that Emilio Orozco finds Lope's description of coloured grapes sensuous, yet regards it as quite natural for the reader to visualize not grapes, but merely colours on reading the passage in question.[32] Similarly, Gerald Brenan in analysing the impressions given by Góngora's *Soledades* finds them so vague that he hesitates to call them images at all:

Out of a cloud of uncertainty come intimations of something different —fleeting sensations that, though they linger in the memory, are difficult to give words to. We catch the flash of a bird's wing, the glint of sunlight on water, the sound of a voice trailing over the sea, the touch of air on the cheek, the red gash of sunset . . . These images, if one can call them by so precise a term, rise between the interstices of the world like aromas, jostled by the sights and sounds of ordinary life and of ancient poetry, and haunt us, like things remembered between waking and sleep with a sort of poignancy.[33]

In practice, then, it appears that the imagination of the pictorialist critics is less vivid than their theories might have led us to believe. This perhaps helps to account for such wildly divergent views as Dámaso Alonso's statement that 'Góngora is the exact opposite of an impressionist poet'[34] and Walter Pabst's that 'Góngora is a great impressionist,'[35] not to mention Gerald Brenan's view that we have in the *Soledades* 'an impressionist landscape with surrealistic features.'[36] Presumably the range of opinions would not have been quite as broad if Góngora had been a painter rather than a poet.

I have so far discussed the theory of sensuousness only in its visual aspects, both because it is this aspect of the theory which is given pride of place by the critics, and also because the range of rhetorical effects attributable to visual images seems to be greater. Probably the bulk of baroque auditory images suggest music or harmony. This certainly seems to be the case with Góngora.[37] The poet's purpose in introducing these images is usually merely to suggest that the sounds mentioned are

[32] See above, p. 30.
[33] Brenan, op.cit. 132.
[34] *Estudios y ensayos gongorinos*, p. 572.
[35] Pabst, op.cit. 97.
[36] Brenan, op.cit. 226.
[37] R.O. Jones has drawn attention to the prevalence of images of harmony in the *Soledades* in his 'Neoplatonism and the Soledades,' *BHS*, 40 (1963), 1–16.

harmonious, whereas, as we have seen, in the case of visual images he is often doing far more than pointing out that the objects he describes are visually beautiful. In Góngora we have references to actual music making—*serranas* singing and playing musical instruments, birds singing —and to sounds of nature which are described in musical terms. Because these images are all examples of music-making, examples of an art, that is, we are obviously invited to look at them as aesthetically important. The equivalent in visual terms would be for the poet to show examples of visual art—Pedro Espinosa's description of nature in terms of painting, for example,[38] or the nymphs' tapestries in Garcilaso's Third Eclogue. Nevertheless, one can find examples of a broader rhetorical function in baroque sound imagery, as may be seen in Góngora's *letrilla* beginning:

No son todos ruiseñores
los que cantan entre las flores,
sino campanitas de plata,
que hacen la salva
a los Soles que adoro.

(It is not only nightingales
that sing amongst the flowers,
but little silver bells
that ring to greet the dawn;
and little golden trumpets
playing a fanfare
for the suns I adore.)[39]

Here the music of the stream (the silver bells) and of the bees (the golden trumpets) are songs of praise. They thus have a panegyric as well as a musical value. We may note, too, in passing, that aesthetes anxious to visualize the shape of the trumpets and the bells are likely to make a nonsense of this poem.

How do the pictorialist critics deal with the question of auditory imagery? Not surprisingly, they are rather less precise about the role played by the reader's imagination when reading these images. For example, Pabst notes Góngora's sensitivity to sound, describing his images as 'descriptive word-music'. But we are not invited to savour each sound, understandably, since it is difficult to even begin to work out a sensible reading technique along these lines. For example, when I see a reference to a gipsy playing a guitar, should I try to imagine the sound of the guitar? If so, what notes should I imagine it to be playing? Should I listen to a whole piece, or should I allow it to fade out after a few bars? But if I do not hear it actually playing precise notes, how

---

[38] See his 'Soledad de Pedro Jesus,' *Obras*, ed. F. Rodríguez Marín (Madrid, 1909), pp. 72–82.
[39] *Letrillas*, ed. R. Jammes (Paris, 1963), p. 8.

can I hear it as the sound of a guitar? And when I see Góngora metaphorically describing birds as 'feathered citharas', should I attempt to
imagine what a host of these stringed instruments would sound like,
despite my suspicion that the effect would bear little resemblance
to birdsong?

The usual escape-route for avoiding considerations of this kind is to
accept that the musicality of the verse itself supplies the necessary
sound picture. But it is straining credulity more than a little to claim
that the sound, or the imagined sound, of a voice reading some lines
of poetry is capable of resembling now the song of a bird, now that of
a gipsy, now the sound of a guitar. And so the theory of sensuousness
receives yet another setback from the problems of giving a satisfactory
account of auditory imagery.

We may summarize the objections to regarding baroque poetry as
sensuous by saying that although the reader's attention is often directed
to beauty of colour and of sound, there is no justification for regarding
the poetry as appealing to our senses like a painting or any other
physical artefact. Our imagination is not a kind of private picture
gallery, nor is it clearly detachable from the understanding and the
emotions. And metaphor, on which so much stress is laid by the pictorialist tradition, is normally incapable of translation into precise
pictorial terms. We are left, apparently, visualizing bright colours, an
experience the reader could easily indulge in without the poet's help,
and one of far less aesthetic interest than the appreciation of the
symmetries and relationships to which the poet draws our attention.
Moreover, the deliberate cultivation of visualization as a reading technique leads all to readily to misreadings, as we have seen. To read
poetry in this way is to approach it with the mind closed to many of
the beauties of baroque imagery.

If a basic misunderstanding of the nature of the visual imagination is
one of the factors responsible for the entrenchment of pictorial theories
of poetry in modern criticism, it is by no means the only one. It remains
for us to consider briefly some of the other contributory reasons.

Firstly, there is the fact, which it would be foolish to deny, that
many readers do find that their imagination is stimulated by baroque
poetry. It is quite probable, though, that at least some enthusiasts of
Góngora would claim to have no visual imagination at all. Galton's
early researches into the phenomenon of mental imagery showed a
remarkable paucity of imagery amongst academics.[40] And that a lack
of visual imagery was compatible with a feeling for descriptive poetry
was recognized by English critics in the eighteenth century when they

---

[40] See G.A. Miller, *Psychology, The Science of Mental Life* (Penguin Books,
1967); P. McKellar, *Experience and Behaviour* (Penguin Books, 1968), pp. 111–35.

came to consider the interesting case of Thomas Blacklock, who was blind, yet wrote creditable nature poetry.[41]

Those readers who do tend to visualize may well find that metaphor, which, as we have seen, has no parallel in painting, stimulates their imagination more than anything else. There is not, I think, any real paradox here, and we are not obliged to conclude that metaphor therefore has a non-intellectual content. In many cases the visual imagination is merely a tool to enable us to grasp the meaning of the metaphor, which may depend on some analogy of colour or shape. For example, when Góngora describes the constellation of Taurus:

Media luna las armas de su frente
Y el sol todo los rayos de su pelo

(The crescent moon the arms borne on his brow,
and all the sun the radiance of his coat),

in order to understand the analogy between the shape of the horns and that of the moon we may find that we need to visualize the relevant shape.

Dámaso Alonso has ingeniously suggested that Góngora is actually describing the astrological sign of Taurus here, which consists of a circle touching a semi-circle.[42] However, the image taken as a whole seems to me to suggest a more substantial beast than one formed from two lines. The fact that the bull has a coat and is described as grazing seems to indicate this.

Pabst, equally ingeniously, has suggested that the image of the sun describes the round shape of the bull's body when seen from the front.[43] But the precise manipulation of the point of view which is required by this interpretation and the difficulty in abstracting this shape even approximately from the total shape of a bull leads one to doubt whether Góngora really had this in mind. Much of the beauty of this conceit lies in the antithesis between 'media luna' and 'el sol todo', and it may well have been an eye for the logic of the conceit rather than for the physical shapes which guided Góngora in his choice of phrase in this passage.[44]

To take another example of a interesting image, the appearance

[41] See Ralph Cohen, *The Art of Discrimination* (London, 1964), p. 163.

[42] 'Góngora y el toro celeste', in *Litterae hispanae et lusitanae*, ed. Hans Flasche (Munich, 1968), pp. 7–15.

[43] Pabst, op.cit. 114.

[44] The reading 'todos' found in the Chacón MS. is clearly inferior to the reading 'todo' found in the Vicuña edition (See the facsimile edition of D. Alonso (Madrid, 1958)). The manuscript Arch. Seld. II, 13, of the Bodleian Library supports the reading 'todo', with the interesting variant 'Y el sol todo en su pelo.' See José Angel Valente and Nigel Glendinning, 'Una copia desconocida de las *Soledades* de Góngora,' *BHS*, 36 (1959), 1–14.

in the second *Soledad* of
> el padre de las aguas, coronado
> de blancas ovas y de espuma verde

> The father of the waters, crowned
> with white seaweed, and green foam)
>   lines 24–25)

may well stimulate the reader's imagination in a complex way. Firstly there is the question of whether the image is to be regarded as iconic, so that we think of the weed as crowning an anthropomorphic Ocean god, or whether we regard it as a more abstract metaphor describing the surface of the sea. In toying with the iconic interpretation, the reader may test it in his imagination and perhaps reject it. Then there is the problem of the description of the surface of the water. The seaweed is white, and the foam green. Why this interchange of the expected colour values? In puzzling out an interpretation the reader may well find himself testing various hypotheses in visual terms. Quite probably Góngora is suggesting here that the foam and the weed are so intermingled that they are not clearly distinguishable from each other. But it is important to note that the reader who takes Góngora at his word and tries to visualize in a precise way green foam and white seaweed, and then attempts to savour the beauty of the colours is likely to make very little progress in interpreting the image.

Another reason why the pictorialist approach to baroque poetry is so persistent is that it seems to be encouraged by the poets and theorists of the seventeenth century. Critics have drawn attention to the seventeenth-century preoccupation with the relationship between poetry and painting, which expressed itself both in theoretical utterances and in practical examples too, when poems were written about paintings.

The general theories linking the arts need not concern us in detail, for the fact that baroque writers may have thought that poetry was like painting is no guarantee that the two arts were in fact closely comparable. But, as Rosemond Tuve has pointed out,[45] the popularity of the Horatian tag 'ut pictura poesis' does not mean that this time the arts were being compared on the same grounds as those adopted by modern critics who ignore the communicative function of painting and talk of it in terms of a mere copy. If poetry was like painting, then painting was like poetry. Luis Alfonso de Carballo, for example, is conscious of the fact that in iconic imagery in poetry the whole point of visualizing is to grasp the author's meaning, so that what is often called the literal meaning is not really a meaning at all, but just an

---

[45] Tuve, op.cit. 50.

image from which the intelligence must extract significance:

And what you wrongly call the literal meaning, which you claim is
conceived immediately from the words, is not conceived by an act of the
understanding—for it would be futile for it to conceive any such thing—
rather it is a fancy of the imagination, by which we imagine and picture
the fiction, for example, that Cupid is blind, this being an act of the
imagination, which is a quite different thing from the understanding,
for it is incorrect that love is blind in the way in which the imagination
pictures it, but the understanding goes on from here to conceive what
the author meant. And if we see an angel painted as a boy with wings,
although our fancy imagines it that way, the understanding of a sensible
person does not therefore conceive that it really is like that in form—for
in fact it is not, but rather is an incorporeal spirit—but from that picture
the understanding grasps immediately the swiftness, the intelligence,
and the eternity of the angel, the figure serving merely as a sign and
symbol by which is expressed this truth rather than the idea that the
angel is a winged boy.[46]

What of the increasing number of poems which appear to be inspired
by paintings, and those poems which have a work of graphic art as
their subject? Jean Hagstrum gives these a very prominent place in the
alleged pictorial tradition, but there is no logical justification for this.
A poem about a painting is not by virtue of its subject matter any more
like a painting than a poem about a melon is like a melon. A profusion
of so-called iconic poetry will not indicate that poetry has become
more like painting, but merely that people have become more interested
in painting as a poetically exploitable subject. For example, Hagstrum
refers to a particular type of Petrarchan poem where the poet will
complain that the painting of his lady does not measure up to the
original, or that the lady is kindlier on canvas than she is in the flesh.[47]
Verse of this kind is hardly likely to concern itself seriously with the
relationship between the arts. The theme of the portrait here is on a

---

[46] 'Y essotro que tu llamas falsamente sentido literal, que quieres que se
conciba inmediatamente de las palabras, no se concibe con obra del entendimiento, que seria vano el que tal concibiesse, antes es fantasia de la imaginatiua,
con que se imagina y fantasea aquella fiction, como q[ue] Cupido es ciego, lo
qual es obra de la imaginatiua differente cosa del ente[n] dimiento, no conuiene
ser el amor ciego, como la imaginatiua lo fantasea, antes passando adelante concibe lo q[ue] el auctor quiso significar. Y si vemos pintado vn Angel a manera de
vn mancebo y con alas, aunq[ue] la fantasia lo imagina assi, no por esso el entendimiento del prudente, concibe ser de aquella forma, como realmente no lo es,
antes es incorporeo espiritu, sino que de aquella pintura el entendimiento concibe
inmediatamente la ligereza, entendimiento, y eternidad del Angel, siruiendo para
ello la figura solamente de characteres, y letras, con que se significa inmediatame
[n] te esta verdad, y no que sea el Angel ma[n]cebo y alado.' *Cisne de Apolo*
(1602), ed. A. Porqueras Mayo (Madrid, 1958), I, 100–1.
[47] Hagstrum, op.cit. 72–3.

par with a thousand and one other Renaissance themes which are used as a pretext for praising or blaming the lady. Perhaps the most famous collection of 'iconic' poetry is Marino's anthology *La Galeria* (1619). But even here one finds the same kind of rhetorical approach to painting, which shows that the author is not attempting to translate paintings into poems.[48] And compiling lists of painter-poets of the seventeenth century[49] will not demonstrate that the sister arts were particularly close at this time. After all, a painter-carpenter is not expected to produce furniture-like painting. Moreover, why should it be assumed that the poet will use painterly techniques in his poetry rather than poetic techniques in his painting? Perhaps the most illustrious Spanish painter-poet of the period is Pedro Espinosa, whose poetry has clearly been influenced by his experience as a painter in that he shows on occasions an unusual precision in his choice of colour words and also uses technical terms from painting in his poetic vocabulary. But this does not make his poetry like a kind of verbal painting.

These links between the arts, then, are significant only in a superficial way. Another rather tenuous link between painting and poetry derives from the attempt to apply Wölfflin's criteria of baroque art to the poetry of the time. Orozco seems to have at the back of his mind Wölfflin's attribution of 'painterly' qualities to baroque art when he writes of the pictorial qualities of baroque poetry.[50] But whether or not one accepts the validity of Wölfflin's categories, it is important to remember that by the term 'painterly' he did not mean simply 'like a painting'. Renaissance paintings, for example, are not 'painterly' according to his criteria, but 'linear'.[51] Is baroque poetry like baroque rather than Renaissance painting? The Abad de Rute saw the *Soledades* as comparable to a Dutch landscape painting of the Renaissance, in which various figures are dotted about.[52] Ironically enough, this would make it non-painterly according to the standard baroque criteria.

These, then, are some of the reasons accounting for the survival of the pictorialist tradition. But, as I have suggested, the theory on which

---

[48] 'One cannot escape the impression that there is much here of an occasional and courtly nature, material that should have gone into another collection of *Rime* (or possibly would have done so had the poet felt free here to leave anybody out). As it stands, *La Galeria* looks suspiciously like many other Renaissance laudatory books, all of which might bear Petrarch's title: *De viris illustribus*,' J.V. Mirollo, *The Poet of the Marvellous: Giambattista Marino* (New York and London, 1963), p. 51.

[49] See, for example, Orozco Díaz, *Temas del barroco*, 55–67.

[50] See 'De lo aparente a lo profundo', in his *Temas del barroco*.

[51] H. Wölfflin, *Principles of Art History*, trans. M.D. Hottinger (London, 1932).

[52] See Andrée Collard, *Nueva poesía. Conceptismo, culteranismo en la crítica española* (Madrid, 1967), p. 83, note.

this tradition is based cannot withstand critical examination. It fails as an account of how language works; it fails on psychological grounds; it fails as an aesthetic theory. And the deliberate cultivation of a reading technique which places the main emphasis on visualization far from enhancing the reader's appreciation of baroque poetry is likely to close his mind to its many subtleties.

In these first two chapters I have tried to justify my concern with the rhetorical purpose of baroque imagery by criticizing the assumptions of two major schools of criticism which, although diametrically opposed to each other, the one stressing the importance of feeling, the other of detachment, are both equally hostile to rhetoric. In the following chapters I consider first what seem to me to be the broad aims of baroque descriptive poetry before going on to analyse more closely the function of specific recurrent images.

III

THE USES OF DESCRIPTION

The emergence of a new genre of Spanish poetry in which the description of nature overstepped its previous restrictive boundaries is something to which I have already drawn attention in the first chapter. But the fact that for the first time natural description may provide the substance of whole poems need not mean that there is in baroque poetry such a thing as 'pure' description, or description for its own sake. The concept of 'pure' description, in so far as it denies poetic imagery a rhetorical function, is very much akin to that of pictorial poetry, and equally hard to defend.[1] Although it may not always follow classical precedent, description always has some function, even if this is not clearly spelled out by the poet. My purpose in this chapter will be to attempt a general survey of the variety of uses to which natural description was put in baroque poetry, and the kinds of poem in which such description was most fully exploited. But first it is advisable to consider what we mean by description, and how far the term is an appropriate one for the nature imagery one finds in baroque poetry.

We have already noted in the first chapter the traditional restrictions placed on poetic description before the seventeenth century. It was seen as a figure which was appropriate in certain places and in certain types of poetry rather than others, particularly in narrative poetry, but which was not an independent technique suitable for providing the very basis of a poem.[2] Descriptive poetry simply did not exist, unless one excepts the *blason*, a genre popular in sixteenth-century France. But even that was regarded by the theorists as an exercise in praising or blaming a chosen subject rather than as an exercise in description.[3] This traditional view of description was put under some pressure by

---

[1] D.B. Wilson's *Descriptive Poetry in France from Blason to Baroque* (Manchester and New York, 1967), is an example of a study which, though otherwise excellent, suffers from an insufficiently clear idea of what we mean by descriptive poetry. The author seems to be in search of a 'pure' description which he never defines: ('It is never easy to isolate examples of what might be described as 'purely descriptive' poetry', op.cit. 1), and which in his final summary he begins to have doubts about ('If *pure* description is possible, let alone a legitimate and pleasing task, then we can only conclude that it is attempted by remarkably few writers', op.cit. 244).

[2] See Tuve, op.cit. 80.

[3] See D.B. Wilson, op.cit. 6–7.

the vogue for nature poetry which developed in England in the eighteenth century under the lead of Thomson. There ensued a very lively debate amongst the English critics and philosophers about the nature and function of description, and this has been admirably documented by Ralph Cohen.[4] Some chose to defend the new poetry on the grounds of its vividness, and its appeal to the imagination: others, like Alexander Pope, who called description 'a feast made up of sauces', were more hostile, and attacked descriptive poetry by reaffirming the traditional rhetorical purpose of description.

In Spain, however, the debate on Gongorism does not seem to have centred on these issues. This leads us to inquire whether there was any awareness in seventeenth-century Spain that a new genre of descriptive poetry had sprung up, and whether, in fact, we are justified in calling the school of poetry inspired by Góngora's major works descriptive.

There are some similarities between the English descriptive poem and the typical large-scale poem which flourished in Spain in the preceding century. Both represent the physical world, and it is with physicality that we primarily associate description. For example, although one may ask a person to 'describe' his feelings, and although one may talk of 'describing' events and actions, most people would probably expect the term 'descriptive poetry' to refer to poetry which largely consists not of the narration of events, nor of psychological analysis, but of the detailed presentation of physical objects and phenomena. Baroque poetry also shares with the later poetry an expansive, leisurely approach to its material, which again we tend to associate with the term 'descriptive'. But there are important differences which cannot be accounted for in terms of what is obviously their radically different approach to style.

It is above all the fondness for periphrasis and the density of metaphor which distinguish the approach to description found in Gongoristic poetry, and which at the same time give rise to a paradox. Gongoristic poetry is full of the physical world. Indeed, one would expect description to bring one into a closer contact with physical realities than other kinds of writing. Yet periphrasis and metaphor are techniques which enable a writer to evade immediate physical facts. They need not be invariably used in this way. For example, if instead of naming an object I introduce it by means of a periphrastic description of its appearance and function this will not mean a flight from the immediate situation. But it has been suggested that they often are used in this way by Góngora. For example, Dámaso Alonso presents a picture of a Góngora who consistently flees reality.[5]

[4] Ralph Cohen, *The Art of Discrimination* (London, 1964). See especially Chapter III.
[5] See his essay 'Alusión y elusión en la poesía de Góngora', in *Estudios y ensayos gongorinos*, pp. 92–113.

Robert Jammes has demonstrated that a close study of the text of the *Soledades* does not in fact bear out the view that the poet finds it distasteful to call a spade a spade, since the poem uses a wealth of ordinary terms from the sphere of human activity.[6] Nevertheless, though we may reject the idea that Góngora is motivated by euphemistic considerations, it seems that he often takes the opportunity of distracting our attention from the immediate facts of a situation. For example, in the well-known opening of his first *Soledad* he sets his story in Springtime. This is just the place in the poem where even the classical writers would be expected to indulge in a little description of the season of the year. And one would expect a poet with a descriptive bent to pass a fairly leisurely eye over all the relevant concomitants of Spring—snows melting, buds bursting, lambs leaping, etcetera. Góngora gives us none of this, but directs our thoughts elsewhere with an ingenious description of the constellation of Taurus. In other words, although the advent of Spring is Góngora's theme, he is busy describing to us something else.

One can find a similar deviousness in the example of *topographia*, or description of place, which begins the second *Soledad*:

Éntrase el mar por un arroyo breve
que a recibillo con sediento paso
de su roca natal se precipita,
y mucha sal no sólo en poco vaso,
mas su rüina bebe,
y su fin, cristalina mariposa
—no alada, sino undosa—,
en el farol de Tetis solicita.
Muros desmantelando, pues, de arena,
centauro ya espumoso el Océano
—medio mar, medio ría—
dos veces huella la campaña al día,
escalar pretendiendo el monte en vano,
de quien es dulce vena
el tarde ya torrente
arrepentido, y aun retrocediente.
Eral lozano así novillo tierno,
de bien nacido cuerno
mal lunada la frente,
retrógrado cedió en desigual lucha
a duro toro, aun contra el viento armado:
no pues de otra manera

---

[6] R. Jammes, *Études sur l'oeuvre poétique de Góngora* (Bordeaux, 1967), pp. 605–17.

a la violencia mucha
del padre de las aguas, coronado
de blancas ovas y de espuma verde,
resiste obedeciendo, y tierra pierde.

(Lines 1—26)

(The sea begins to enter a small stream
which in its thirst to meet it, hastes to leap
down from its natal rock
and drinks not only in a little glass much salt,
but its own ruin too,
and seeks its end, a crystal butterfly,
with waves instead of wings,
in the lantern of the ocean goddess.
Dismantling walls of sand,
the Ocean, a centaur made of spume,
half sea, half estuary,
twice a day sets foot upon the lowland,
seeking in vain to scale the mountainside
of which the torrent is
a vein of water fresh, repentant now,
although too late, and even drawing back.
Just as a lusty bull of tender years,
his brow as yet ill-mooned
by horns new-born to him,
withdrawing might concede the unequal fight
against one armed to toss the very wind,
the selfsame way the stream
the great violence of
the father of the waters, crowned
with white weed and green foam,
resistantly obeys, and loses ground.)

This series of images describing the meeting between stream and ocean
has considerable vigour yet in fact gives relatively little indication of
the physical appearance of things. Góngora's themes here are relatively
abstract—the extinction of the stream in the sea, the ill-defined nature
of the meeting point between the two, the struggle between opposing
forces. The concrete images which he uses to put across these ideas
direct our attention towards objects—the glass, the moth, the centaur,
the bulls—which in physical terms have at best only a tenuous resemblance to the stream or the sea.

First comes the ingenious metaphor of the stream dying from salt
poisoning. The idea of the stream drinking develops from the adjective
'sediento' which Góngora chooses to describe its eager advance. The

image of the glass does have a physical basis in that it represents the mouth of the stream into which the sea-water has flowed. But can one really say that it gives an accurate description of what an observer might see? There is an analogy between the shape of a stream as it broadens, and that of the cross-section of a glass broadening out from its base. The transparency of both water and glass is another connecting link. But the shape has to be abstracted from the continuous stretch of water in which there is nothing which obviously corresponds to the clearly defined top and bottom of a drinking vessel. The idea of the stream drinking places the image under further strain. If we are thinking in physical terms, the glass would appear to be facing the wrong way for the stream to drink out of it. Or did Góngora have in mind for his drinking vessel a hollow in the bed of the stream? In any event, the very irony of a watercourse feeling thirsty is liable to divert our attention from physical situation to more abstract considerations.

Góngora's second image, that of the moth irresistibly attracted towards a flame in which it can only meet destruction is one which it is even more difficult to pursue in physical terms. We no longer have the analogies of shape and of physical appearance, and the theme is the abstract one of inevitable death. Indeed, part of the wit of Góngora's image lies in the physical contradiction between the moth suffering death by fire, and the stream death by water in 'Tethys lantern'. Again, the image of the centaur which follows has a logical rather than a physical basis, as does the simile of the two bulls fighting which concludes the passage.

Baroque description of this kind, then, does not correspond entirely with the traditional concept. But it is explicable in terms of the seventeenth century's preoccupation with wit. As wit attempts to link disparate objects and surprise us, so we find deliberate tensions created between that which is formally being described and the other objects to which it is being related by the poet. At times so much attention will be given to these peripheral objects that it seems more appropriate to say that it is they that are being described. We have, then, a poetry which has its roots in the physical world, and which is in that sense descriptive, but which has a density of metaphor which tends to disturb the continuity of situation, whereas one normally expects description to offer a sustained presentation of a particular situation.

The reactions to Góngora's poetry show that the critics were aware that he was overstepping traditional rhetorical boundaries, but description itself does not seem to have been a controversial issue. Apart from the question of vocabulary and syntax, the critics concentrated mainly on metaphor and periphrasis, which are precisely the techniques whose systematic use distinguishes baroque poetry from what one might call normal descriptive poetry.[7] Nevertheless, there is common ground in the attitude of the English critics of eighteenth-century descriptive poetry, and the Spanish opponents of extreme Gongorism. Just as Pope criticized descriptive poetry as 'a feast made up of sauces', so Lope de Vega upbraided the new Spanish poetry in the following delightful way:

For to make the whole composition nothing but figures of speech is as wrong and unworthy as if a woman making herself up, instead of putting the rouge on her cheeks, a wholly appropriate place for it, were to put it on her nose, forehead, and ears. For that, Sir, is what a composition full of these Tropes and Figures is—a ruddy face, like those pictures of angels blowing the last trump, or the winds on maps, without any spaces for pale, white, or crystalline tints, or for the veins, or highlights, or what painters call flesh tint.[8]

Although there may be little critical discussion about description as a genre in seventeenth-century Spain, some of the titles given to baroque poems nevertheless give us a clear indication that poets were aware of the existence of such a genre. The two poems about nightfall by Francisco de Trillo and Hortensio Paravicino mentioned in Chapter One reveal their descriptive intentions in their titles.[9] Trillo calls his a 'Pintura de la noche desde vn crepsuculo a otro' ('A painting of night, from twilight to twilight'), and Paravicino calls his a 'Romance, descruiuiendo la noche, y el dia, dirigido a don Luis de Gongora' ('A ballad, describing the night and the day, addressed to Don Luis de Góngora'). In some cases we have what appears to be an early use in the Spanish language of the adjective 'descriptivo' itself.[10] For example, Juan Ruiz de Alarcón entitled his poem recounting the celebrations in honour of the betrothal of the Infanta María and the Prince of Wales in 1623 an *Elogio descriptivo*. This earned him the disapproval of Quevedo, who, in his petty attack on this poem criticizes not so much the intent to write descriptively, but the mixing of narrative and panegyric genres within a single

---

[7] Díaz de Rivas offers a very clear summary of the principal objections to Góngora's poetry in his *Discursos apologéticos*. See the edition of E.J. Gates in her *Documentos gongorinos* (Mexico, 1960), pp. 35–6.

[8] 'Pues hazer toda la composicion figuras, es tan vicioso, y indigno, como si vna muger que se afeyta, auiendose de poner la color en las mexillas, lugar tan propio, se la pusiesse en la nariz, en la frente, y en las orejas, pues esto, señor excelentissimo, es vna composicion llena de estos Tropos, y Figuras, vn rostro colorado, a manera de los Angeles de la trompeta del juyzio, ò de los vientos de los Mapas, sin dexar campos al blanco, al candido, al cristalino, a las venas, a los realces, a lo que los pintores llaman encarnacion...': 'Respuesta a un papel que escribió un señor de estos reinos'; in *La Filomena* (Madrid, 1621), fo. 195.

[9] See pp. 15–16.

[10] Martín Alonso's *Enciclopedia del idioma* (Madrid, 1958), dates the usage of this term from the eighteenth century onwards.

poem.[11]

Another example is a poem by Miguel de Colodrero Villalobos, published in 1639, and entitled 'Tercetos descriptivos, hablando con vn amigo' ('Descriptive tercets, addressing a friend'). This is an interesting poem in praise of nature, cast in the form of a monologue addressed to a friend, proposing a closer inspection of some of the beauties visible from a mountain-side, and beginning:

Ya estamos e[n] el mo[n]te Celio amigo,
Dime de su belleza lo que sientes,
O escucha de la misma lo que digo.

(We are now on the mountain, Celio, my friend.
Tell me what you think about its beauty,
Or listen to what I say about it.)[12]

Similarly, the term 'Canción descriptiva' is used to describe one of the fascinating pair of odes in honour of Saint Jerome by Adrián de Prado, appearing in a seventeenth-century manuscript belonging to the Biblioteca Nacional, Madrid.[13] The poem remained unpublished until J.M. Blecua's edition in 1945, and the text has unfortunately not survived in its entirety.[14] Presumably it dates from about the same time as the other poem of Adrián de Prado which was published in 1619 and which enjoyed an immediate success. The manuscript anthology in which this latter poem appears, and which provides the text for Blecua's *Cancionero de 1628*, shows a quite unmistakable taste for

[11] Esto es desatino; que no hay elogio descriptivo, como no hay hombre y caballo, ni tragicomedia, por ser diferente especie, y aun en el estilo ha de haber diferencia en el elogio, que es alabanza, y en la narración de unas fiestas; porque tres estilos hay ínfimos: el primero es doctrinal, el segundo descriptivo, y el tercero laudatorio; y uniendo y confundiéndolos, vino a formar un monstruo'. *Comento contra setenta y tres estancias que hizo don Ruiz de Alarcón*, in *Obras completas*, ed. F. Buendía, Vol. 1 (Madrid, 1958), pp. 354–62 (p. 355).

[12] *El Alpheo, y otros assuntos, en verso, exemplares algunos* (Barcelona, 1639), fo. 32.

[13] MS. 3795. J.M. Rozas confirms that it is written in a seventeenth-century hand, *El Conde de Villamendiana. Cuadernos Bibliográficos*, 11 (Madrid, 1964), p. 16.

[14] For the text and some introductory remarks, see J.M. Blecua, *Cancionero de 1628* (Madrid, 1945), pp. 26–35. Blecua does not mention the cause of the lacuna, but an examination of the manuscript shows that a number of pages have been torn out after binding. A portion of the following poem is also missing, and since according to the index this begins on folio 16 and the lacuna begins at folio 13, one may deduce from the approximate number of lines per page that there are between 100 and 130 lines of Adrián de Prado's poem missing, depending on whether the following poem begins on the recto or verso side of folio 16. The lacuna is the more disappointing since it begins just after the appearance on the scene of a nymph of considerable charms whose relevance to the saint's ascetic existence is not obvious. Might one deduce that a prudish hand tore out a passage which seemed insufficiently decorous in a religious poem?

descriptive nature poetry, although satirical poetry also has a prominent place. In this same volume are to be found, for example, the poem by Paravicino, mentioned earlier in this paragraph, Góngora's *Soledades*, *Polifemo*, and *Angélica y Medoro*, and his *romance* 'Esperando están la rosa', and Valentín de Céspedes' fable of Atlanta.

Despite the lack of theoretical pronouncements about description, then, there was at the practical level not only a taste for descriptive poetry, but also a clear awareness of its existence as a new genre in sevententh-century Spain. In France too, as Antoine Adam has shown,[15] there was a flourishing descriptive school of poetry between the 1620s and 1650s, so that even the young Racine tried his hand at baroque description with his *Promenade de Port Royal*. The new poetry did elicit a response from the critics. Jean Chapelin, the President of the French Academy, for example, praised Saint Amant for his descriptions, acknowledging in effect that this was descriptive poetry.[16] The Chevalier du Méré, on the other hand, was somewhat less than complimentary about the whole idea of descriptive poetry, declaring, 'Les descriptions sont des torcheculs'.[17] But perhaps the most important comments about description are made by one of its apologists, J. de Bussières, who in the preface to his own volume of poetry, entitled *Les Descriptions poétiques* (Lyons, 1649), gives an interesting defence of descriptive writing, and one which is worth quoting at length because of its relevance to the possible motives behind Spanish baroque poetry:

...La Poësie prenant beaucoup de liberté dans ses Descriptions, où elle semble estre sans contrainte, et suivre son caprice, plus qu'en nulle autre de ses matières. Et où ne recevant aucune reigle que de son Genie, sans se mettre en peine de la bien-seance qu'elle garde dans le Poëme Epique, ou dans le Tragique, elle ne songe qu'à se divertir. C'est là proprement où elle se monstre, telle qu'elle est, où ses beautez naturelles paroissent à nud. Où sans se contraindre par l'artifice, elle n'a point de loix que la vigueur de sa boutade; imitant la Nature dans les choses qu'elle décrit, et leur donnant autant de paroles, que cette Mere des Creatures leur donne d'ornements divers. C'est à mon avis ce qui doit me faire pardonner si ces Descriptions sont un peu longues, et si elles paroissent vides de quelques pensées, dont nos Poëtes ravissent aujourd'huy les Esprits: Certes il me semble qu'on ne doit point reprocher la longueur à la Poësie, à l'endroit où elle se contente et où elle satisfait pleinement; et qu'on ne doit point la gesner dans la

---

[15] 'Le Sentiment de la nature au dix-septième siècle en France,' *Cahiers de l'Association Internationale des Études Françaises*, 6 (1954), 1–14.

[16] 'Saint-Amand s'est sanctifié par l'entreprise de son Moÿse dont il fait un idille heroïque tout rempli de descriptions, et belles en vérité,' Chapelin, *Lettres*, ed. Tamizey de Larroque (Paris, 1880), Vol. 1, 253–4.

[17] See A. Adam, op.cit.

contrainte des Antitheses, lors qu'elle ne suit que son humeur, et qu'elle veut estre le Tableau de la Nature, qui nous donne ses productions toutes simples, sans autres beautez que les siennes. Que si cette sorte de Poësie me rend excusable, le dessein qui me l'a fait entreprendre demande bien quelque pardon, puisque c'est pour renouveller le dessein de Dieu dans la formation des Creatures, et pour enseigner aux moins savans le moyen de trouver cette Cause universelle dans tous ses effets . . . J'ay tasché de le faire par les conclusions des Pieces principales de ce petit Ouvrage, y laissant comme l'aiguillon de l'Abbeille, ou comme l'espine des Roses. . .[18]

Despite De Bussière's apparent distaste for antithesis and other manifestations of poetic artifice, which no Gongorist is likely to have shared, his defence against the possible accusation that descriptive poetry is capricious and lacking in substance is pertinent to Spanish poetry, particularly if one bears in mind the charge of vacuousness levelled against Góngora's *Soledades* by Jáuregui, and in more recent times, by Menéndez Pelayo in a purple passage in his *Historia de las ideas estéticas en España*.[19] De Bussières argues that since the descriptive nature poet is re-enacting the creation, it is reasonable that his writings should reflect the wantonness of nature herself. Interestingly enough, the seventeenth-century theorist Roger de Piles makes out a similar case for landscape painting, which he regards as rich in possibilities:

Dans la grande variété dont il [le paysage] est susceptible, le Peintre a plus d'occasions que dans tous les autres genres de cet Art de se contenter dans le choix des objets. . .de toutes les productions de l'Art & de la Nature, il n'y a aucune qui ne puisse entrer dans la composition de ses Tableaux. Ainsi la Peinture, qui est une espece de creation, l'est encore plus particulierement à l'égard du Païsage.[20]

De Piles thus defends in a similar way a new genre which judged by traditional standards might have been regarded as lacking in substance and design.

Although De Bussières does not seem to be an advocate of poetic wit, to judge by his implied criticism of those who set out to 'ravir les esprits', one can find parallels to his approach in some of the seventeenth-century thinking about wit. For example, Abraham Cowley in an ode on wit writes:

> In a true piece of *Wit* all things must be,
> Yet all things there *agree*
> As in the *Ark*, joyn'd without force or strife,
> All *Creatures* dwelt; all *Creatures* that had *Life*.
> Or as the *Primitive* Forms of all

---

[18] As quoted by D.B. Wilson, op.cit. 206–7.
[19] Madrid, 1947, Vol. 2, p. 329.
[20] *Cours de peinture par principes* (Paris, 1708), pp. 200–1.

(If we compare great things with small)
Which without *Discord* or *Confusion* lie,
In that strange *Mirror* of the *Deitie*.[21]

There is much common ground here, in that wit, like description, is seen as embracing the whole range of creation, whilst at the same time finding some pattern in the multiplicity. But whereas De Bussières seems content to translate into poetry what he regards as the simple, naked beauty of the natural world, leaving the question of the ultimate significance of nature as a sting in the tail left until the end of the poem, the advocates of wit seem to have had a rather different attitude. For them, the beauties of nature are not simple and naked, but often subtle and occult, so that by highlighting unsuspected patterns in nature wit may go some way towards revealing the divine plan.

The ways in which Spanish poetry portrays both nature's infinite variety and nature's subtle patterns will be examined in later chapters, as will the question of the relevance of the theory of wit to poetic practice. In the remainder of this chapter we shall be concerned in a more general way with the whole range of rhetorical objectives of poetic description. We may then see how the various objectives are balanced in different types of poem. In the process we should achieve a clearer picture of what constitutes the novelty of poetry in the age of Góngora.

The various uses of description may be broadly classified under six headings, each of which I shall consider in turn. These general aims are:

1. To narrate, or inform.
2. To praise or blame.
3. To persuade or dissuade.
4. To move or awaken sympathy.
5. To amuse.
6. To surprise or arouse wonder.

These are not, of course, mutually exclusive aims. Indeed, in baroque poetry they are more often than not mixed. Nor would I claim that the list is an exhaustive one. But it seems to me to be a useful tool for distinguishing between the main kinds of poem in which the description of nature plays a prominent part.

1. NARRATION

One of the commonest functions of the description of nature in pre-seventeenth-century poetry is simply to tell a story, or lay facts before the reader. As we have already seen in the first chapter, the traditions of narrative poetry usually demanded that the poet describe

---

[21] Text taken from *The Metaphysical Poets*, ed. Helen Gardner, (Penguin Books, 1966), p. 225.

both the time and the place of the events he is recounting. Particularly in pastoral poetry this provided an opportunity for the description of nature.

Baroque poets often extended such introductory descriptions far beyond the bounds of what Renaissance writers expected of the topoi of *cronographia* and *topographia*. The opening of Góngora's second *Soledad*, examined earlier in this chapter, is a case in point. Not content to describe the stream flowing into the sea from just one point of view, Góngora pursues all the descriptive possibilities, producing now the image of the moth, now that of the centaur, now that of the fighting bulls, before pressing on with his narrative. A description like this tends to lose its purely preparatory function, for the author presents nature in a surprising way, rather than merely factually.

A good example of a poem which stretches the introductory description virtually to breaking point is a pastoral ode by Pedro de Godoy which is unremarkable save for its opening description of the riverside scene, which lasts for some fifty lines, and in which there is such a welter of subordinate adverbial clauses as detail is added to detail that the reader begins to wonder if he will ever reach the main verb. The following extract from this passage is wholly characteristic of the seventeenth-century approach to description:

Donde la guinda roja,
con la cermeña verde entretejida,
en el peral arroja
las ramas de su fruta, que engerida
parece en su verdura,
y no son sino mezclas por natura;
  do la abierta granada
por resquiebras el fruto nos descubre,
al agua tan llegada,
que, del viento impelida, en sí la encubre
y con ella jugando
los cristales están de en cuando en cuando;
  adonde la manzana,
enferma en el color, sana en el gusto,
está verde y lozana,
debido premio y por belleza justo
a Venus, una diosa,
por ser de tres opuestas más hermosa.

(Where the red cherry tree,
intertwined with the green musk pear,
thrusts into the latter
its fruit-laden branches

so they seem grafted to its greenery,
though this is no more than a natural blend;
  Where the pomegranate,
open, through chinks reveals to us its fruit
which hangs so near the water that
the wind-blown water covers it
and the crystals play with it from time to time;
  where the apple,
sickly in colour although sound in taste,
is green and vigorous,
a worthy prize, apt in its handsomeness,
for Venus, a goddess,
fairest of three rivals.)[22]

Here the poet seeks to surprise the reader with some unusual circumstances—the interlaced trees, the pomegranate in the water—and with
phenomena which arouse wonder because they are not what they
seem—the apple, whose taste belies its looks, the cherry and pear trees
which are so interwoven that they look like a new species of tree
combining the properties of both. The level of detail in the description
of items such as the split pomegranate, and the enumerative approach
of this passage is also characteristic of the baroque poets' approach as
we shall see in the next chapter.

Not only were poets extending the introductory descriptions of
Renaissance narrative poetry, and, as in the examples above, introducing
the new rhetorical ingredient of surprise, but they were also introducing
narrative themes which gave a far greater scope for the description of
nature, not merely at certain set points in the poem, but throughout.
Hence the flowering of the *fabula mitológica* at this time, following the
lead of Góngora's *Polifemo*. The classical legends were well suited to a
descriptive treatment, since they often concerned semi-human figures
who were in close contact with nature, and who became transformed into
plants, animals, rivers, and trees. The descriptive possibilities are obvious
in myths such as the rape of Europa, carried out to sea by Jupiter in the
form of a bull, or Phaeton, who tried to drive the chariot of the sun, or the
Phoenix, reborn from the flames in which it dies. And these are all
subjects to which Villamediana, for example, devoted full-scale poems.
Particular descriptive traditions began to build up around particular
myths. For example, an integral part of the story of Phaeton is the
description of the scorching of the earth when the sun's chariot passed
too close, and of the chariot itself, and the temple of the sun.[23] In the

[22] *Cancionero antequerano*, ed. D. Alonso & R. Ferreres (Madrid, 1950),
p. 296 ff., lines 19—36.
[23] A. Gallego Morell notes the recurrence of such themes in his *El mito de
Faetón en la literatura española* (Madrid, 1961), pp. 57—81.

case of the last two themes mentioned we have in a sense descriptions of nature, for their acceptability depends partly on their correspondence with our impressions of the dawn sky.

In addition to reworking the classical legends, baroque poets were also creating stories of their own in which the plot was suitably manipulated in order to allow the maximum opportunity for natural description. The plot of Góngora's *Soledades*, in which our young shipwrecked courtier is taken on a guided tour, is a case in point. Taking a leaf out of Góngora's book, Miguel de Barrios also wrote a *sylva* on a theme of his own invention, in which the outrageous manipulation of plot which allows full play to description, and the slightly too mechanical use of some of Góngora's formulae suggest that the poet was in a deliberately jocular vein. The poem describes how a lady who had set sail in search of her lover was shipwrecked on an island on which, as luck would have it, he was living. The opening shipwreck gives the poet ample opportunity to display his descriptive powers:

La derrotada Nave,
Delfín de pino, si entre espuma Ave,
Saltando sobre el cuello de una Roca,
(Por furia mucha, si por dicha poca)
Con alas de cañamo rompidas
En solo un golpe pierde muchas vidas.

(The battered ship,
A pine dolphin, though a bird amongst the foam,
Leaping upon the neck of a rock,
(Meeting great fury, though little luck)
Its canvas wings now smashed,
In one fell blow lost many lives.)[24]

When the lady eventually comes ashore, she is conveniently attacked by a serpent which is eventually killed by her lover—again a splendid subject for description.

These, then, are some of the ways in which description developed in narrative poetry. And the pattern which we shall see repeated in other kinds of poem, is the combination of different functions of description in a single poem. The one more or less constant function which is present in so many baroque poems that it may be regarded as the most characteristic feature is that of arousing surprise or wonder, as I hope to demonstrate.

2. PRAISE

Probably the commonest situation in which one finds description

---

[24] Miguel de Barrios, *Flor de Apolo* (Brussels, 1665), 35–43.

used to praise, is in love poetry where the lady's beauty is being praised. The tradition is basically Petrarchan, and begins in Spain in the sixteenth century, since the earlier *cancionero* school of poetry had interested itself far more in abstract psychological analysis than in physical description. It is because these amorous descriptions so often draw on images from nature that they fall within the scope of our investigation. The basic themes are too commonplace to need much illustration here. Eyes are stars, lips are carnations, etcetera. But one special feature of baroque poetry is the integration of these metaphors with other themes from nature. For example, in a poem such as Góngora's *Polifemo*, after the description of the island of Sicily, the description of Galatea in terms of nature seems wholly appropriate.[25] But as far as isolated images are concerned, the progress since Petrarch is not so very remarkable, bearing in mind that already in the fourteenth century he was writing:

> La testa òr fino, e calda neve il volto,
> Ebeno i cigli, e gli occhi eran due stelle,
> Ond'Amore l'arco non tendeva in fallo;
> Perle e rose vermiglie, ove l'accolto
> Dolor formava ardenti voci e belle:
> Fiamme i sospir, le lagrime cristallo.[26]

> (Her head was pure gold, her face hot snow,
> Ebony her eyebrows, and her eyes two stars,
> Wherein Cupid did not draw his bow in vain;
> All pearls and crimson roses was the place
> Where pain gathered to form ardent, lovely cries:
> Flames were her sighs, her tears, crystal.)

Apart from love poems, epithalamia and panegyrics also gave a chance to poets to praise a person by associating him with the natural world. These two genres, which were not all that often practised, though Góngora set the lead with his nuptial song in the *Soledades* and his panegyric to the Duke of Lerma, were a speciality of Francisco de Trillo y Figueroa. Trillo's poetry is not easy to read, and the notes he gives to some of his own poems show him to be the most erudite of Gongorists. His epithalamium to Francisco Ruiz de Vergara, of 1649, is a typical poem in which he exploits natural description to the full. Here his praise and his good wishes are amplified by invocations to nature to witness the marriage ceremony and to bless the couple, although it is often to the mythological representatives of natural forces that he turns. It is through fusion with the natural world that the human events gain significance, although, of course, the panegyrist

---

[25] I leave for a later chapter the question of how far there is a philosophical purpose behind this.

[26] Sonnet 157 ('Quel sempre acerbo ed onorato giorno').

will by his sophistry hint that the reverse is the case, and that nature is ennobled by its association with his illustrious patron. Thus at the start of his poem Trillo urges the river Genil not to fear meeting its end as it flows into the sea, for its waters will be reborn as the nuptial torch melts the ice on the shore, and these fresh streams, bearing the ceremonial ash, will then enrich the ocean.[27] Trillo's panegyric on the birth of the Marques de Montalbán also keeps the accent on natural description, imagining the child's future career, whether he be hunting at home, or avidly travelling to far-flung regions in pursuit of military glory. The poet is obviously conscious that some of this description might seem superfluous, as he observes of the opening of the poem in his own commentary: 'If anybody objects that this seems to be a large digression for so short a poem, let him note that it is all necessary and not superfluous, in order to introduce our subject and the causes that made him desirable.'[28] The following passage from this poem is an example of how the dynamism of Trillo's imagery heightens the impression of the marvellous which is never far from the surface in poems recounting heroic deeds:

Despues a mas edades ascendido,
quien duda que siguiendo al duro Marte,
tremolar tu Estandarte,
mas allá de si mismo vea el viento?
O bien el mar en esquadrones ciento
de Euripos inquiétos se desate,
sorviendo las montañas espaciosas,
freno poco a sus planttas tormentosas,
si el ya piadoso Cielo
no le huuiesse en la arena
empuesto feroz yugo, alta cadena,
ó bien la tierra enjugue
sus terminos prolijos dilatando
el Occeano fiero,
ya bebiendo los golfos errabundos,
hidropicos tambien ya de sus venas,
ò ya donde primero
desobauan fecundos,
numerosos aun mas que las arenas
de las arenas los sedientos hijos,
sucediendo ferozes, ò prolijos,
ya el que manchado de colores ciento,
Argos su piel, si no custodia, es graue

[27] *Obras*, ed. A. Gallego Morell (Madrid, 1951), p. 284.
[28] 'Y si alguno reparare en que parece mucha digresion en tan pequeño poema, advierta que toda es menester sin ociosidad, para poner el sugeto y causas que le hizieron deseable.' Ibid. 360.

de amante rezelosa, o fugitiua,
escandalo es del viento,
opression de la tierra,
el redil buele transformado en ave,
ó en sombras el cayado soñoliento.
Ya el que mas impaciente,
y sediento no menos,
besa la arena de la Lybia ardiente. . .

(Then, having reached maturer years,
who doubts but that as you follow hardy Mars,
the wind will see your standard flying
beyond the reach of its own bounds?
Whether the sea in a hundred squadrons
of restless Euripi becomes unleashed,
engulfing mighty mountains,
a useless barrier to its stormy path,
unless the heavens in their mercy
had not placed on it in the sand
a fierce yoke, and a lofty chain;
or whether the earth
its spacious boundaries spreading
dries up the cruel sea,
now drinking up its wandering gulfs,
now thirsting for its inmost springs;
or even if, where once
there spawned prolifically,
more numerous than the sands themselves,
the thirsty offspring of the sands,
there now replace them, fierce or huge,
now the beast who, coloured with a hundred hues,
an Argos by his coat, if not his vigilance,
laments his lover who, untrusting, flees him,
he who astounds the wind,
and subjugates the land,
whether he flies into farm pens,
transformed into a bird,
or now changed into shadows,
slips the shepherd's sleeping crook;
now the beast who, more impatient,
and no less bloodthirsty,
kisses the burning Libyan sands. . .)[29]

---

[29]   Ibid. 345. In the interests of meaningfulness I have amended to 'ya el que',
the beginning of the tenth and the third lines from the end of this extract, which
in Gallego Morell's text read 'Y a el que'.

Trillo's theme here is that his hero's prowess will triumph in any place and under any circumstances. And to exaggerate his theme he chooses some impossible places—territory beyond the reach of the wind—and some impossible circumstances. In his commentary, the poet seems rather pleased with his *argumentum ab impossibili*, and explains that the beasts alluded to near the end of our passage are tigers and lions, taking over the territory once occupied by fish.[30]

A more popular type of descriptive poem in which praise is an important rhetorical aim is the religious poem in honour of a particular saint or of Christ. An outstanding example is Adrián de Prado's *Canción Real a San Jerónimo en Suria*. The rhetorical purpose is made clear in the penultimate line:

[Canción]. . .al santo mío, que alabar pretendes, . . .'

(Ode. . .you who aim to praise my saint. . .)

And the method is to emphasize the saint's virtue by portraying in detail the austere desert scenery in which he has chosen to live as a hermit, and by describing his physical condition. But the poem is rich with fantasy. Adrián de Prado is obviously as interested in revealing nature in an exciting new way as he is in praising his saint. Nothing is too humble for the poet's attention, and he weaves fantasies around the very rocks:

Ay en aqueste yermo piedra rubia
que jamás la cabeça se a mojado,
ni su frente adornó bella guirnalda;
antes, para pedir al cielo pluuia,
tiene, desde que Dios cuerpo le a dado,
la boca abierta en medio de la espalda;
y de color de gualda,
por entre sus dos labios,
a padecer agrauios
del rubio sol y de su ardiente estoque,
sale en lugar de lengua vn alcornoque,
cuios pies corbos como pobre[s] sabios,
porque a los cielos pida agua la roca,
no le dexan jamás cerrar la boca.

(lines 43–56)

(In this wasteland stands a golden stone
whose head no rain has ever soaked,
whose brow no garland ever decked;
instead, to pray to heaven for rain,

---

[30] See op.cit. 371–2.

it has since God first gave it shape
held its mouth open in the middle
of its back; and, yellow coloured,
between both lips,
to suffer damage
from the golden sun with its burning sword
there springs a cork tree for a tongue
whose feet, as bent as wise old men,
to make the rock beg heaven for water
never let it close its mouth.)[31]

The hermit himself is described in considerable anatomical detail, but in a way which de-humanizes him and makes him just another interesting feature of the landscape:

Pensará quien le viere
en aquel sitio bronco,
que es algún seco tronco. (160–2)

(Anybody seeing him
in that rough place would think
he was some shrivelled tree-trunk.)

In a poem like this, description serves a dual purpose: to honour a saint, and to reveal at the same time a fresh and surprising picture of the natural world. This is a duality which is typical of baroque poetry, and the reader may at times find it difficult to decide whether the poet is genuinely attempting to kill two birds with one stone, or whether, although his interest is basically in the phenomena of nature, he has introduced a subsidiary rhetorical theme as a concession to literary convention. In the case of Adrián de Prado's poem there is most probably a genuine desire on the part of the poet to praise the founder of his own religious order. But it is the kind of poem which might perhaps have raised an eyebrow amongst the guardians of religious standards, if the following remark about the writers of Gongoristic sermons is to be believed:

The sermons there, falsely christened spiritual and holy, seem just like a Dutch painting, full of birds and rustic animals, of forests and woods, of gardens, springs and brooks, where just because in the corner of the canvas there is depicted, doing penance beneath a rock, a Saint Jerome no bigger than your finger, and barely noticeable, they call it the painting of Saint Jerome.[32]

[31] Blecua, *Cancionero de 1628*, pp. 207–19. See above, p. 47. The text is also available in Blecua's *Floresta de lírica española*, (Madrid, 1963), I, 258 ff.

[32] 'Aun las [pláticas] que falsamente se bautizaron con nombres de espirituales y santas aparecen allí pintadas como en paño de Flandes, que estando él lleno de pájaros y animales campesinos, de florestas, arboledas, jardines, fuentes, arroyos,

Adrián de Prado's desert landscape is something of an exception amongst poems which picture saints in a natural setting. The majority of poets, instead of showing nature as an obstacle or a test of moral fibre, amplify the praises of their saint by portraying a glorified nature which reflects the perfection of the saint or offers him its own tribute. The hermit honoured in Andrés Melero's *Canción real a San Joan Clymaco*,[33] for example, is seen as a beautiful youth in a perfect natural setting. The saint's austerity and devotion appear as an additional decorative feature rather than as something whose intensity we are asked to witness. He is described as 'bordando de aljófar sus mexillas' (line 315) ('embroidering his cheeks with pearls'), and we have the following picture of his asceticism:

Y de vno y otro poro
con la sangre que vierte en las espaldas,
de las yerbas las verdes esmeraldas
en rubíes pareçe que conuierte.

$$(318-21)$$

(And as from every pore
the blood streams from his back,
he seems to change to rubies
the emeralds of the grass).

One might question the rhetorical effectiveness of such a prettified approach to the subject, which is probably more suited to love poetry. It may be that in this particular poem the poet is primarily interested in the mechanics of ingenious description. But that a successful balance of rhetorical objectives is possible in descriptive poems of this kind is admirably illustrated by Pedro Espinosa's ode *A la navegación de San Raimundo*.[34] This poem is particularly significant since it was written before 1605, and shows that there was already a taste for descriptive poetry developing before Góngora wrote his major poems.

The poem concerns the story of Saint Raymond of Peñafort, confessor to the King of Mallorca in the thirteenth century. Legend has it that he urged the King to give up his mistress, and threatened to leave unless he did so. The king retaliated by closing all ports to him to

---

sólo porque al rincón del paño está pintado, haciendo penitencia, debajo de una peña, un San Gerónimo del tamaño de un dedo, que apenas se ve, le llaman el paño de San Gerónimo.' P. Bernardino de Villegas, *Vida de San Lutgarda* (1635), as quoted by Andrée Collard, op.cit. 83 n. In the note the text of a similar complaint by Benito Carlos Quintero is given.

[33] Blecua, *Cancionero de 1628*, pp. 418–27.

[34] *Obras*, ed. F. Rodríguez Marín (Madrid, 1909), 22–5). Blecua includes this poem in his *Floresta de lírica española*, Vol. 1, p. 224 ff.

prevent his escape, whereupon the saint made the crossing to the mainland on his cloak, and this miraculous crossing led the king to repent.[35] Espinosa takes full advantage of the dramatic possibilities of the story in the last two stanzas where there is the excitement of the pursuit, and the king's fury at his frustration, contrasting with the humility of the saint when he reaches land. And although these stanzas are less concerned with the descriptions of the seascape than the preceding ones, they offer a good example of the narrative function of description in which the excitement of the moment is captured through the visual characteristics of the scene: the billowing sails, the mass of foam as the boats rush through the water, the way the oarsmen dig their oars in, the sweat streaming from their brows, and the rage showing itself on the king's red face. But even in the first four stanzas, which form a coherent group and describe the colourful scene at sea, the poet maintains a sense of drama through his portrayal of the rather daunting figure of Neptune who rushes to meet the saint.

On the one hand, then, Espinosa offers a vivid and dramatic narrative, and on the other, he delights in describing in an exciting way the colours of the sea and sky at dawn, this latter aspect of his poetry being the one which is usually concentrated on by the critics. But this description is none the less directed towards perhaps the poet's main rhetorical objective in the poem—his desire to praise the saint. What the reader witnesses is not beauty for its own sake, but a scene in which nature is self-consciously beautiful, and in which all the participants are deliberately displaying their most splendid attributes in order to honour the saint. The point of all this splendour is summarized at the end of the fourth stanza:

> Y tu, Raimundo, sobre el pobre manto,
> Miras la fiesta, en tanto,
> Que hace a tu santísima persona
> El turquesado mar de Barcelona.

> (And you, Raymond, on your humble cloak,
> observe the while the fiesta given
> to your most holy person by
> the turquoise Barcelona sea.)

We have, in fact, a celebration. Thus, when Neptune's chariot plunges into the sea, throwing up foam, this is not seen as a haphazard occurence, but as something deliberately done—'por más gala' ('for greater display'), the poet tells us. And when the dolphins throw up spouts of water we can be sure that they are doing so as a salute to the saint. Even the old

[35] See Fray Andrés Pérez, *Historia de la vida y milagros del glorioso Sant Raymundo de Peñafort* (Salamanca, 1601).

man himself enters into the party spirit:

Las canas, por más ornato, aforra
de una arrugada concha, en vez de gorra.

(To add to the splendour, he tucks his white hair
in a curly shell instead of a hat)

So far we have discussed poems in which the objects of praise are people. But the baroque fascination with nature is revealed even more strongly in the emergence for the first time of poems in which natural phenomena themselves are praised and provide the overt subject. It is not easy to find examples of such poems before the end of the sixteenth century,[36] but in the following century they abound.

A number of Francisco de Rioja's *silvas* fall within this category, as is revealed by their titles—'A la rosa', 'Al clavel', 'Al jazmín', 'Al verano'.[37] Rioja seems to have been something of a pioneer in the field, and his relative simplicity and directness probably place him nearer to Meléndez Valdés than to Góngora.[38] One may contrast Rioja's *silva* 'Al verano', for example, with that of the Aragonese Gongorist, Matías Ginovés. Rioja's poem begins with a description of relatively general characteristics of Summer, some of which seem more appropriate to Spring than to Summer as such. But there is some attempt to build up a sense of situation when he talks of the blossom on the trees which promises fruit to come:

En la copia de flores que aparece
por los troncos desnudos
que rara y breve hoja cubre apenas. . .[39]

(In the host of blossom that appears
along the bare tree-trunks
scarcely covered by the sparse, small leaves)

It would, of course, have been more convincing if Rioja had referred to the branches rather than the trunks as being covered in blossom, and if his poem had been about Spring rather than Summer. The poet then bursts out with enthusiasm:

Oh, cómo es el verano
Tiempo el más genial y más humano
Que otro alguno que da el volver del cielo!

[36] One may perhaps regard Fray Luis de León's ode, 'Cuando contemplo al cielo', as one such poem, although it has an obvious didactic function, and does not merely praise the heavens.

[37] See *Poetas líricos de los siglos xvi y xvii*, I, ed. A. de Castro, *BAE*, 32 (Madrid, 1950), pp. 381–2.

[38] See L.A. Cueto, 'Bosquejo histórico-crítico de la poesía castellana en el siglo xviii', *BAE*, 61, cxxxiii.

[39] Castro, op.cit. 383.

Oh cuál número y cuánto trae de flores!
Oh cuál admiración en sus colores!

. . . .

Oh florido verano!
Si a mi afecto se debe,
Camina a lento paso. . .

(Oh, how much more genial and human a season
is the Summer time
than any other which the turning heavens bring!
How many and varied are its flowers!
How wonderful their colours!

. . . .

Oh flowery Summer,
if my fondness merits it,
pass by slowly. . .)

The poem then concludes with the familiar 'Carpe diem' theme, encouraging a friend to enjoy himself while he may. There is nothing here
which would have seemed out of place in an eighteenth-century context.

The approach of Matías Ginovés in his ode to Summer is quite
different, and far more typical of the seventeenth-century treatment of
nature.[40] There is little direct expression of the author's enthusiasm,
but the enthusiasm is nevertheless very strongly communicated by his
treatment of his theme. Every aspect of nature he considers gives rise
to an ingenious metaphor, so that we are presented with a world full
of surprises. Nearly two-thirds of the poem consists of a list of fruits
and flowers, the characteristics of each of which are described in a
novel way. And the sense of delight which communicates itself to the
reader is partly due to the fact that the Poet does not complicate the
syntax, and derives his metaphors not so much from the world of
learning as from witty observation and fantasy. For example, in the
following passage the apricot is described as a kind of frustrated peach,
and the variety of plums is described satirically in terms of variations
in human society:

Y[a] entre las esmeraldas de sus ojas
de púrpura se tiñe el albercoque,
tan grande y tan sabroso,
que por dulçe y loçano
pretende ser melocotón temprano,
(que al fin asta los árboles pretenden

---

[40]   For the text see Blecua, *Cancionero de 1628*, 194–207.

ya aun para bien lograr sus pretensiones
ramirrotos reparten varios dones);
pero los albercoques,
aunque a melocotones aspiraron,
al fin se contentaron
con ser enanos, que preceden antes
de los melocotones más jigantes.
Luego, la multitud de la ciruelas,
varias en el pellejo,
comiença a colorar su verde hollejo;
vnas por ser de monjas enfadosas,
otras por ser de damas melindrosas
y otras que, patitiessas,
por lo que son de frayles, viuen gruessas.

(lines 261–280)

(Now among the emeralds of its leaves
the apricot is tinged with red,
so large and luscious
that in sweetness and profusion
it aims to be an early peach
(for even trees can be ambitious,
and to achieve their aims they even
hand out, broken-branched, assorted bribes);
but the apricots,
though they aspired to peachdom
in the end were satisfied
with being dwarves who come before
the more gigantic peaches.
Then the multitude of plums
all varied in their skins
begin to tinge the greenness of their skin;
some, as vexatious as nuns,
others, as prudish as ladies,
and others which, stiff-limbed,
like monks live a fat life.)

Ginovés' poem is one of four he addressed to the seasons,[41] and there were other poets equally eager to pay their homage to the seasons. For example, Juan Montero's 'Silva a el otoño' is a descriptive poem full of nature's riches, though lacking much of the ingenuity of Ginovés. One of the problems for the poet writing in the new descriptive genres seems to have been how to bring his poem to a convincing conclusion.

---

[41] All four were published anonymously in 1688, and later appeared amongst an eighteenth-century edition of Gracián's works. See Blecua, op.cit. 24.

All Montero can do at the end of his poem is to declare rather tamely:

Con esto me pareze ya que puedo
diuino Otoño recojer mi Pluma.[42]

(And now I think, sweet Autumn,
I can lay down my pen.)

Gutierre Lobo, a fellow poet from Granada, concludes his 'Silva a el estío' with a reference to his cruel lady, which, coming as it does at the end of three hundred lines of unrelated description, fails to make much impact.[43] Again, we can sense the awkwardness experienced by the poet in tackling a new genre.

A poet more adept at handling the theme of the praise of nature was Miguel Colodrero de Villalobos, who seems to have been friendly with Lope de Vega, Pérez de Montalbán, and Soto de Rojas, to judge by the prefatory sonnets they wrote for him.[44] His *silva* beginning 'Albergaban al Sol, ledos fulgores' is a good example of a descriptive poem of over 300 lines which starts off with no definite explicit theme, which accumulates many examples of the richness and variety of nature in a series of images some of which convey a strong feeling of wonder,[45] and which ultimately goes on to make explicit the implicit theme of the praise of nature, linking it with the idea of the morally improving effect of rural solitude. For example, the poet, admitting his own predilections, says: 'Muchas vezes montañas, me dedico/A la alabança vuestra.'[46]

He returns to the plains in the closing lines of his poem, and this enables him to finish on the paradoxical theme of the lowlands as a route to heaven:

O llanos, encumbradamente hermosos
Que para el cielo sois itinerosos.

---

[42] *Las estaciones del año*, ed. A. Rodríguez Moñino (Valencia, 1949), p. 63. This is one of four poems selected from a whole collection about the four seasons appearing in the manuscript *Poetica Silva*.

[43] *Las estaciones del año*, 41–53.

[44] Miguel Colodrero de Villalobos, *Varias rimas*, (Córdoba, 1629).

[45] e.g.   El Sylgero de plumas ramillete
            Que parece bolando
            Sonoramente Rosicler errando,
            Aui culto promete,
            Suspension al oydo menos blando.

      (The goldfinch, a bouquet of feathers,
      which seems as it tunefully flies
      like the pink of the dawn on the move,
      promises with his polished song
      to enrapture the harshest of ears.)
                                        Colodrero, op.cit. 51.

[46] Colodrero, op.cit. 61 ('Mountains, how often I devote myself/to your praise').

(Oh plains, loftily beautiful,
who offer us a route to heaven!)

We have seen poems in praise of people and those in praise of nature. One way in which the two could be combined is illustrated by a poem of Quevedo's describing the country retreat of a nobleman, his *silva* beginning 'Este de los demás sitios Narciso'.[47] Here we have another poem in which the rhetorical aim of surprising the reader is just as prominent as the desire to praise. The conceits show a Gongoristic side to Quevedo's poetic personality which is often ignored. See, for example, lines 26–32:

Sus calles, que encanecen azucenas,
de fragrante vejez se muestran llenas,
y el jazmín, que de leche perfumado
es estrella olorosa,
y en la güerta espaciosa,
el ruido de sus hojas en el suelo
la Vía Láctea contrahace al cielo

(Its paths, which are white-haired with lilies,
are full of a fragrant old-age,
and the jasmine is a scented star
of perfumed milk,
the sound of whose petals on the ground
within the spacious orchard
imitates the Milky Way in heaven.)[48]

These, then, are some of the ways in which the description of nature was used to praise people or things. Often this rhetorical aim is combined with that of surprising and delighting. And the special contribution of the baroque is the development of the type of poem in which nature herself is the primary object of praise.

3. PERSUASION OR DISSUASION

Of those poems in which the rhetorical purpose of natural description is to persuade, probably the bulk have a moral purpose. On the small scale, one can find a number of relatively short poems which take phenomena of nature as *exempla*. Francisco de Trillo's fourth sonnet is an example:

En vna sobre el mar caida roca,
Que vn monte de las ondas carcomido
Auia de su cumbre sacudido,
Much auiso escondiendo en ruyna poca. . .

[47] *Obras completas*, ed. J.M. Blecua, I (Barcelona, 1963), 233–6.
[48] The presumably inaudible sound is akin to that of the music of the spheres, which was so fine as to be inaudible to man's gross hearing.

(On a rock now fallen in the sea,
which a mountain gnawed at by the waves
had buffeted down from its peak
concealing in a little ruin a great lesson. . .)[49]

Trillo seems to have been particularly fascinated by the sea, which he never tires of describing. Another marine poem of his with a moral slant is his fourth *romance*, entitled 'A la ambición de los que nauegan', in which a fisherman attempts three times unsuccessfully to reach an underwater cave by diving, whereupon a mermaid delivers him a lecture on the folly of attempting to penetrate the sacred house of the sea-god, and points out the wreckage of ships which have previously come to grief on the same rocks.[50]

On the large scale, there are poems which set out to persuade the reader of the moral and other benefits of life in the country. The poets are here building on the tradition of which Fray Luis de León's ode 'A la vida retirada' is an obvious example. But the novelty of the seventeenth-century poets in this field is that they stress the positive attractions of the country in a way which makes nature seem completely fresh and surprising. Pedro Espinosa's *Soledad de Pedro Jesús* is an example of a didactic poem of this kind. It takes the form of an ode addressed by a hermit to a friend, and contains some genuine devotional material, including a colloquy to Christ in the fifth, sixth, and seventh stanzas, and a prayer to the Virgin later in the poem, with a psalm which was later added to the text. But in the centre of the poem there are eleven stanzas describing what delights nature has to offer. One can see a conscious pursuit of novelty in the descriptions, and the fusion of the two rhetorical functions of persuading and surprising. But the two objectives are perfectly fused, since it is precisely through revealing the surprising novelty of nature that the poet makes it seem persuasively attractive. Rather than opposing the riches of nature with those found in civilized society, Espinosa links the two, and describes nature in terms of civilization. Thus the creepers which entwine the trees are seen as a kind of fantastic art form, and here he draws on a technical vocabulary with which his practice as an artist had doubtless acquainted him:

Ven y verás por estos valles frescos
Ensortijados lazos y follajes
Y, brillando, floridos arabescos
Prender espigas, trasflorar celajes;
Estofados subientes de grutescos
Arbolando cogollos y plumajes;

[49]   Trillo, *Obras*, p. 6.
[50]   Trillo, op.cit. 49–52.

Prósperos tallos de elegantes vides
Trepando en ondas el bastón de Alcides.[51]

(Come, and you shall see in these cool valleys
curly knots and leaf motifs,
and, brightly shining, florid arabesques
dressing flower spikes, and tracing cloud patterns;
gilt ornaments in grotesque ascending
supporting relievos and crests;
thriving shoots of elegant vines
climbing in waves up Hercules' stick.)

The ingenuity of this passage lies in the double meaning of some words. *Cogollo*, for example, means both a tree-top and a particular type of architectural ornament. *Follaje* is both a botanical and an architectural term. Similarly, what more appropriate verb than *arbolar* to describe the raising up of these various ornaments, since it is the trees—*los árboles* —which provide the support? And the plumage referred to may be thought of as an artistic crest, or we may think of it in terms of the plumage of the birds who are up in the trees.

Espinosa goes on to describe the view from a high rock in terms of a Dutch oil-painting:

Y siendo superior de cosas grandes
Habrás visto pintado vivo a Flandes.

(op.cit. 75)

(And finding yourself above great things,
you will have seen all Flanders painted live.)

And the cave is seen as civilized accommodation, with its floor of jasper, and its tapestry of ivy. In the poem as a whole, the impression of strange beauty is enhanced by the vocabulary, which is very exotic by the standards of the time.

Another remarkable poem, which seeks to persuade a friend to join the poet and his companion in the countryside is Polo de Medina's *Ocios de la soledad* (1633). The poem is brimming with ingenious images, discussion of which I defer until later chapters where specific techniques of arousing wonder are discussed. Suffice it to say here that this is another poem in which persuasion and surprise are combined.

Góngora's *Soledades* is another poem in which one can see the same fusion of rhetorical objectives. The freshness of Góngora's vision of nature enhances the moral theme of the superiority of country life. It is not easy to judge how important the moral aspect of the *Soledades* was to Góngora, for the theme of rural superiority was commonplace

[51] *Obras*, ed.cit. 73–4.

enough for it merely to have been used as a peg on which to hang other ideas. And when in the first *Soledad* we see the old man complaining bitterly about the greed of modern society, we do not of necessity have to regard this as Góngora's own view. It is just as feasible to accept this as a character sketch of a rather bitter old man who is biased against sailing because he has lost a son at sea. But it is reasonable to assume that Góngora is inviting us to share some of the wonder of the shipwrecked youth, and hence to be persuaded that there is something admirable in the simple way of life.

Persuasion is also a common feature in the imagery from nature found in love poetry. For example, one may find in the pastoral love poem a lover offering fruits and flowers in order to persuade his lady to accept him. There is a classical tradition here, derived from Virgil, and from the song of Poliphemus in Ovid's *Metamorphoses*. In the seventeenth century, the treatment becomes more expansive, and the list of natural products become longer, so that one has once again a balancing of different rhetorical objectives, and a desire to reveal nature in a new light as well as to offer an exercise in persuasion. Since this enumerative tradition is examined in some detail in the next chapter, precise examples are deferred until then.

4. AWAKENING SYMPATHY

The use of natural description to move or arouse sympathy is again something found quite frequently in sixteenth-century poetry, particularly in the pastoral. One of the most common themes is the description of nature in order to stress the lover's isolation from the world in his misery. Petrarch's *canzone*, 'Nella stagion che'l ciel rapido inchina' is a model for this particular theme. On the whole, baroque poets contribute little of value to the tradition, since where the descriptions become longer the rhetorical purpose tends to get forgotten, until one finds the extraordinary imbalance of a poem like Francisco de Trillo's 'pintura de la noche', already mentioned, where the primary aim is obviously to describe nature rather than the poet's amorous sentiments.

Another method of using natural description to heighten the emotions is for the poet to emphasize his plight by portraying himself in a gloomy or hostile environment. Fernando de Herrera was particularly adept at depicting barren, often deliberately symbolic, landscapes, albeit within the narrow confines of the sonnet.[52] The tradition is again a Petrarchan one.[53] Luis de Ulloa y Pereira shows how this

---

[52] See, for example, sonnet 35 ('Por un camino, solo, al Sol abierto'), *Poesías*, ed. V. García de Diego (Madrid, 1952), p. 72., the opening of which is rather reminiscent of La Fontaine's fable 'Le coche et la mouche'.

[53] Compare Petrarch's sonnet 'Solo e pensoso i più deserti campi/Vo misurando a passi tardi e lenti'.

theme could be developed in a way which exploited the descriptive
possibilities to the full in a poem in which, an exile in misery, he
addresses 'una dama muy entendida, y de muy buena voz.'

Atiende aora las humildes vozes,
Que el sentimiento anima,
Entre la escarcha del vezino Polo,

. . . .

Con pavorosos silvos amenaça
El aire, de suaues,
Y numerosos ecos despoblado,
Y solo le embaraça,
De las nocturnas aues,
El bolar triste, y el gemir pesado,
El misero ganado,
Que en el hielo sediento,
De la inundada tierra
Los manantiales yerra,
Y por la selva ignora el alimento,
oculta de la niebe.
Pace en el agua, y en la tierra bebe.
Emulo siempre de mi amargo llanto
El cielo proceloso,
No se despeja de nubes frias,
Y si se serena tanto,
Que al semblante nubloso,
Luzes permite escasas, y sombrias
En los lobregos dias,
Tan veloz al Ocaso
El Sol se precipita,
Y quando resucita,
Tan lento mueue el pereçoso paso,
Y tan tarde amanece,
Que todo es noche, ó todo lo parece.[54]

(Attend now to my humble words,
emotionally inspired
among the nearby Pole's hoar-frosts.

. . . .

The wind with terrifying whistles
threatens, now bereft

[54] *Prosas y versos* (Madrid, 1674), 152–3.

of sweet and tuneful echoes,
and plagued instead with the sad flight
and the baleful moan
of nocturnal birds.
The miserable herd,
wandering thirsty on the ice
cannot find the springs
of the flooded land,
And in the woods it does not see the food
hid beneath the snow.
It tries to eat the water and drink the land.
Ever emulating my harsh tears,
the tempestuous sky
is never free from clouds.
And if it clears enough
to allow on its cloudy face
some shadowy, meagre lights,
in these dark days
the sun doth plunge
so swiftly in the sea,
and moves its way so slowly
when it doth revive,
and dawns so late,
that everything is night, or so it seems.)

The 'nocturnas aues' have obviously migrated from Polifemo's cave, and other aspects of this passage reflect an approach to description similar to that of Góngora. Ulloa, like Góngora, surprises his readers with paradoxes and seeming impossibilities. There is the irony of the animals being thirsty although the land is flooded, and the strong metaphors used to describe the herd's confusion on finding the snow hiding everything—'Pace en el agua, y en la tierra bebe'—shows a confusion between different elements which, as we shall see in Chapter Five, is a powerful source of wit in many baroque poems.

Ulloa's interest in the gloomier aspects of nature perhaps reflects a genuine distaste for country life.[55] It is interesting to see him take a stand quite contrary to that of most poets in seeking to argue that life lived close to nature is dull, uncivilized, and a waste of man's talents:

Aquellos en Abril verdes despojos,
Que se miran teñidos del Estio,
En el Octubre palidos y rojos,
Y cuanto viue del humor del rio

[55] See Josefina G. Araez, *Don Luis de Ulloa y Pereira* (Madrid, 1952), p. 70.

En la buelta del Sol accelerada
Lo matiza el calor, lo borra el frio.
Y una vez aduertida, ó contemplada,
La nouedad malogra los primores,
Y queda la atencion desconsolada,
Descifrando a las fuentes los rumores,
Entendiendo por señas a las plantas,
Oyendo por alientos a las flores.
Y contemplando variedades quantas
Se ven de brutos tardos, y velozes,
Que pueden enseñar rudezas tantas.
Bramar, ladrar, gemir; son vnas vozes,
Que contienen aguero en el sonido,
Y solo pronunciadas son ferozes:
Daráse entre las fieras por vencido
Lo racional, y para introducirse,
La humana voz se bolverá bramido.[56]

(Those once green spoils of April
you see tinged in the Summer,
and in October, pale and red,
and all things that depend upon the river-water,
as the sun hastens through its cycle
are browned by the heat, then destroyed by the cold.
Once noted or considered, novelty
no longer can achieve its master-strokes,
and our attention's left disconsolate,
deciphering the murmurings of the springs,
and grasping the sign-language of the plants,
and listening to the flowers with our noses,
gazing, too, upon as many species
as can be seen of swift or sluggish brutes,
each with coarse habits no less numerous.
Roars, barks, and howls are utterances
that bring foreboding with their sound,
ferocious in themselves, whenever voiced.
Amongst wild beasts, the rational
must count itself defeated, and man's voice
must take to roaring, if it would be heard.)

As far as Ulloa is concerned, then, nature's secrets are soon exhausted, and man puts his rationality in jeopardy by consorting with sub-human creatures. Ulloa goes on to criticize the traditional view that the

---

[56] Ulloa, op.cit. 80.

countryside is the most appropriate place for moral reflection by arguing that human nature remains the same even in less peaceful surroundings:

No menos que en los paramos remotos
de nuestras almas las celestes lumbres
lucen entre tumultos, y alborotos.

(No less than in the wilderness
our soul's celestial light shines forth
mid tumults and disturbances.)

He concludes that since man is the noblest part of the creation he is in any case a more worth object of study than, for example, plant life.

5. AMUSEMENT

One novel feature of baroque poetry is the use of natural description in satirical poetry, where its function is to amuse the reader. Sometimes the humour is that of parody, in which descriptive techniques are themselves held up to ridicule. For example, one industrious poet produced a quite creditable satire on the Gongorist descriptive poem, in which he describes in an inflated style the flooding of the river Tormes. The author's purpose is perhaps not merely to poke fun at pomposity of style, but also to attack the whole attempt to write poems of stature about natural phenomena.[57]

Another interesting work, with a particularly revealing title, is Agustín de Salazar y Torres' four burlesque *silvas* in which the poet 'discourses on the theatre of human life, from dawn to dusk, through the four seasons of the day, not forgetting the harsh ingratitude of his beloved Marica, to whom he dedicates this treatise'.[58] The fact that in the very title the poet's reference to his cruel lady has no obvious relevance to such a grandiose scheme and seems to be added almost as an afterthought is surely a comment on the kind of descriptive poems we have already noted in which the poet, very late in the poem, makes the feeble gesture of referring to his beloved after many lines of totally unrelated natural description. The major source of humour in the text of Salazar's poems themselves is in the use of a low style and anthropomorphic images to describe natural phenomena. At the start, for example, Dawn is described as a housewife dressed in a slipshod manner, doing the cleaning.

---

[57] See Blecua, *Cancionero de 1628*, 467–73 for the text—some 200 lines long—of this anonymous poem.

[58] 'Discurre el autor en el teatro de la vida humana, desde que amanece hasta que anochece, por las cuatro estaciones del día, no olvidando la fiera ingratitud de su amada Marica, á quién ofrece este tratado,' *Cythara de Apolo* (Madrid, 1681), pp. 67–104.

Quevedo, too, poked fun at descriptive poetry, and at the kind of poem which he himself was not averse to writing. There is a series of four satirical poems addressed to beasts celebrated in legend—the Phoenix, the Pelican, the Basilisk, and the Unicorn.[59] Each of these *romances* begins by listing a whole string of attributes belonging to the relevant beast, each wittily expressed.

> Tú, que vuelas con zafiros;
> tú, que con rubíes picas,
> guardajoyas de las llamas,
> donde naciste tan linda;
> tú, que a puras muertes vives,
> los médicos te lo invidian
> donde en cuna y sepultura
> el fuego te resucita. . .

> (You, who fly with sapphires;
> you, who peck with rubies,
> jewel-cases for the flames
> in which was born your beauty;
> you, who live from pure deaths,
> the doctors envy you
> when in cradle and grave
> fire revivifies you.)

Thus runs part of Quevedo's poem on the Phoenix. After some seventy lines of description in this vein, he adds:

> ansí de cansarte dejen
> similitudes prolijas
> que de lisonja en lisonja
> te apodan y te fatigan.

> (Enough of lengthy similes
> that tire you in this way,
> with flattery on flattery
> dubbing you, exhausting you.)[60]

Other satirical descriptive poems can be found which unlike our earlier examples, are not so much concerned with satire of the descriptive genres as with describing in a humorous way fantasies involving flowers or other creatures of nature. For example, Quevedo stages a slanging match between the flowers and the vegetables, a contest which might seem medieval in its conception, but which in so far as the descriptions go is wholly characteristic of the seventeenth century in its ingenious humour. For example, one of the protagonists is

[59] *Obras completas*, I, 790–7.   [60] Ibid. 792.

La Azucena carilarga,
que en zancos verdes se sube
y, dueña de los jardines,
de tocas blancas se cubre.[61]

(The long-faced lily,
high on green stilts,
duenna of the gardens,
dressed in her white bonnet.)

This kind of humorous attribution of human qualities to some of nature's humbler products can be seen in the tradition of Góngora's charming *Romance del Palacio de la Primavera*, an immensely popular poem, in which the Rose is pictured as a queen surrounded by her courtiers.[62]

Once again, in this kind of poem we can see that the rhetorical aim of surprising the reader by presenting a fresh vision of nature is very much to the fore.

6. SURPRISE AND WONDER

I have left until last discussion of the function which seems to me above all to characterise the descriptive poetry of the period. We have already seen how persistent and important an ingredient is a sense of surprise or wonder in baroque descriptive poems which seek to narrate, praise, persuade, move, or amuse. Many of our examples might equally well have been included in this section. Many more examples I defer until Chapters Four and Five in which I examine specific techniques of conveying wonder which again are common to the different kinds of poem we have outlined. I shall therefore restrict myself here to considering just a few examples of poems which do not obviously fit into the categories we have already discussed.

One kind of poem which seems to have as its main function the excitement of wonder is that which takes as its theme some single aspect of the creation—a flower, a bird, the stars—and describes it with little or no comment with a whole string of conceits. We have already seen comic examples of this kind of thing in Quevedo's four *romances* devoted to mythical beasts. But some other poems take themselves a little more seriously so that one cannot really say that their primary aim is to amuse. A good example of the genre is the anonymous *Romance a las estrellas* in the *Cancionero de 1628*:

Innumerables estrellas,
ornamento al alto Olimpo,

---

[61] Ibid. 1014.

[62] Góngora, *Obras completas*, ed. Millé, No 61. See also D. Alonso, *Góngora y el Polifemo*, I, 308.

ministrando claues de oro
a sus puertas de Jacinto.
Flores al celeste campo,
y diamantes al vestido,
de la noche vagas luces
al monumento de Cintio,
. . . .[63]

(Innumerable stars,
ornament of high Olympus,
providing keys of gold
to its gates of hyacinth.
Flowers in the celestial field,
and diamonds on the gown of night,
wandering lights upon
the monument of Cynthus,
. . . .)

The poem continues in similar vein for eighty lines, concluding thus:

Y con tantos atributos,
más, estrellas, os estimo,
por imitar vnos ojos,
dulçe objeto de los míos.

(Despite these many attributes,
I think more of you, stars,
for copying two eyes,
sweet objects of my own.)

The phrase 'os estimo' at the end of the poem makes explicit the sense of admiration which has progressively built up in the course of the poem as compliment succeeds compliment, and the concluding lines ingeniously seek to divert all this admiration to the poet's lady.

Quevedo's own *Himno a las estrellas*, although it is nearer to a love poem than the anonymous *romance* already quoted, has the same unmistakable tone in its opening stanzas, and the same rhetorical aim:

A vosotras, estrellas,
alza el vuelo mi pluma temerosa,
del piélago de luz ricas centellas;
lumbres que enciende triste y dolorosa
a las exequias del difunto día,
güérfana de su luz, la noche fría;
ejército de oro,
. . . .[64]

---

[63] Blecua, op.cit. 437.   [64] *Obras*, I, 428–30.

(To you, oh stars, my quill
takes off in timorous flight,
rich sparks within the sea of light;
funerary torches
for the departed day
lit sad and mournfully
by the chilly night,
the orphan of its light.
Golden host. . . .)

Quevedo's *décima* to the nightingale is in the same familiar vein:

Flor con voz, volante flor
silbo alado, voz pintada,
lira de pluma animada
y ramillete cantor.[65]

(Vocal flower, flying flower,
wingèd whistle, painted voice,
lyre of animated feathers,
singing nosegay.)

It is significant that the Italian poet Giambattista Marino, who was highly conscious of wonder as a primary rhetorical aim, seems to have directly influenced these poems with his *canzonetta, Le Stelle*, and his *Adone*.[66]

Brilliant but lightweight might be a fair verdict on these poems which consist in the enumeration of attributes. But for an example of a full-scale poem of greater depth which also has the same aim of arousing wonder we need look no further, I believe, than Góngora's *Soledades*. Clearly with a poem of such seminal importance as this, if we can demonstrate that the marvellous is one of the primary preoccupations of the poet this will be an important step in our argument. The remainder of this chapter, then, will be devoted to this question.

If poetic wit entails the tracing of surprising relationships, then in saying that Góngora was preoccupied with the marvellous we might seem to be merely restating the obvious—that he, like so many of his contemporaries, enjoyed wit. But my argument aims to take matters much further than this. Firstly, there are conceits and conceits. The sense of the marvellous is not equally strong in all, and, as I hope to demonstrate in Chapter Five, one notable feature of Góngora's imagery

---

[65] *Obras*, I, 238.

[66] See J.V. Mirollo, *The Poet of the Marvelous: Giambattista Marino* (New York and London, 1963); Marino, *Poesie varie*, ed. Croce (Bari, 1913), pp. 361–2; and J.G. Fucilla, who notes the influence of a passage from the *Adone* on Quevedo's poem to the nightingale, 'Riflessi dell' Adone di G.B. Marino nelle poesie di Quevedo', *Romania* (1962), 279–87.

is his use of conceits which epitomize the marvellous. Secondly, wit is not the only vehicle for communicating wonder: another approach is indicated in my next Chapter. But in the following paragraphs I shall restrict myself to the most obvious method which Góngora uses to suggest to the reader that wonder is an appropriate response to the things he describes. This is to show us the reactions of the characters in the poem to what they see, and in particular the reactions of the young courtier whose shipwreck has thrust him into a completely new world.

The very suggestion that the young man in the *Soledades* might show any reaction at all appears to be something of a novelty. Traditionally, he has been viewed as a neutral observer, acting out his role without any display of emotion. For example, Dámaso Alonso writes that Góngora 'does not present us with the wanderer's emotions as he faces the natural world; he leaves him vague, as merely the thread holding together the sketchy plot, and places directly before our eyes nature herself.'[67] M. Molho similarly states that there is nothing human about Góngora's world, and goes on to describe the wanderer as a 'protagoniste mystérieux, spectateur neutre dont l'intériorité échappe.'[68] Such beliefs seem to be based more on *a priori* considerations than on a reading of the text. In view of the general insistence on the impassivity of Góngora's poetry, it is worth stressing that the emotional attitudes of the characters in his poetry are generally quite clearly defined, and are not noticeably abnormal or inhuman. Robert Jammes has rectified some of the old prejudices in his analysis of Góngora's *Polifemo* as a poem showing considerable subtlety in its psychology.[69] The poet's interest in his characters' psychology is no less important in the *Soledades*.

Firstly, we have the wanderer's emotional reactions to his past life, and his sensitivity in matters of love. It is with a tearful lament that he first enters the poem (line 10), and his tears all but flow again when later the sight of the beautiful peasant bride reminds him of his own unrequited love (I, 734–49). The tearful song he sings when he sets out in a boat in the second *Soledad* (II, 115–172), is far from impassive.

[67] *Estudios y ensayos gongorinos*, 71.

[68] 'Soledades', *Bulletin Hispanique*, 62 (1960), pp. 250–1.

[69] 'Que Góngora ait consacré 160 vers–160 vers denses comme l'or–à décrire et prolonger cet instant délicieux, la naissance de l'amour dans le coeur d'une vierge, prouve à quel point il était séduit par ce thème: on s'étonne, que toute une critique moderne s'entête à faire de lui, unilatéralement, une espèce de Parnassien avant la lettre, un poète marmoréen et insensible, uniquement préoccupé de sonorités et de couleurs,' *Études sur l'œuvre poétique de Don Luis de Góngora y Argote* (Bordeaux, 1967), p. 543.

The peasants in the *Soledades* are equally sensitive. For example, the goatherd who shows the visitor some ruins from a hilltop does so 'con muestras de dolor extraordinarias' (I, 214) ('with extraordinary signs of pain'). The old man who buttonholes the young man at the wedding feast, and who might be described as the Ancient Non-mariner, is quite unable to control his emotions in his vigorous outburst against seafaring. Not only is he described as 'de Lágrimas los tiernos ojos llenos' (I, 360) ('his tender eyes filled with tears'), but he is unable to complete his speech because he breaks down:

> En suspiros con esto,
> y en más anegó lágrimas el resto
> de su discurso el montañes prolijo
>
> (I, 503–5)

> (whereupon with sobs and further tears
> the garrulous man of the mountains
> blotted out the rest of his harangue)

Góngora pursues the old man's emotional state in some detail, and shows how he is so disturbed that he is unable to appreciate the delights of nature:

> No céfiros en él, no ruiseñores
> lisonjear pudieron breve rato
> al montañés, que—ingrato
> al fresco, a la armonía y a las flores—
> del sitio pisa ameno
> la fresca hierba, cual la arena ardiente
> de la Libia. . .
>
> (I, 592–8)

> (No zephyrs in the trees, no nightingales,
> were able to distract even a while
> the mountain-dweller, unreceptive to
> the shade, the harmony, the flowers,
> walking the green grass of that beauty-spot
> as if it were the burning sands of Libia.)

And while the other guests are enjoying the celebrations, he is pessimistically considering the risk of fire from the nuptial torches.[70]

The presence of all these negative emotions should not, however, draw our attention from the very positive reaction of the wanderer to his new environment. His response in one of gratitude,[71] and, above all, of pleasant surprise. For example, his first excursion is with the goatherd, who takes him to a nearby hilltop, where he is amazed by

---

[70] *Soledades*, I, 653–8.
[71] See *Soledad* I, 182, 531.

the view:

Llegó, y, a vista tanta
obedeciendo la dudosa planta,
inmóvil se quedó sobre un lentisco,
verde balcón del agradable risco.

(I, 190–3)

(Now having reached the top,
his halting steps obedient to the view,
he stood stock-still above a mastic tree
that formed the pleasant cliff's green balcony.)

The strength of the reaction is suggested by the words 'dudosa planta' and 'inmóvil', which indicate that the experience has a physical impact. This point emerges even more strongly a few lines later, where, referring directly to the stranger's amazement, Góngora picture him as dumbstruck:

Muda, la admiración habla callando.

(Wonder, dumbstruck, speaks by keeping silent.)

This image, which is an interesting indication that people at this time did have their breath taken away by a good view, is not the only one in which Góngora introduces a strong metaphor personifying wonder. The reaction of those watching the athletics display in the first *Soledad* is described thus:

La admiración, vestida un mármol frío,
apenas arquear las cejas pudo.

(I, 999–1000)

(Wonder, frozen into marble,
scarce could even raise its eyebrows.)

Góngora could scarcely have pitched it higher. Here, the amazement is so extreme that even the normal physical sign of surprise is inhibited, and the personification of wonder makes the image even stronger. Again, the expression of wonder when the young man and his companion pause during their boat trip to admire a beautiful building is heightened by the use of a physical image:

La admiración que al arte se le debe,
áncora del batel fue.

(II, 706–7)

(Their boat was anchored by the wonder
which we owe to art.)

These images were all too much for Jáuregui, who scorned them in his attack on the *Soledades*.[72] But they are not the only ones which seek to show surprise. For example, Góngora describes the young man's surprise when the goatherd, whose speech he has been enjoying,[73] joins a passing wolf-hunt with great abandon:

Bajaba entre sí el joven admirando,
armado a Pan o semicapro a Marte.

(I, 233–4)

(The youth descended, inwardly amazed,
to see Pan bearing arms,
or Mars become half goat.)

Another source of wonder for him is the sumptuous scenery, rivalling the finery of the court:

...Admira cortesano
—a pesar del estambre y de la seda—
el que tapiz frondoso
tejió de verdes hojas la arboleda.

(I, 714–17)

(Despite being a courtier,
used to fine wool and silk,
he wondered at the frondent tapestry
woven by the wood with its green leaves.)

In the second *Soledad*, he is enthralled by the beauty of the fisherman's daughters:

La vista saltearon poco menos
del huésped admirado
las no líquidas perlas...

(II, 230–2)

(Amazed, the guest thus found his gaze
no less captured by
these non-liquid pearls...)

The verb *admirar* is again used a few lines later to indicate his reaction to their radiant beauty.[74] A little later it is the rabbits on a hillside that attract him.[75]

Even if we restrict ourselves to considering the reactions of Góngora's characters, then, it becomes clear that wonder is a key emotion in the

---

[72] See *Documentos gongorinos*, ed. E.J. Gates, p. 124.
[73] 'Con gusto el joven y atención le oía' (I, 222): another instance of the stranger's positive reaction.
[74] II, 240.
[75] 'A pocos pasos le admiró no menos/montecillo...' ('A few steps later he was no less amazed,/to see a hillock...'), II, 275.

Soledades. Moreover, the general air of breathlessness in the poem is increased by the very suddenness of so many of the events which Góngora describes. In the course of the poem the wanderer meets a barrage of interruptions. More than one speech is broken off by some sudden interruption. For example, the goatherd's speech is brought to a halt by the sudden arrival of the hunt (I, 222–3); a conversation with the old man is cut short by the departure of other peasants for their celebrations (I, 507–13); a sudden gust of wind curtails the fisherman's account of his daughters' exploits (II, 512–15). When the stranger is beginning to mope about his unrequited love, his black thoughts are suddenly stopped by the sound of merrymaking (I, 747–54); and when he is busy paying attention to the fisherman's guided tour of the island, he is pulled up short by a tree in his path (II, 314–18). Elsewhere, Góngora uses such expressions as 'apenas' ('scarcely had. . .') to suggest the rapid succession of events:

Apenas reclinaron la cabeza,/cuando. . .

(I, 616)

(Scarce had they reclined their heads, than. . .)

Llegó la desposada apenas, cuando. . .

(I, 963)

(Scarce had the bride arrived, before. . .)

No bien, pues, de su luz los horizontes. . .
desdorados los siente, cuando. . .

(I, 42)

(No sooner had he sensed the golden light
fade from the horizon, than. . .)

All these details heighten the drama of events, and we see Góngora using a similar technique in his *Polifemo* when the giant's love-song is interrupted by goats trampling the vines (lines 465–6). The giant then throws stones to frighten off the goats, interrupting in his turn the lovers.

The *Soledades* is full of surprises, then, more of which we shall be examining later. Góngora actually goes out of his way to show the wonderment of the young stranger, a response which I believe he hopes the reader will share. The inhuman neutrality which some critics would like to see in his poetry is simply not there.

We have seen how the descriptive poem emerged as a recognizable genre, how it developed and exploited to the full some of the traditional functions of description, and in particular, how it added to and combined with these a sense of wonder, and a desire to reveal nature in a new light. The combination of different rhetorical aims within a single poem is very characteristic. Sometimes the result can be a lack of proportion, as when the poet, in a kind of deathbed repentance, attempts to convert into a love poem an extensive work which until its final lines has shown no intention of being anything other than an ingenious description of nature. Perhaps poems like this reflect a lack of confidence felt by the poet in trying to free himself from previous tradition. But sometimes the poetic aims are so finely and teasingly balanced that we may be unable to say with confidence what the main theme of a particular poem is. Renaissance poetry rarely causes this kind of problem. But although each individual baroque descriptive poem may cause different problems of interpretation, we can see in most of them a common thread in their approach to natural description. It is to the more detailed tracing of this thread that my remaining chapters will be dedicated.

IV

NATURE'S PLENTY

The fact that baroque poets indulged in more extensive descriptions than their predecessors is in itself likely to make their world seem richer and more varied to the reader. But the theme of nature's plenty is not one which emerges by accident, as it were, as a consequence of the use of longer descriptions which more or less obliged the poets to describe a wider range of things. It is a theme which we can often see quite deliberately followed, and is, I believe, an important source of wonder for the poet.

The immense profusion of nature has the power to excite wonder by virtue of its sheer magnitude. If physical or numerical magnitude tends to amaze people this is perhaps because it presents the human mind with more than it can assimilate at once. A degree of uncertainty or confusion caused by the inability to take things in fully often seems to be an important ingredient in wonder. It certainly seems to be present in the mind of the wanderer in Góngora's *Soledades* whose hesitant footsteps betray his doubt as he glimpses the vastness of the hilltop panorama which confronts him.[1]

How could poets give an impression of the confusing variety of the natural world and place the reader in an analogous situation to that of an observer bombarded with such a wealth of experiences that he is left in a state of bewilderment? There is one descriptive method which became very popular in the seventeenth century, particularly in Spain, which gets as close as any to doing this, and which may be regarded as the very embodiment of the theme of nature's plenty. The technique consists in the systematic listing in a more or less leisurely fashion of a multitude of different natural products and creatures, such as animals, flowers and fruits. At first glance, this might not seem to be a very promising way of approaching description, for one could envisage it leading to a kind of poetry which makes no more compulsive reading than the telephone directory. Yet at times it provided the vehicle for some highly original poetry. It is with this enumerative approach to natural description that this chapter is concerned. First by tracing its history I hope to show how it enjoyed an unparalleled vogue in the seventeenth century. I then go on to consider in more detail what

---

[1] See above, p. 79.

constitutes the originality of baroque versions of the theme.

The cataloguing of natural products was not unknown in Latin poetry, and indeed was widespread enough to be recognizable as a topos. Ernst Robert Curtius devotes a section of his well-known study of the traditional themes of Latin literature to examples of the topos in which different species of tree are listed.[2] One fact that emerges from the four examples he cites—from Ovid, Statius, Claudian, and Seneca—is that the topos gets off to a rather late start in Latin literature. Moreover, the lists are not very extensive if one compares them with the more rambling versions of some later poets. Admittedly Ovid offers us a 'mixed forest' of as many as twenty-six different species of tree.[3] But the other Latin versions of the topos do not aspire to even half that number of trees, and even in Ovid the whole passage lasts a mere twenty lines.

Although Curtius is concerned only with catalogues of trees in his study, it seems likely that this restriction is due to a lack of plentiful examples of lists of other natural products. In Ovid's *Metamorphoses* (XIII, 792—820), the giant Poliphemus in his love-song to Galatea enumerates all the fruits and the animals that could be hers. This was a passage which inspired many later European poets, but it seems to be an isolated example in Latin literature. It is significant that the topos is absent from Virgil's Second Eclogue in what is otherwise a very similar love-song.

In the Middle Ages the theme lies more or less dormant. That is not to say that enumeration was not a favourite technique with medieval writers. Indeed, the reverse is the case. But where they do make lists, it is not usually the theme of nature's plenty that concerns them. For example, in the *Laberinto de Fortuna*, Juan de Mena devotes nineteen stanzas to the list of places which could be seen from the lofty vantage point to which Fortune had transported him.[4] And Santillana's *Triunphete de Amor*, a similarly visionary poem, displays a long list of names of legendary figures.[5] But such examples have nothing to do with the treatment of nature. One could say the same of the splendid enumeration of the ranks of combatants in the battle between Don Carnal and Doña Cuaresma in the *Libro de Buen Amor* (Coplas 1081—1129). In a sense the Arcipreste's theme is the plenitude of nature, but his thoughts are very much centred upon man, and upon man's stomach in particular. One may perhaps question whether this butcher's-eye-view of the animal world reflects a genuine interest

[2] Curtius, op.cit. 194—5.

[3] *Metamorphoses*, X, 86—105.

[4] *Cancionero castellano del siglo xv*, ed. R. Foulché-Delbosc, I, 156—7 (Nueva Biblioteca de Autores Españoles, 19, Madrid, 1912.)

[5] Ibid. 542.

in nature. Where the naturalist would see a pig, the Arcipreste sees pork, bacon, and ham:

En pos los escudados están los vallesteros,
Las ánssares, çeçinas, costados de carneros,
Piernas de puerco fresco, los jamones enteros.

(After the shield-bearers come the crossbowmen:
geese, cured meats, sides of lamb,
fresh legs of pork, and whole hams.)[6]

We may compare this *bon viveur*'s approach with that of Rabelais in the *Quart Livre* in which there are exuberant lists of foodstuffs.[7]

It is to the medieval French poets rather than the Spaniards or Italians which one must turn for evidence of the survival of our topos of *Cornucopia*, as I shall call it.[8] There are interesting examples in the *Roman de la Rose*, and in Jean Lemaire des Belges, a poet who despite his relatively late date is usually thought of in a medieval context along with the *rhétoriqueurs*. I shall be referring briefly to these versions of the theme later in the chapter. But the over-all picture which we get of the development of the theme up to the Renaissance is that having got off to a modest start in late Latin literature, it barely survives in the Middle Ages, despite the medieval poets' fondness for enumeration.

In Italian literature, the classical 'mixed grove' is revived in the opening description of Sannazaro's *Arcadia* (1504). But more significant than this are two earlier examples of enumerative description in which the range of items referred to is noticeably broader than in Latin versions of the topos. Luigi Pulci in his *Morgante* (1478) had regaled readers with an extensive list of precious stones, birds, and animals when describing the design of a pavilion given by Rinaldo to his lover.[9] And Angelo Poliziano, who enjoyed the friendship of Pulci at the court of Lorenzo Il Magnifico, followed this with an equally varied treatment of the topos in his *Stanze* (1494) in honour of a tournament held in Florence in 1475. Here, Poliziano's description of the natural setting of the Palace of Venus is remarkably lush, and includes a passage of some ten stanzas listing not only trees, but also animals and birds.[10]

In Spain, the influence of Ovid's account of the love-song of the

---

[6] Copla 1084. I quote from the text of J. Cejador y Frauca (Madrid, 1959).

[7] See, for example, Chs. LIX and LX, which list the offerings of the Gastolatres. Rabelais is a compulsive cataloguer, and obviously found in such lists the ideal vehicle for his verbal virtuosity.

[8] After Soto de Rojas, who gives his enumerative Third Eclogue this title. See his *Obras*, ed. A. Gallego Morell (Madrid, 1950), p. 274.

[9] *Morgante*, ed. Franco Ageno (Milan and Naples, 1955), pp. 363–83.

[10] *Stanze*, ed. G. Carducci (Florence, 1863), I, 82–92.

giant Poliphemus seems to have been an important factor in the introduction of enumerative natural description. Perhaps Juan del Encina had Ovid in mind when in his Seventh Eclogue he portrayed the shepherd Mingo proudly listing all the gifts he was prepared to offer to his beloved, beginning with clothes and trinkets, but going on to add nuts, fruits, and herbs in profusion.[11] The theme is handled in such a rudimentary fashion here, however, that it could hardly be called a description. It is literally a catalogue, in which unlike in Ovid, nearly all the items are starkly listed without adjectives or qualifying phrases. But it is interesting to note that the reaction which the shepherd expects from his audience to his display of wealth is amazement.[12]

It is not until a century later that we being to see the theme of *Cornucopia* expanded and developed in Spanish poetry. The first signs of this are in Luis Barahona de Soto's *Primera parte de la Angelica* (1586) in which the legend of Orlando is retold. In Barahona's poem, the giant Orco becomes conflated with Ovid's Poliphemus, and sings a love-song in which he lists all the natural riches which await his lady if she will be his:

> Ni la ciruela endrina, ò la melosa,
> Que dizen que en color vence à la cera,
> Ni la màs tiessa, larga y generosa,
> Que, al Sol enxuta, largo tiempo espera,
> Ni la castaña ò nuez, ni la preciosa
> Guinda, y cereza, y la bellota, y pera,
> Pueden faltarte, ni la almendra y higo,
> Si con diuido [*sic*] amor biues comigo.
> Pues la Zamboa dulce, y menos tierno
> Membrillo agudo, y la peraza acerua,
> El vil madroño, y datil casi eterno,
> Y la almezina y nispera, y la serua
> Y la açofeyfa blanda, y como cuerno
> Torcido la algarroua, y la proterua
> Y armada piña, y la naranja, y lima,
> Y cidra, que yo tengo en màs estima:
> Pues el durazno, aluerchigo y mestizo
> Melocoton, y prisco, y frutos ciento
> (Qu'el fertil año en varios tiempos hizo)
> No faltaran. . .[13]

---

[11] See *Eglogas completas de Juan del Enzina*, ed. H. López Morales (Madrid, 1968), pp. 152–4.

[12] 'Cómo no te maravillas?' Ibid. 154.

[13] *Primera parte de la Angelica* (Granada, 1586), fos. 52v–53. See A. Vilanova, *Las fuentes y los temas del Polifemo de Góngora* Madrid, 1957, I, 522–3, who notes this as the first example in Spain of this Ovidian theme. Com-

(You shall not lack the sloe, or the sweet plum
whose colour, people reckon, outshines wax,
nor the firmer, longer, more abundant prune
which takes a long time drying in the sun,
nor the chestnut, walnut, or the precious
heart-cherry, the standard cherry, acorn,
also the pear, the almond and the fig,
if you will live a life of love with me.
For the sweet samboa, and the firmer,
acid quince, the bitter grafted pear,
the mean arbutus, and the long-lived date,
the sorb- or service-apple and the medlar
the soft jujube and the carob fruit,
like a twisted horn, and the perverse,
prickly pineapple, the orange, the lime,
the citron, which I prize most highly,
the persicary and the apricot,
all kinds of peaches, and a hundred fruits
the fertile year produced at different times
will not be lacking. . .)

It is noteworthy that Barahona's giant, unlike Ovid's, includes items like acorns, not noted for their edibility (*pace* our Golden-Age ancestors who, legend has it, ate little else), as well as some very exotic fruits. So that here we have the impression that Barahona is not selecting merely the most appetizing of nature's fruits, but is attempting to build up a picture of the immense range of the creation.

From this time onwards, the theme of *Cornucopia* underwent a remarkable expansion in Spanish poetry, thanks in no small measure to the efforts of Lope de Vega who returns to the topic time and time again.[14] In his *Arcadia* (1598), for example, he uses it not once but a number of times. The opening passage of descriptive prose embodies a long list of flowers,[15] and shortly afterwards there is recounted Olimpio's tale, which includes the song of the giant Alasto for Crisalda,

pare the opening reference to plums in our passage with Ovid, *Metamorphoses*, XIII, 817—8.

[14] Lope's fondness for enumeration has already attracted the attention of the critics. See José F. Montesinos, in his edition of the *Poesías líricas* (Madrid, 1963), II, xxii—xxiv; A. Vilanova, op.cit. I, 522—9; N. Salomon, *Recherches sur le thème paysan dans la 'comedia' au temps de Lope de Vega* (Bordeaux, 1965), pp. 281—306. Examples of the topos have been noted in the following works of Lope: *Los amores de Albanio e Ismenia*; *Angelica* (1604); *Arcadia* (1598); *Belardo el furioso*; *Circe* (1624); *Descripción de la Abadía* (1604); *Descripción de la Tapiada*; (1621); *El galán de la membrilla*; *Isidro* (1599); *La madre de la mejor*; *Pastoral de Jacinto*; *El vaquero de Moraña*.

[15] *Obras completas*, ed. J. de Entrambasaguas (Madrid, 1965), I, 9—10.

where once again the theme of *Cornucopia* appears, as the giant lists
the gifts of birds, fruits, animals, and fish that he has to offer:

> Perdizes te ofreciera,
> Biuas en la misma percha,
> Con el pico y los pies roxos,
> Que estampan en el arena.
>   Las calandrias que madrugan
> Las mirlas a quien enseña
> Naturaleza a caçar,
> Las ormigas con las lengua.
>   El gauilan pardo y libre,
> La filomena parlera,
> Que el verano alegre anuncia.[16]

> (Partridges I'd offer you,
> alive upon their perch,
> red-beaked, and with red feet
> whose imprints mark the sand,
> and larks, those early risers,
> blackbirds, taught by nature
> to catch ants with their tongue.
> The tawny sparrow hawk,
> the chattering nightingale
> who gaily heralds Summer.)

Again, Anfriso's farewell to Belisarda which ends Book IV contains
what may be regarded as a further example of our topos. All five
stanzas adopt the same repetitive enumerative pattern, and one
of the five lists is of animals.[17] Finally, in Book V we have a farmers'
calendar listing the crops appropriate to each season of the year.[18]

In general, Lope handles his catalogues somewhat mechanically,
passing from one item to the next after a perfunctory epithet or two
at most, or, as at the start of his Arcadia, after a brief reference to
the classical myth with which each item is associated. In the passage
from Alasto's song cited above, we see him at his most adventurous.
Here we see him take an interest in detail—footprints in the sand
the catching of ants—which, whether ornithologically accurate or
not, is a sign of a more careful and more imaginative approach. As
the topos became more firmly established, other poets moved further
in this direction, doubtless inspired by the example of Góngora's
inventive genius to exploit the technique in a far more original way

---

[16] Ibid. 23. The list continues in similar vein for more than a hundred lines.
[17] Ibid. 128
[18] Ibid. 131.

than hitherto.[19]

Although in his individual poetic enumerations Góngora accumulates less items than some poets, the enumerative tendency in his *Soledades* is nevertheless very important, and as Dámaso Alonso has noted in drawing attention to some of his most significant enumerative descriptions, the effect is to leave us with an impression of the plenitude of nature:

Already one can see how rich in incident and how full of life the *Soledades* are. But one can deduce this much more clearly from the last group of descriptions: that of enumerations. These constitute one of the most brilliant aspects of Góngora's art ... Many of these series could be cited ... But especially interesting are those which amount to a rapid and precise description of the most varied of natural forms: those of the gifts which the mountain folk take to the wedding, the food for the wedding-breakfast; the fish provided by the estuary; the birds carried by the falconers. Here, that seething, that swarming of natural forces and forms which is ever present in the *Soledades* reaches its peak ... The most faithful symbol of this poetry is the horn of plenty.[20]

Any of these examples furnishes evidence of Góngora's originality, but for a brief sample I turn to his *Polifemo*, where he enumerates the fruits in the giant's bag. The tenth stanza, with which the description begins, had already been revised by Góngora because one of its metaphors had seemed too audacious to Pedro de Valencia.[21] In the final version, the poet describes:

La serba, a quien le da rugas el heno;
la pera, de quien fue cuna dorada
la rubia paja, y—pálida tutora—
la niega avara, y pródiga la dora.[22]

(The sorb-apple, all wrinkled by the hay;
the pear, who had the golden straw to serve
as cradle, and as her pale governess,
who avariciously hides her away,
yet generously covers her with gold.)

---

[19] Note Robert Jammes's comment on an enumerative passage from Lope's *Isidro* contrasting Lope and Góngora: 'Cette poésie n'est sans doute pas dépourvue de charme, mais la multiplicité des objets qu'elle évoque, si elle produit un certain effet, lui interdit par ailleurs tout effort d'originalité dans la manière de les évoquer; il est significatif que Lope, dans le dernier passage cité en soit la plupart du temps réduit à décrire à l'aide d'un seul adjectif (généralement de couleur) les fruits qu'il énumère...La poésie rustique...tend toujours chez Lope à une certaine superficialité, alors que chez Góngora elle se tourne vers la recherche de l'intensité et de la profondeur.' Jammes, op.cit. p. 549.

[20] *Estudios y ensayos gongorinos*, pp. 85–6.

[21] See A. Vilanova, op.cit. I, 538.   [22] Lines 77–80.

Here not only does Góngora note detail, such as the wrinkling of the sorb-apple as it ripens, but gives a boldly original account of the relationship between the things he describes. Thus he suggests that it is the hay which has actually caused the wrinkling of the sorb-apple, perhaps inviting the reader to imagine that the strands of hay have left their imprint on the fruit. And in describing the humble straw Góngora switches from the metaphor of the straw as an inanimate protector to that of the governess in whom he wittily combines the contradictory qualities of meanness and generosity.

The use of light-hearted anthropomorphic imagery as in this last example was a method of handling the topos of *Cornucopia* which appealed to a number of poets. Góngora himself had adopted this approach systematically in an earlier poem, his *romance, Del Palacio de la Primavera* (1609). This highly popular enumerative description of the many flowers at the court of Queen Rose must have awakened many poets to the descriptive possibilities of our topos.[23] Góngora gives us not a dry factual list, but a series of conceits all beautifully connected by a central theme. In some of the images active fantasy is combined with an almost scientific interest in the objects he describes. For example, we have the following satirical description of the iris:

Oh, qué celoso está el lilio,
un mal cortesano que
calza siempre borceguí
debe de ser portugués![24]

(How envious the iris is
an ill-bred courtier, who is
forever shod in common boots;
He surely must be Portuguese!)

Presumably this image, which refers to the physical appearance of the plant, depends upon direct observation. It seems likely that Góngora is referring to the characteristic shape of the calix which is rather long and covers the base of the petals, just as a boot extends beyond the ankle.

However, one should beware of concluding that there was any widespread move to reject bookish learning in favour of the direct observation of nature. For example, one might assume that Góngora's conceit about the hyacinth in this poem was the result of reflection on the physical appearance of the plant:

En viéndola, dijo: 'ay!'
el jacinto, y al papel

[23] D. Alonso comments on the popularity of this poem, *Góngora y el Polifemo* (Madrid, 1967), II, 57.

[24] D. Alonso, op.cit. II, 55.

lo encomendó de sus hojas
porque se pueda leer.

(On seeing her the hyacinth
let forth an 'Ay!', and wrote it down
upon the paper of his leaves
in order that it could be read.)

Although this image must refer either to the shape or to the markings
of individual petals or leaves of the plant, or to its over-all shape, it does
not follow that Góngora has been carefully observing the hyacinth.
It is far more likely that he is recalling the legend of Hyacinthus as
recounted by Ovid in Book X of his *Metamorphoses*, where it is stated
that the petals of the new flower bore the signs of Apollo's grief, AI.[25]
In general, the pursuit of wit seems to have led to the exploration of
all possible sources of conceits, including information derived both
from recondite books and from direct experience of the phenomena
being described.

Valuable evidence of the popularity of *Cornucopia* in descriptive
poetry is provided by the manuscript anthology of poetry compiled in
1628, a substantial part of which has been edited by Blecua under the
title *Cancionero de 1628*. The manuscript includes not only all the
poems of Góngora in which we have noted examples of the topos,
but also notable instances of enumeration in no less than five other
poets: Villar, Bartolomé Argensola, Matías Ginovés, Adrián de Prado,
and Andrés Melero.[26] One of these poems—a light-hearted epistle in
verse by Argensola, in which is told Aesop's story of the eagle summon-
ing a council of birds, more than thirty varieties of which are named
by the poet—may be dated between 1600 and 1605.[27] All the others
are of later date. Three examples drawn from Matías Ginovés, Adrián
de Prado, and Andrés Melero, will serve to illustrate how Góngora's
example was followed.

The *Selva al verano* by Matías Ginovés is a good example of the
imaginative handling of a list of flowers. Such is the care taken with
each item that the poet builds up a witty story about each plant:

De que tantos la miren vergonçosa,
purpúrea nace la virjínea rosa,
mostrando en sus viuísimos colores,

---

[25] *Metamorphoses*, X, 215.
[26] In Blecua's index (op.cit. 68—151), the relevant poems are numbered 7,
16, 20, 23, 35, 104, 242, 250. Poem 20, one of Adrián de Prado's *Canciones a
San Jerónimo*, although showing enumerative tendencies, does not contain such a
clear-cut example of our topos as its sister poem, which does not appear in the
Zaragoza manuscript, but which is reproduced by Blecua in his introduction, pp.
29—35.
[27] Blecua, op.cit. 221 (note). For the enumeration, see lines 340—91.

ser flor del alua y alua de las flores,
si no pauón soberuio
de la verde floresta,
que sin embargo de la bronca planta
de su pie espinoso
descoje altiua el círculo pomposo,
que aunque encojida es, por ser doncella,
también es arrogante por ser bella.

Como galán de la fragrante rosa,
el clauel boquirubio
ámbar respira, bálsamo derrama,
de púrpura vestido
por sacar las colores de su dama,
si bien sobre sus sienes de escarlata
dos cuernecillos de bruñida plata
le naçen de la roja cabellera,
porque aun entre las flores, a quien sobran
próuidos jardineros y guardianes,
no se escapan de cuernos los galanes.

La mosqueta olorosa,
tercera entre el clauel y entre la rosa,
si ya no entre el jaçmín y açuçena,
paga sus liuiandades,
con que el vulgo viento
la dexa a la vergüença en vn momento
desnuda de sus cándidos vestidos,
si no de infames plumas guarnecidos,
de miel tan bien vntada
quanto de abejas visitada.[28]

(All coy because so many gaze at her
the virgin rose is born a blushing red,
in her bright colours showing that she is
a flower of the dawn, a dawn of flowers
if not a peacock proud
from the verdant woodland,
who, notwithstanding the unsoftened sole
of her so thorny foot,
haughtily unfolds her pompous tail-fan,
for though she is a maiden, therefore shy,
her beauty also makes her arrogant.

[28] Ibid. 200–1.

Just like a suitor of the fragrant rose,
the glib young carnation
breathes amber everywhere, and exudes balm,
decked out in purple clothes,
favouring the colours of his lady,
although upon his scarlet brows appear
two little horns of silver shining bright
that emanate from his red head of hair,
for even among flowers, who are not short
of gardeners and keepers who protect,
gallants may none the less be cuckolded.

The sweet-smelling musk-rose,
the carnation and rose's go-between,
if not that of the jazmine and the lily,
pays for her wantonness;
the wind, *vox populi*,
makes her at once a spectacle of shame,
stripping her naked of her pure white clothes,
abandoning her feathered shamefully,
as tarred with honey as
she is sought out by bees.)

Góngora's influence is apparent here not only in the poet's style but
also in the general conception of the poem, which is reminiscent
of the *romance Del Palacio de la Primavera*. We have only to compare Ginovés' conceit about the carnation with Góngora's to see that
the earlier poem was probably being used as a model.[29] Nevertheless,
Ginovés contributes some brilliantly original images. In the parallels
he draws between plants and people, the poet satirizes human society
while at the same time drawing attention to some interesting botanical
detail. His allusion to the small white stamens which are visible in
the red carnation, which he describes with the metaphor of little
horns, shows a precision of observation which no poets before Góngora's
time could match. The image of the tarring and feathering of the
musk-rose is quite brilliant, and again has an observational basis, since
presumably the feathering was suggested by the appearance of a flower
stripped of its petals. For poets of an earlier age a flower without
petals was not the kind of object to be considered worthy of precise
attention.

A list of fruits, trees, animals, and birds, is included in Adrián de
Prado's incomplete ode to Saint Jerome, beginning 'En vna soledad que

---

[29] See Góngora, *Obras completas*, p. 169:
   Las colores de la Reina/vistió galán el clavel/Príncipe que es de la sangre/
   y aun aspirante a ser rey.

el Nilo riega'.[30] Although the passage is not Prado's most inventive, he nevertheless describes the products of nature with epithets which characteristically are the product of independent thought. For example, he writes:

El alcornoque pálido y poroso,
espeso, coruo, denso y intrincado;
el verde pino que los cielos toca,
estéril, melancólico y humbroso;
el tosco roble, montaraz, armado
de cortezas más fuertes que vna roca,
la zarza seca y loca
aquí nunca habitaron,
ni su pie soterraron
entre la yerba y flores olorosas
ni estendieron sus ramas espaciosas.[31]

(The cork tree, pallid, porous, broad, and bent,
and dense and intricate,
the green pine tree that reaches to the sky,
barren, and melancholy, and shady,
the tough oak from the mountains, armed with bark
so hard that it is stronger than a rock,
the dry and wayward bramble,
not one of them dwelt here,
nor ever hid its foot
mid grass or fragrant flowers,
nor ever stretched its spreading branches forth.)

Once again we see humanizing imagery in the adjectives 'melancólico' and 'loca', and in the verb 'habitar'. And the thoroughness of detail is particularly noticeable in the description of the cork tree in which the poet's use of adjectives reflects an almost scientific interest in nature, as he considers the tree's colour, its texture, its shape, and the way in which its branches interweave.

Another example of *Cornucopia* is found in Andrés Melero's *Canción a San Juan Clímaco*. Melero was a professor at the University of Huesca, and his poem is another of those devoted to hermit saints. Although Melero dispatches the items on his list more briskly, and is therefore closer to Lope de Vega in his approach, nevertheless we still see the characteristic use of imaginative anthropomorphic adjectives:

Está a vn lado el nogal presuntuoso
con su pálido fruto encarcelado,
junto al castaño tosco y auariento

---

[30] See above, p. 000.　　　　[31] Blecua, op.cit., 32–3.

el almendro florido y ambicioso,
el pino erguido y el ciprés copado
y el moral descolado y corpulento.[32]

(On one side, the presumptuous walnut stands,
with its pallid, incarcerated fruit,
by the chestnut, tough and avaricious,
the flowering and ambitious almond tree,
the upright pine, the cypress densely leaved,
the mulberry tree, docked and corpulent.)

The main weakness of this passage is that Melero does not explain
to us in what way his walnut tree is presumptuous, or his almond tree
ambitious.

The *Cancionero de 1628* was not the only seventeenth-century
anthology to contain a variety of examples of our topos. For instance,
the manuscript anthology, *Poetica silva*, extracts from which were
published by Gallardo,[33] contains a number of poems on the four
seasons. Three of the four poems from this anthology published by
Rodríguez Moñino under the title *Las estaciones del año* include
examples of *Cornucopia*.[34] Doubtless some of the unpublished material
in the codex offers similar examples. Another version of the topos
is to be found in an ode by Pedro de Godoy in the *Cancionero antequerano* (1627–8). An extract from this passage was included in
Chapter Three.[35]

It is quite probable, in view of the wide range of as yet unpublished
poetic anthologies of the period that remain to be examined, that as
far as the popularity of the theme of *Cornucopia* amongst the lesser
writers is concerned, we have only seen the tip of the iceberg. Among
the better known writers, we find examples in Gabriel Bocángel's
Egloga amorosa, where fruits and flowers are enumerated,[36] Soto de
Rojas' *Paraiso cerrado*, where the extensive list of flowers in the final
part of the poem shows the familiar influence of Góngora's *romance,
Del palacio de la primavera*,[37] and also Soto's Third Eclogue, discussed
later in this chapter. One of the most original enumerative descriptions
is Polo de Medina's delightful invitation to the country life, his *Ocios
de la soledad* (1633). In the following brief sample he admirably
exploits, in Gongoristic manner, the poetic possibilities of the reflection

---

[32] Ibid. 421.
[33] *Ensayo de una biblioteca española de libros raros y curiosos*, I, 1051.
[34] These are Juan de Arjona's *Silva al Hibierno*, Gutierre Lobo's *Silva a el
Estío*, and Juan Montero's *Silva a el Otoño*. See A. Rodríguez Moñino, *Las
estaciones del año* (Valencia 1949), pp. 16 ff., 46 ff., 60 ff.
[35] See above pp. 51–2.
[36] Bocangel, *Obras*, ed. R. Benítez Claros, (Madrid, 1946), I, 79.
[37] Soto de Rojas, *Obras*, pp. 413–15.

of a flower in a stream:

El armiño verás de una azucena,
en el margen hermosa,
y otra dentro el cristal, floresta amena,
fragante espuma es, cisne de Flora,
y caducando en olas repetidas,
tembladera es de plata, donde bebe,
la abejuela sutil perlas de nieve.[38]

(Behold the ermine of a lovely lily
upon the bank, and here another one
within the crystal—such a nice bouquet—
is aromatic foam, is Flora's swan,
and as it in the frequent ripples fades,
it is a silver drinking-cup wherein
the subtle bumble-bee sips pearls of snow.)

The reader may envisage the second lily, 'dentro el cristal', either as a plant growing in the water, or as a reflection of the first lily. Having sharply drawn attention to the ambiguous semi-floral, semi-aquatic status of this second flower in the two images 'fragante espuma' and 'Cisne de Flora',[39] Polo develops his idea in a way which suggests that the more attractive interpretation is to think in terms of a reflection in the water. The lily's reflection, although blurred by the ripples ('caducando'), deceives the bee, who sips from this white, vessel-shaped reflection not nectar, but snow-white water ('perlas de nieve').

The same exquisite care is lavished on Polo's description of the fruits. For example, he describes the pomegranate in these terms:

Con triunfante corona
la granada verás que te abre el pecho,
pelícano en el prado de Pomona,
y en panal de rubí, miel de colores.[40]

(With its triumphal crown
see the pomegranate open you its breast,
a pelican in Pomona's meadow,
and offer in a ruby honeycomb,
bright coloured honey.)

Here brilliant invention is combined with acute observation. The characteristic shape of the skin peeling back at the end of the fruit suggests to the poet the image of a crown. This natural peeling in

---

[38] Polo, *Obras completas*, ed. A. Valbuena Prat (Murcia, 1948), p. 168.

[39] Compare Góngora's description of the water-nymph Galatea as a 'Cisne de Juno', *Polifemo*, line 104.

[40] Polo, op.cit., 169.

turn suggests that the pomegranate is offering up its flesh within, just as in legend the Pelican was reputed to open up its own breast, sacrificing its own blood for the sake of its offspring. The redness of the pomegranate's flesh makes the image the more appropriate. Finally, Polo's series of images culminates in the perfect one of the honeycomb. The fruit is sweet, and hence suggestive of honey. But more than this, both the membranes which divide the inside of the fruit and the appearance of the individual flesh-covered seeds clustered together in the pomegranate are reminiscent of the compartments within a honeycomb. With such an inspired approach to description we are obviously a far cry from some of the more mechanical enumerations produced by Lope.

More examples of our topos can be found in some of the lesser-known poets mentioned in our previous chapter, such as Miguel Colodrero,[41] and Luis de Ulloa. Ulloa develops quite an original idea in describing the ravages of a drought upon the flowers in his garden. His poem in epistolary form begins with some military news, and continues the military imagery when describing the flowers.[42]

From the examples we have examined in this chapter, it is clear that the theme of *Cornucopia* had developed to one of major importance in seventeenth-century Spain. By the 1620s it was so firmly established that poets had no hesitation in using it as extensively as they could. And some went to extraordinary lengths to demonstrate their virtuosity. The catalogue to end all catalogues is surely Soto de Rojas' Third Eclogue (1623), which he himself entitles *La Cornucopia*.[43] His list of precious stones, flowers, fruits, animals, and fish sprawls over four hundred lines of verse. So many species are mentioned that there is scarcely space for him to say much about each, and the display is perhaps more of erudition than of ingenuity. The notes in fact invite the reader to consult Pliny and other natural historians for an exposition of the properties of the various items. In all, there are some forty fruits, forty-five animals, forty-five fishes, and nearly thirty birds named. Nevertheless, wit and sharp observation still have a place in the poem. Witness the following extract:

---

[41] See Colodrero, *El Alpheo*, f.3.
[42] *Obras de Don Luis de Ulloa y Pereira, prosas y versos* (Madrid, 1674), p. 196 ff. For a further example in Ulloa, see p. 201. Note also Ulloa's reference to wonder as a reaction to the vision of cornucopia:

> Tan fertil se descubre la campaña,
> Que mas vezes mirada, mas admira
> . . . .
> Esteril es, si solo es abundante,
> no satisface aqui, quando no vierte,
> El marfil de la copia redundante. (pp. 114–15)

[43] See his notes on the poem, *Obras*, p. 274.

De su piel despojado
entre el aniexo vino, en vaso hermoso,
te seruiré el Melocoton sabroso,
que despues de cortado,
sangre derrama en su color dorado.
  Desnuda y sin camisa
bien que casta nadante, en linfa pura,
a tomar de tus labios su dulçura
vendrà la Almendra lisa
con blanco orgullo derramando risa.[44]

(Denuded of its skin,
in a fine glass, amid the vintage wine,
I'll set before you the delicious peach,
which when it has been cut
displays its golden colour steeped in blood.
  Naked, without her shift,
though chastely swimming in pure liquor she,
to take her sweetness from those lips of yours
the smooth Almond will come,
in her proud whiteness bringing merriment.)

In the same year as the publication of Soto de Rojas' works there
appeared in Paris Marino's *Adone*, the seventh canto of which contains
a list of birds with even more specimens than Soto's eclogue.[45] Marino
was obviously attracted to the topos as he had already used it in other
major poems.[46] His *Orfeo* provides the most ambitious example, with
a catalogue of trees, animals, and birds stretching over three hundred
lines of verse.[47]

Marino's visit to Paris increased his popularity in France, and French
baroque poetry too was affected by the vogue for *Cornucopia*. See,
for example, the extensive catalogue in Tristan l'Hermite's *Orphée*
(1641). He has some interesting specimens in his collection, and even
adds a unicorn for good measure at the end.[48] Scudéry is another poet
using our topos.[49]

So far our survey has demonstrated the vastly increased popularity

---

[44] Ibid. 179.

[45] Canto VII, 20–32. See Marino, *Opere scelte*, ed. G. Getto (Torino, 1962),
pp. 482–6.

[46] Notably in the following works from *La Sampogna* : *Europa*, lines 48–130;
Proserpina, lines 715–27.

[47] Marino's fondness for the topos did not pass unnoticed by his imitators.
See, for example, Stigliani's singularly unimpressive version in his *La Primavera,
Marino e i Marinisti*, ed. G. Guido Ferrero (Milan and Naples, 1954), p. 649.

[48] *Poésies*, ed. P.A. Wadsworth, (Paris, 1962), pp. 68–72.

[49] *Poésies diverses* (Paris, 1649), pp. 116 ff.

of the topos of *Cornucopia* in the seventeenth century, and has indicated
some of the new directions which it took in Spanish baroque poetry.
It remains for us to look a little more closely at some of the differences
between earlier and later versions of the theme and to offer an assessment of their significance.

Comparing the fully developed enumerations of the seventeenth
century with those of earlier times one can in general see the transition
from a certain neatness, almost pettiness at times, to a freer, more
capricious treatment of the topos. In medieval times, the enumeration
of natural objects, or indeed any kind of cataloguing, tends to be
associated with the poet's role as chronicler. Because the narrative
poet is enacting the role of a witness to the events he describes, or of
one who claims to have a true knowledge of them, he will sometimes
attempt to demonstrate this 'knowledge' by enumerating as many
facts as he can muster. The catalogue, in other words, gives an air of
authenticity to his poem. One can see this pursuit of a feigned authenticity in the list of fruit trees in Guillaume de Lorris' *vergier d'Amour*:

Ce bel vergier par compassure
Estoit trestout d'une quarrure
Par tout autant long comme large
De fruict estoit plain le rivaige
Au moins excepté ung ou deux
Ou quelque mauvais arbre hideux.
Les pommiers estoient au vergier
Bien m'en souvient pour abrégier
Qui portoient les pommes grenades
Proffitables pour les malades

. . . .

Des arbres divers y eut tant
Que me seroit grant encombre
De les vous déclairer par nombre.[50]

This whole passage deliberately avoids generalized statement in order
to give an impression of accuracy and to persuade the reader that the
author has actually seen the orchard in question and is merely acting
as a reporter here. Thus he cunningly qualifies his statement about the
abundance of fruit by noting that there is the occasional barren tree.
The phrase 'Bien m'en souvient' is there to confer further authenticity
on the list. Finally, when the list is complete, the poet gives the impression that there were more things he might have mentioned, but that
he or the reader might be bored if the account were protracted any
further.

[50]   As quoted by D.B. Wilson, *Descriptive Poetry in France*, pp. 4—5.

This medieval approach to enumeration still survives in the fifteenth and sixteenth centuries. Pulci in his *Morgante*, for example, for all the richness of his version of the topos, is describing not the big open world, but a work of art, the design on the pavilion given to Rinaldo, an object with physical limitations (like Guillaume de Lorris' square orchard) of which he is feigning to give an accurate description.

As for the neatness of pre-baroque enumerations, it would be hard to beat Jean Lemaire des Belges who adopts the extraordinarily mechanical method of listing his natural products in alphabetical order.[51] Even Sannazaro in his *Arcadia* describes an impossibly neat copse with an accuracy worthy of the medieval veridical tradition. One might imagine, taking the passage out of its context, that as Sannazaro lists each species of tree, that we are to envisage several specimens of each dotted about the wood. But his introduction leaves no scope for such an interpretation: 'On the summit of Partenio there lies. . .a delightful plain. . .where, if I am not mistaken, there are some twelve to fifteen trees.[52] When one comes to count up the number of species of tree mentioned in the list, remarkably there happen to be thirteen, a number falling precisely within the numerical limits set by the author in the passage quoted where he is pretending to be vague. The implication is that there is only one specimen of each species in the copse. True, Sannazaro has them 'in ordine non artificioso disposti' ('disposed in an artless arrangement'), but even this randomness is deliberately planned. One hesitates to apply too freely to literature Wölfflin's criteria for distinguishing baroque and Renaissance art, but here, if anywhere, is an example of the Renaissance 'linear' style.

By contrast, characteristic seventeenth-century Spanish enumerations have a more generous conception. Often the lists are much longer, and often the poet will pause to give special attention to individual items, clothing them with rich fantasies. As a result, the baroque poets are much better able to convey a sense of wonder. Firstly, by their approach they give the impression that they themselves have been captivated by their subject. Secondly, by making their enumerations more extensive they are able to convey more effectively the immense profusion of nature. Thirdly, by taking care over their descriptions of individual items, they show how small things can be just as worthy of wonder when viewed in isolation as when considered *en masse*. These were important innovations, and I shall illustrate them in a little more detail in the following paragraphs.

The poet's apparent attitude to his subject can have an important bearing on the impact of his poem. Neatly ordered descriptions, like Jean Lemaire des Belges' alphabetical catalogue, are far less likely to

---

[51] See D.B. Wilson, op.cit. 4.   [52] Sannazaro, *Opere volgari*, p.5.

convey a sense of mystery or wonder than those in which the poet moves from item to item as a bee from flower to flower. Excessive neatness conveys the impression that the writer is in full control over a subject which he thoroughly comprehends. It suggests that the writer himself does not share any of the doubt or confusion that one associates with wonder. This is why the full flourishing of the topos of *Cornucopia* was tied up with the development of a new descriptive poetry which overthrew some of the restraints inherent in earlier poetry. To produce an impressive enough enumeration one had to introduce a certain abandon. It is interesting to note how self-conscious Lope is in explaining, perhaps with humorous intention, that the long enumerative description which begins his *Arcadia* is justified because it is an obligatory part of the storyteller's art to set the scene.[53] But ultimately *Cornucopia*, like other types of description, was to become a viable basis for an entire poem instead of remaining always a set-piece forming a relatively small part of a longer work.

Because in their enumerations baroque poets are sometimes prepared to abandon the sense of proportion to be found in earlier poetry as they accumulate detail after detail, the question arises as to how far they were interested in the composite picture arising from their descriptions. If the over-all picture seems confusing, this may be because the poet is only interested in individual items, so that the reader may be adopting a perspective which the writer had not envisaged, looking through a telescope, as it were, at what was intended to be seen only through a microscope, and finding the picture blurred. On the other hand, it may be that the poet is perfectly well aware that his picture might look blurred at the macroscopic level, and is content that his reader should experience some degree of confusion. If poets were consciously pursuing wonder, then the second of these attitudes seems the more likely. Moreover, it is hard to believe that a poet of Góngora's stature was not fully conscious of the general impact of his descriptions. The French baroque poets make an interesting point of comparison here, providing as they do an outspoken statement of their poetic attitudes.

In a poem which is sharply critical of the school of Malherbe, Théophile openly declares his deliberate rebellion against traditional poetic discipline:

Je ne veux point unir le fil de mon subjet,
Diversement je laisse et reprens mon objet,
Mon ame imaginant n'a point la patience,

---

[53] 'Ya saueis que es obligacion del q[ue] comiença alguna [historia], la descripcion del lugar...Dexa[n]do os pues aduertidos, y primero del referido mo[n]te, bosque, y prado; sabed...' *Obras completas*, vol. 1, p. 10.

De bien polir les vers et ranger la science:
La reigle me desplaist, j'ecris confusément,

. . . .

Je veux faire des vers qui ne soient pas contraincts,
Promener mon esprit par de petits dessains. . .[54]

He sees his imagination as determining the course his poem takes, leading
at times to a concentration on small detail—his 'petits dessains'. But he
is quite conscious that the result may seem capricious.

Saint Amant is equally frank about his rebellion against any form of
constraint, picturing his poem *La Solitude* as inspired by a Platonic
frenzy:

Tu vois dans cette poesie
Pleine de licence et d'ardeur
Les beaux rayons de la splendeur
Qui m'esclaire la fantaisie:
Tantost chagrin, tantost joyeux,
Selon que la fureur m'enflame,
Et l'object s'offre à mes yeux,
Les propos me naissent en l'ame,
Sans contraindre la liberté
Du demon qui m'a transporté.[55]

Again, Saint Amant is fully aware that the product of this inspiration
may seem whimsical. This kind of self-analysis shows that the poet has
in fact considered the over-all effect of what he has written, and is
expecting his reader to have done so too.

If one accepts, then, with Odette de Mourgues and previous critics
that the baroque poets have a 'myopic and disjointed vision', one
should beware of pushing the analogy too far and assuming that they
were incapable of seeing beyond individual objects and were unaware
of the perspective they were adopting.[56] The inconstant flitting from
object to object reveals a mind which is always searching for fresh
experiences. Saint Amant shows us that, however disjointed he realizes
his poetry may be, he is trying in it to give an impression of the mystery

---

[54] Théophile de Viau, *Oeuvres Poétiques*, ed. Jeanne Streicher, (Geneva, and
Lille, 1951), I, 11, 12.

[55] *Oeuvres Poétiques*. Texte choisi et établi avec une introduction, des notes
et une bibliographie par Léon Vérane (Paris, 1930), p. 8 (First edition 1629).

[56] See Odette de Mourgues, *Metaphysical, Baroque and Précieux Poetry*
(Oxford, 1953), pp. 93–9. Note her quotation from Croce on Marino and the
Marinists (p. 94). Antoine Adam, *Théophile de Viau et la libre pensée française
en 1620*, p. 447, draws an analogy with *pointillisme*, which is perhaps less appropriate in that the pointillist technique requires quite the reverse of a myopic
outlook. The collection of dots on the canvas seems incoherent when seen at
close range, but makes sense when the viewer stands back.

and breadth of the universe. In his poem, *Le contemplateur*, he writes:

Nature n'a point de secret
Que d'un soin libre, mais discret,
Ma curiosité ne sonde;
Ses cabinets me sont ouvers,
Et, dans ma recherche profonde,
Je loge en moy tout l'univers.

. . . .

Celuy que l'Euripe engloutit
Jamais en son coeur ne sentit
Un plus ardent desir d'apprendre.[57]

But he goes on to admit his over-confidence in suggesting that this is a task which can ever be completed:

Mais quand je veux bien l'esplucher,
J'entens qu'on n'y peut rien entendre,
Et qu'on se pert à le chercher.

This is precisely the attitude which one sees epitomized in the Spanish baroque poet's fondness for *Cornucopia*. The desire to cram as much of the physical world as possible into their poetry,[58] a sense of the wonder of nature, and at the same time an ardent curiosity which reflects itself in a concern for detail which is lacking in earlier poetry.

This new eye for detail was in part the automatic consequence of the increasing part played by nature in poetry. Just as those who pursue research in a well-tried sphere may find themselves limited to a restricted area, so those who sought to write within an established and thriving school of nature poetry might have felt that their best opportunity to say anything new was to concentrate upon nature *in parvo*. Now, for the first time, one could find poems written in honour of nature's humbler products. Rioja, for example, writes poems about individual species of flower. And Adrián de Prado, in one of the most delightful poems of the century, his ode to Saint Jerome beginning 'En las desierta Syria destemplada', shows an unprecedented appreciation of the unpromising desert landscape, considering in detail the lives led by spiders, lizards, wasps, ants, snails, and beetles, and even looks at the rocks with a sympathetic eye.[59]

One can find examples of a similar trend in other European literatures. For instance, in his Ode 'Perside je me sens heureux', Théophile reflects on the beauty of pebbles:

---

[57] Saint Amant, op.cit. 12–13.
[58] Compare C. Jannaco's description of Marino as a 'cataloguer of reality', *Il Seicento* (Milan, 1963), p. 155.
[59] Blecua, *Cancionero de 1628*, pp. 209 ff.

Ces petits cailloux bigarez
En des diversitez si belles,
Où trouveroient-ils des modelles
Qui les fissent mieux figurez?
La Nature est inimitable. . .[60]

Marino writes *capricci* about the ant and the mosquito.[61] The English
poets, too, took delight in small things.[62]

Not only do the baroque poets concern themselves with small or
humble creatures, they write of these things in a sometimes unexpected
level of detail. Matías Ginovés' observation of the stamens on the
carnation, or Polo de Medina's description of the peeling skin of the
pomegranate are examples of this kind of thing, as is Adrián de Prado's
depiction of the life of insects. The pursuit of wit helped to stimulate
this natural curiosity, for in their search for conceits the poets projected
themselves imaginatively into the situations they depicted. In order to
make a conceit about an ant, one has to know some of its characteristics
and may find oneself working through its everyday life in one's imagination in order to find the basis of an ingenious comparison. But this
approach to description could also affect poetry which was not constantly striving to produce conceits. For example, the anonymous poem
'corona de rubíes' in Blecua's *Cancionero de 1628* (p. 349), in which
the poet as absent lover expresses the hope that the whole world of
nature will reflect his own misery, takes things a stage further than one
might have expected:

Corona de rubíes
no saque el sol, en braços de la Aurora. . .

. . . .

ni las parleras aues
canten motetes dulçes y süaves.

(May the sun in the arms of dawn not display
his crown of rubies

. . . .

nor the chattering birds
sing their motets, mellifluous and gentle)

Not content to say just this about the birds, the poet stretches the
imagination further by wishing disaster upon them:

---

[60] *Oeuvres poétiques*, II, 42.
[61] *Opere scelte*, 257.
[62] See Kitty Scoular, *Natural Magic. Studies in the Presentation of Nature
in English Poetry from Spenser to Marvell* (Oxford, 1965), Ch. 2.

antes, si con su buelo
bolar quisieren por el ayre vago,
con tempestad el cielo
en ellas haga miserable estrago,
quebrantando sus alas
con gruesas piedras, con menudas balas.

(Instead, if they would fly
and try to wing their way through the wandering wind,
then let a storm from heaven
wreak havoc upon them,
smashing their wings to bits
with great boulders raining down and lesser stones.)

The awareness of nature in miniature, then, is one of the original features of seventeenth century poetry. And it is possible that we see reflected in this poetry a new spirit of curiosity in small things shared by many at this time. In France, the appeal to man's sense of wonder at nature's minutiae played an important part in the argument of the religious apologist Louis Richeome, (1544–1625).[63] Similarly, Pascal in his *Pensées* introduced into his argument the novel concept of the infinitely small as well as the infinitely large, seeking thereby to arouse wonder and confusion. Having reflected on the vastness of the universe Pascal suggests that man then turn his thoughts to a mite: Mais pour lui présenter un autre prodige aussi étonnant, qu'il recherche dans ce qu'il connaît les chose les plus délicates. Qu'un ciron lui offre dans la petitesse de son corps des parties incomparablement plus petites, des jambes avec des jointures, des veines dans ses jambes, du sang dans ses veines, des humeurs dans ce sang, des gouttes dans ses humeurs, des capeurs dans ces gouttes, que, divisant encore ces dernières choses, il épuise ses forces en ces conceptions, et que le dernier objet où il peut arriver soit maintenant celui de notre discours; il pensera peut-être que c'est là l'extrême petitesse de la nature. Je veux lui faire voir là dedans un abîme bouveau.[64]

We can summarize the development of the topos of *Cornucopia*, then, by saying that not only did it become more popular than ever before in the period we are discussing, but there were significant changes in the way it was handled. Enumerations became longer, more detailed, and more surprising. There was less sense of proportion. The result of all these developments was to draw more attention to the wonder of nature's infinite variety. This simple technique, then, is one which epitomizes the baroque poets' approach to description.

---

[63] See Henri Bremond, *Histoire littéraire du sentiment religieux en France* (Paris, 1916), I, 36–46.

[64] *Pensées*, ed. L. Lafuma (Paris, 1960), p. 216.

V

PATTERNS IN NATURE

The descriptive technique of enumeration studied in my previous Chapter was a means of arousing wonder which was more concerned with the confusing complexity of nature than with its unifying patterns. But in this chapter we shall be examining some typical metaphorical techniques, again expressing wonder, where it is precisely to patterns in nature that the poet directs the reader's attention, albeit to reveal a world in which conventional boundaries are overstepped, and where an unexpected, and therefore potentially confusing, order of things prevails.

It is already widely accepted that one of the main functions of baroque imagery is to trace interesting new patterns in the universe. But I believe that traditionally critics have exaggerated the extent to which the poets of the period show us a carefully structured universe by means of their metaphorical technique. In order to demonstrate more clearly what is special about the imagery I shall be discussing later in the chapter, it will be necessary first to consider some of the objections to the critical commonplaces about baroque metaphor.

Some would claim that it is the very frequency of metaphor in baroque poetry which by itself demonstrates that poets of the time were concerned with the unifying design of the world. For metaphor by its very nature could be regarded as a cohesive force in that it unites separate things, linking the object represented by the metaphorical term with that represented by the suppressed proper term. Hence the richer the poetry is in metaphor, the more concepts it will link together, and the more structured will its picture of the world be. This certainly seems to be the sort of view of metaphor implicit in a criticism often made of Gracián's theory of wit, namely, that by defining the witty conceit in terms of the finding of correspondences between objects, he fails to make an adequate distinction between conceit and metaphor.[1]

But does it really make sense to think of ordinary metaphors in which there is no strong sense of wit in terms of a kind of link? Can metaphors which consist of a simple substitution and no further elaboration be

---

[1] See, for example, A. Coster, *Baltasar Gracián (1601–1658)* (New York and Paris, 1913), p. 288.

convincingly analysed in terms of the bringing together of two previously separate concepts? In the case of the most ordinary of metaphors, those which through constant use have become idioms in their own right and are now 'dead', such an analysis goes counter to the psychological facts. It is simply that in the mind of a writer using such commonplace metaphors there is no thought of unifying a previously existing duality. For example, it would be idiosyncratic to interpret an isolated metaphorical reference to a scholar 'ploughing through' a book as an attempt to forge a link between the academic life and life in an agricultural community. And it would be equally fanciful to assume that I had the blacksmith in mind when using the word 'forge' in the preceding sentence. Yet in baroque poetry there is a hard-core of metaphors of simple substitution, particularly among the images used to describe feminine beauty, which if not stone-dead, are at least sufficiently commonplace to have lost much of their original vigour. The assimilation of this kind of metaphor into Góngora's ordinary poetic language removes all sense of duality from the simplest metaphors of the kind found, for example, in his sonnet beginning:

Ya besando unas manos cristalinas,
ya anundandome a un blanco y liso cuello,
ya esparciendo por el aquel cabello,
que amor sacó entre el oro de sus minas,
ya cogiendo de aquellas perlas finas
palabras dulces mil sin merecello. . . ,[2]

(Now planting kisses upon crystal hands,
now clasping mine around a smooth white neck,
now loosening about it that fine hair,
the very gold extracted from love's mines,
now garnering from those exquisite pearls
a thousand undeserved sweet utterances. . .)

Here there is little attempt to add to the Petrarchan tradition. The metaphor *perlas finas* has the function of praising the lady's beauty in a more forceful way than literal language, but it does not really encourage the reader to explore the relationship between pearls and teeth. The preceding images of crystal and gold lead one quite naturally to expect a metaphor in which colour and preciousness are significant, and in which other factors are irrelevant. Knowledge of the traditional significance of this particular metaphor will reinforce this expectation, so that in practice, the mind is most unlikely to consider the pearls as independent entities with a range of attributes amongst which the

---

[2] I adopt here the text of the Vicuña edition (fo. 18), whose reading of line 5 makes far more sense than that of the Chacón manuscript, followed by Millé in whose edition this is poem No. 224.

solution to the metaphor is to be found, but instantly translates the metaphor without even pausing to notice that pearls are round, whilst teeth are sharp. Since the pearls and the teeth are never really separate in the reader's mind, he is not conscious of any linking process.[3]

With highly complex or original metaphor, however, the situation is rather different. Here the poet is often drawing attention not only to the dominant trait associated with the metaphorical term, but also to the secondary characteristics associated with the suppressed proper term, so that, paradoxically, the reader becomes more aware both of the separateness and of the unity of the two terms. A good many baroque metaphors are derived from the extension in a new direction of the familiar Petrarchan images. James Mirollo has noted Marino's use of this technique:

Metaphors like milk, snow, and ivory have, in addition to their dominant trait, qualities of fluidity or solidity, of surface texture, of thermal degree, not to mention personal associations that may cling to them. And since metaphor is based on a degree of resemblance rather than a point to point correspondence between two objects, many of these other qualities are habitually ignored by the poet and suppressed by the reader—provided the two objects do not clash violently and the poet has been able to make the reader forget that they do so clash . . . Marino extends the utility of the traditional metaphor by concentrating on other traits than the dominant, by exploiting those qualities and associations which had not been so thoroughly exhausted by past poets.[4]

Commonplace metaphors, then, are not really concerned with tracing patterns unless in using them the poet has complicated them and pushed a traditional idea in a new direction. Yet it is the whole range of commonplace baroque images of brilliant colour, whether simple or complex, which critics have regarded as one of the means by which the poets present a structured view of the universe. Granted that stylistic unity is brought about by the constant repetition of images of snow and crystal, silver and gold, roses and lilies, diamonds and pearls, rubies and emeralds, in European poets of the seventeenth century, are we justified in concluding that these poets are able by these very means to present a more coherent view of the world? To judge by the remarks of some critics, there is a danger of accepting

---

[3] See Christine Brooke-Rose, who has criticized I.A. Richards's division of metaphor into 'tenor' and 'vehicle', because it artificially separates two terms which are united in metaphor, in her *A Grammar of Metaphor* (London, 1965), p. 9. She also observes (p. 33) that 'most Simple Replacement metaphors—before the advent of the literal symbol—are banal or so self-evident that one is hardly aware of the metaphor. . .or they refer us clearly back to the general context. . .or they are well-known emblematic symbols.'

[4] J.V. Mirollo, op.cit. 154, 156.

automatically that this is so, thereby confusing two distinct things—the structure of the poetry, and the structure of the world about which the poet is writing. For example, Odette de Mourgues writes of Crashaw's metaphors forming a 'shimmering screen made of one material,' and she compares his 'universe' with that of the French baroque poets, which, she says, has 'a sort of glittering solidity ... the facets of the piecemeal composition being the more sparkling as a great number of the metaphors are borrowed from jewellery and precious metals.'[5] When reading statements like this, one needs to bear in mind that it is only metaphorically that one can talk of 'screens', 'solidity', or indeed of 'universes' in poetry. For it is words, not things, which go to make up poems, whilst universes consist of matter rather than of language. Probably many would understand the poet's 'world' to consist neither of words nor of material objects, but of imagined objects. The poet's words refer to things, and it is the inventory of all these objects named by the poet, together with his conception of how they appear and how they behave, which may be said to constitute the poet's universe.

But in practice, this concept of the poet's so-called universe can lead to confusion. The difficulty arises when the poet names one thing but signifies another which he does not name. Such is the case with irony, where what is said may be the exact opposite of what is meant. Such is also the case with metaphor. With each new metaphorical reference to a jewel it seems to be assumed that another gem has been added to the baroque poet's world. But the weakness of this assumption is that it ignores the poet's meaning. When he says 'pearls' but means 'teeth', is there any clear justification for adding pearls rather than teeth to one's inventory? And yet it is all too often upon the domain of thought from which baroque metaphors are drawn that critics have concentrated, ignoring the imagery's meaning and rhetorical function. This general approach has strong affinities with the theory that baroque poetry has a primarily sensuous appeal, a theory which also tends to ignore the meaning of images.

The use of many metaphors drawn from the same domain, then, cannot in itself be taken as evidence that baroque poets seek coherent patterns behind the diversity of natural phenomena. But what of the fact that a poet like Góngora not only draws images from the same domain, but often uses a single metaphorical term to describe a whole range of objects? Dámaso Alonso has drawn attention to this aspect of Góngora, stressing its unifying function, and his view has become something of a critical commonplace:
One searches in vain in the *Soledades* for river-water, sea-water, or the

---

[5] De Mourgues, op.cit. 80, 97.

water of springs or lakes: *crystals* is the label which covers them all.
But crystals also happens to be the image used to refer to a woman's
beautiful limbs. And so we see how not only does individuation dis-
appear within a generic idea, but also how two distinct concepts of
physical matter go on to form a single aesthetic concept, a single
image. As a result we have in Góngora's art some remarkable series
in which the most disparate elements are brought together under a
single term.[6]

Attractive as this point of view is, I believe it is fallacious, simply
because it assumes that in this context metaphor is performing some
special function which lies outside the power of literal language. But
a moment's thought will show that the uniting of disparate objects
by means of a repeated vocabulary is a perfectly normal feature of
everyday language. For example, Góngora's metaphors 'nieve hilada',
'volante nieve', 'la nieve de sus miembros', and so forth ('woven snow',
'flying snow', 'the snow of her limbs'), unite a number of white things
under the single term 'nieve'. But it is doubtful whether in such cases
the poet unites anything which is not already united in ordinary language. What these objects have in common is that fact that they are
very white. Translating the images into literal language, one arrives
at 'white cloth', 'white birds', 'white limbs', and so on. And in all these
cases one has the repetition of the same word, 'white', to describe,
and presumably unite, a number of quite disparate objects. There is
no mystery here, other than that of language in general, and no mental
acrobatics are required; this is a perfectly normal function of the
adjective. In the metaphorical version the function of noun and adjective has been reversed, and this results in a more forceful expression
of the whiteness of the objects involved. But it is hard to see how it
unites the various objects more closely than the literal version.

There are, however, cases where the use of repeated metaphor cannot be so easily translated into literal language. This is where in different
instances of the same metaphorical term different aspects of the object
which it represents are highlighted. For example, 'pearls' may refer
not only to teeth and to a girl's complexion, but also to tears and dew-
drops. In these latter examples it is the shape of the pearl rather than its

---

[6] *Estudios y ensayos gongorinos*, p. 72. C.C. Smith testifies to the widespread acceptance of this view when he writes, 'I have deliberately left out of
account those images of simple equivalence such as 'carne = nieve' which are a
constant, even too constant, feature of Góngora's manner. These figure in all
the textbook accounts of his language... Such series as *carne = nieve ... lana =
nieve* ...are one of the ways in which the poet tries to make us see the oneness
of creation.' 'An approach to Góngora's *Polifemo*,' *BHS*, 42 (1965), 229.

colouring which is relevant, although it could perhaps be argued that the colour is not wholly irrelevant. But to take another example, Góngora refers metaphorically to both streams and poisoned arrows as 'snakes'. In the case of the poisoned arrows, described in the first *Soledad* as 'áspides volantes' ('flying asps'), it is the venomousness of the snake, not its shape, which provides the basis of the analogy. In the case of the stream, described, for example, in Góngora's *Romance* 'Cuatro o seis desnudos hombros' (Millé, No. 70) the analogy is purely one of visual appearance. Even if we met these images in the same poem, could we really claim that the poet had bridged a gap, and brought together two disparate objects?[7] (Question: 'Why is a poisoned arrow like a stream?' Answer: 'Because they are both snakes') I am not convinced that any effective link would have been made between stream and arrow when the only thing that they seem to have in common is the fact that each shares one of its properties—a different property in each case—with a snake. It seems more convincing to claim that the poet, far from uniting stream and arrow, has split the snake! One could make out a reasonable case for the disintegrative rather than the unifying function of repeated metaphors of this type.

Sheer repetition of the same poetic vocabulary, then, is no guarantee that a poet has a structured view of the world. We cannot simply take in the whole of baroque metaphor at a glance and draw any significant structural conclusions of this kind. We need to distinguish more carefully between different types of metaphor, looking at the structure of thought they involve. The metaphorical technique which we shall be examining in this chapter, singled out because it seems to convey a sense of wonder more powerfully than any other, has both a disintegrative and a unifying function. On the constructive side, we see the poet revealing interesting patterns in nature; but on the destructive side, these new patterns are only possible through the breaking down of normal patterns.

This dual aspect of some metaphors is best illustrated by considering first some of Góngora's images of colour before showing how he applies the same basic idea in other spheres. In general, the metaphors of colour of Góngora and his contemporaries have a common rhetorical objective, which is to suggest that what they describe is in some sense exceptional. Thus it is because snow epitomizes whiteness that it is so often used as a metaphor to describe white objects. This pursuit of the extreme in colour, this preoccupation with the remarkable, is one of the simple ways in which the sense of the marvellous is heightened in

---

[7] Góngora's stream = snake images in the *Soledades* unfortunately cannot serve as illustrations here, since he brilliantly works into them the idea of venomousness. See his *Soledades*, I, 509–601; II, 320–4.

baroque poetry. However, the colours described in terms of simple metaphors of this kind are exceptional only in the sense that they are on the high point of a scale. An even stronger sense of the marvellous would result from implying that what is being described is so exceptional that it is right off the end of the scale, and cannot be fitted into accepted categories. Such is the effect of Góngora's well-known description of Galatea's complexion:

Duda el Amor cuál más su color sea,
o púrpura nevada, o nieve roja.

(Polifemo, lines 107–8)

(Love cannot say which better fits her hue,
if it be snowy purple, or red snow.)

His image here is worth analysing in some detail. Galatea's dumbfounded admirers (it probably makes most sense to read 'el Amor' as a metonymic reference to those who have fallen in love with her) waver between two opposite and equally unbelievable versions of what they see. Góngora's juxtaposition of two mutually contradictory contradictions—*púrpura nevada* and *nieve roja*—gives maximum point to an image which epitomizes the marvellous by suggesting that the impossible has come true. Góngora's meaning is probably that two colours grace Galatea's cheeks, red and white, but that these are so closely intermingled that the eye cannot separate them and is deceived, as with a pointillist painting, into seeing only one colour—pink. But there are other possible interpretations, one being that in reality there is only one colour—pink—hence the eye is not deceived, although what it sees is not some pale compromise between two basic colours, red and white, but a colour of redoubled brilliance which miraculously combines the virtues of both. A further possibility is that the eye can in fact distinguish between two colours, but that Galatea's beholder is rather like Buridan's ass, finding himself confronted by two equally exciting attractions, the red and the white, and unable to concentrate on the one because the other cries for attention at the same time. But on any of these readings of the passage, Góngora's metaphor is strongly expressive of wonder.

A further aspect of this passage is the doubt and hesitation in the face of the remarkable which I singled out as an important ingredient in the psychology of wonder in the previous chapter, and which is here made explicit in the verb 'dudar'. But it is also implicit in many other passages in which Góngora offers two or more images to describe a single phenomenon. The feeling that an object defies adequate description, or that the poet does not wish to be dogmatic about what he describes, is conveyed by the poet offering now one image, now another, as if none were definitive. See for example, the description of the ill-defined meeting point between a stream and the sea which

opens the second *Soledad*.[8] That this use of alternative images is an
integral part of Góngora's way of thinking is shown by his easily recognized mannerism of using *si* and *si no* as a link between images.[9]

Two other images of colour cast in the same mould as his description
of Galatea's complexion are worthy of mention. One is in the concluding
lines of the description which opens the second *Soledad* (see above,
p. 37). Here the reversal of the expected colour values is probably
intended to convey the confusion of the seething waters where seaweed
and foam are intermingled in a constantly shifting pattern, so that the
eye is not able to distinguish clearly the one from the other. Another
comparable image is Góngora's delightful description of a poplar tree
in the first *Soledad*:

Músicas hojas viste el menor ramo
del álamo que peina verdes canas.

(lines 590–1)

(Musical leaves bedeck each little branch
of the poplar, grooming its green white hair.)

Again, Góngora's image is open to a variety of interpretations. The
'músicas hojas', for example may refer literally to the leaves of the tree
moving in the breeze, or it may refer to birds hidden in the foliage
whose sound seems to emanate from the very leaves themselves. By the
image 'verdes canas', Góngora may mean that there are two colours in
reality, white and green, but that the eye is deceived by the constant
movement of the leaves (suggested by the verb *peinar*) into seeing only
one. Pellicer suggests, not very credibly, that both the bark and the
leaves on poplar trees are green and white in colour. But certainly
the leaves are paler on one side than on the other. More important than
the botanical facts is the over-all colour effect described by Góngora
which is of a light green, and which seems remarkable in that it is
expressed in terms of a contradiction. Góngora implies that what he
is describing in this and the other colour images of this type violates
the rules, or goes against accepted patterns. He adopts the stance of a
person who is expecting to see only certain fundamental colours—white
and black, and the primary colours. To a person conditioned to think
only in terms of such a clear-cut range of colours, a shade like pink or
pale green may seem like the impossible come true.

We perhaps should not rule out the possibility that the word 'canas'
describing the poplar's foliage may be intended in an abstract sense to
symbolize venerable old age. Góngora may be saying that the tree is
old, but that whereas we would expect a normal person's hair to go

---

[8] See above, p. 43.
[9] See D. Alonso, *Góngora y el Polifemo*, I, 156–61.

white with age, the poplar's hair is green. But even on this less likely
interpretation there is an element of surprise, and the reader would
be expected to note the contradiction between the literal meaning of
'canas' and the value which it has in this passage.

The use of contradictory metaphors of the kind we have seen is
not restricted to images based on colour patterns. Perhaps those most
frequently met take as their starting point the idea of the universe
being built upon the basic structure of the four elements of earth, air,
fire, and water, each element having characteristics of its own which
quite clearly distinguish it from the others. This basic structure is
sufficiently commonplace for its currency in seventeenth-century
Spain not to need much demonstration. Apart from all else, the account
of the creation in the Book of Genesis was sufficient to ensure that
thinking in terms of the various elements came naturally to people.
But it is worth showing how the basic structure was very much in
the mind of baroque poets before we go on to consider how through
their metaphors they sought to show surprising deviations from the
traditional pattern.

In a simple way Góngora affirms the elemental structure of the
world in his sonnet beginning:

Ni en este monte, este aire, ni este río
corre fiera, vuela ave, pece nada,
de quien con atención no sea escuchada
la triste voz del triste llanto mío.[10]

(On this hillside, in this air, this river,
no beast runs, no bird flies, and no fish swims,
but listens fully and attentively
to the doleful sound of my sad sobbing.)

Here, to amplify the theme that the whole world is affected by the
lover's lament, the poet splits the world up into the constituent elements
of earth, air, and water (*monte, aire, río*) and selects a representative
inhabitant of each. The same basic method is used in a later sonnet
of Pedro Espinosa:

Selva, viento, corriente, que jüeces
os mereció en mi mal el llanto mío;
Verde calle, luz tierna, cristal frío,

. . . .

Ancha selva, aire fresco, claro río,
De alta sombra, luz nueva, alegre brío,
De animales, de pájaros, y peces.[11]

---

[10]   *Obras completas*, ed. Millé, No. 232.
[11]   *Obras*, ed. F. Rodríguez Marín, p. 34.

(Wood, winds, and stream, which I in my sad plight
deserve as judges in my tearful cause,
green pathway, gentle light, and chilly quartz,

. . . .

broad forest, cooling air, and limpid stream,
with lengthy shadows, new light, and joyous verve,
with animals, and feathered friends, and fish.)
This rather mechanical approach left little room for further development along the same lines. Even so, Góngora had the imagination
to exploit the same idea in a new way in another of his sonnets:

No destrozada nave en roca dura
tocó la playa más arrepentida,
ni pajarillo de la red tendida
voló más temeroso a la espesura;

bella Ninfa, la planta mal segura,
no tan alborotada ni afligida,
hurtó de verde prado, que escondida
víbora regalaba en su verdura,

como yo, Amor, la condición airada,
las rubias trenzas y la vista bella
huyendo voy, con pie ya desatado,

de mi enemiga en vano celebrada.
Adiós Ninfa crüel; quedaos con ella,
dura roca, red de oro, alegre prado.[12]

(Never vessel, smashed on a hard rock,
reached the shore more humbled and repentant,
nor any little bird more fearfully
flew from the outstretched net into the woods,
never maiden, stepping gingerly,
displayed more shocked alarm or more distress
in taking to her heels in a green field
which hid a viper in its greenery,
than I, Love, from the overbearing mien,
the golden tresses, and the lovely looks
of the enemy I vainly courted,
go running headlong upon flying feet.
And so, cruel nymph, farewell: remain with her
hard rock, gold net, and pleasant meadow.)

[12] *Obras completas*, ed. Millé, No. 239.

In this poem, the dangers of love are compared with the hazards to be found in the various elements: in the water, the rock which threatens the ship; in the air, the net which threatens the bird; on land, the snake which endangers the nymph. The fact that the net referred to in the last line is of gold gives us a key to the conceit on which the poem is based. The snare is provided by the lady's golden hair.[13] Completing the equation, we see how the 'dura roca' represents the harshness of the lady's 'condición airada', and the 'alegre prado' the deceptively pleasant appearance of her 'vista bella'. Small wonder that the poet flees from this example of universal danger.

One might conclude that the sort of symmetries illustrated in the foregoing examples could be the result of the poets' concern for the stylistic structure of their poems rather than of their interest in the structure of the world. Yet there are other examples in which it is quite clear that the poet has in mind a natural law which maintains the separation of the four elements, and ensures that each finds its own appropriate level. For instance, Soto de Rojas uses this theme in his *Faetón*, where he describes the impetuous Phaeton's irresistible urge to see his father in terms of the attraction which leads each element to seek its own natural level:

Agua a su curso assi, llama a su esfera
Piedra, se inclina a su natiuo assiento.[14]

(Thus water to its course, flame to its sphere,
stone to its seat, by nature are inclined.)

The same theme is found in one of Soto's sonnets, where the frustrated attempt of a flame to regain its distant sphere is taken as an example:

Subes ò llama con veloz carrera,
Destos cansados leños desatada,
Solicitando en humo transformada
El distante reposo de tu esfera;
Pero al subir por la region ligera
Te buelue el viento burlador en nada.

(*Obras*, p. 42)

(You rise aloft, oh flame, in rapid flight,
liberated from the exhausted timber.
Now changed to smoke, you diligently seek
the restfulness, far distant, of your sphere;
but as you soar through the region of air,
the tricky wind converts you into nought.)

---

[13] Compare Garcilaso's fourth *canción*, lines 101–2: 'De los cabellos de oro fue texida/ la red que fabricó mi sentimiento'.

[14] *Obras*, ed. A. Gallego Morell, p. 307.

Góngora had also given poetic expression to this elemental law:
Desde su barca Alcïón
suspiros y redes lanza,
los suspiros por el cielo
y las redes por el agua

. . . .

En un mismo tiempo salen
de las manos y del alma
los suspiros y las redes,
hacia el fuego y hacia el agua.
Ambos se van a su centro,
do su natural les llama,
desde el corazón los unos,
las otras desde la barca.

(Millé, No. 5)

(From his boat Halcyon
disperses sighs and nets,
the sighs towards the heavens,
the nets towards the sea.

. . . .

At the same time there leave
his hands and his spirit
the sighs and the fish-nets
for the fire and water.
Both make for their centre,
in natural response,
the one from his heart,
the other from the boat.)

Here, with a certain amount of poetic licence, Góngora embellishes the basic idea that in the sub-lunary world each element tends to seek its natural level.[15] His originality lies in his seeing the nets as natural to the element of water, and the passionate sighs of the lover as akin to fire rather than air. We have a different variation on the theme elsewhere in the poem, when the fisherman himself describes his lamentations as 'dar viento al viento, y olas a las olas' ('giving wind to the wind, and waves to the waves'), where this time his complaints find

[15] See E.M. Tillyard, *The Elizabethan World Picture* (London, 1963), p. 79. The theory was elegantly expressed by the seventeenth-century moralist, Francisco Garau: 'Rodará despeñandose entre riscos por toda la tierra, el Nilo, para hallar en el mar su quietud: y se dexará caer del Cielo mismo, un jaspe, en busca de su centro la tierra, i romperá con un monte el fuego, para subirse à su esfera; y se desprenderá de jaulas de oro, y diamantes, el ave, para echar mil puntas en el aire,' *El Olimpo del sabio. Segunda parte* (Barcelona, 1691), p. 39.

their centre in the wind, and his tears in the sea. The poetic effect of this alternative version of the theme, is, like the first one, to unite the lover with nature.

Seventeenth-century poets were quite familiar, then, with the convention of thinking of the structure of the universe as based on the contrasted elements. And the repeated parallelisms adopted by the poets in the examples we have cited give the impression that it was a structure with a reassuring sturdiness about it. The structure of these poems echoes the structure of the world, as if to affirm that there is a place for everything, and that everything is in its place. Hence it was all the more exciting when, under Góngora's lead as ever, poets began to adopt imagery in which the expected divisions between the four elements were rejected in the same way that the basic pattern of simple colours was overturned by Góngora in some of his images. The technique used was to describe one element metaphorically in terms of another, or to refer to the characteristic inhabitants of one element in terms more usually associated with those of another. For convenience I shall refer to these images of interchange between the elements as trans-elemental images.

Trans-elemental imagery is a phenomenon already familiar to the critics, especially since E.M. Wilson's study of it in Calderón's theatre,[16] but there seems to have been no comprehensive investigation of its function. In discussing Góngora's *Soledades*, R.O. Jones has interestingly analysed some of these images, but his aim is not to generalize about all trans-elemental imagery, and his conclusions as to the moral function of the metaphors he discusses are not readily applicable to the whole range of examples found in Góngora and other poets.[17] Wilson's article, on the other hand, although giving a bird's eye-view of the whole phenomenon, is largely unconcerned with its function. He describes his article as a contribution to the study of Calderón's diction, and is more concerned with the classification and the formal characteristics of these images than with their poetic effect. His conclusion that they are a manifestation of 'the rise of the baroque spirit in literature, with its emphasis on force and passion, and its tendency to overflow the natural bounds', even if one were to accept its assumptions, could not really serve as an explanation of all trans-elemental imagery. What of the typical floral images, for example? It does not seem very appropriate to think of these in terms of force, passion, or an overflowing of natural bounds. My aim in the remainder of this chapter is to offer an account of this type of metaphor which will be applicable to the whole range. At the same time I hope to suggest a wider

---

[16] 'The four elements in the imagery of Calderón', *MLR*, 31 (1936), 34–47.

[17] See R.O. Jones, 'The poetic unity of the *Soledades* of Góngora', *BHS*, 31 (1954), 189–204.

interpretation of individual images by showing not only their negative
aspect—the way in which they show the breaking down of normal
patterns in nature—but also their positive aspect, which has tended
to be ignored, namely the way in which they show us new patterns.

We may begin by considering those images in which the negative
idea of disruption is strong. One context in which trans-elemental
imagery is used appropriately is in the description of catastrophes in
which the normal balance of nature is overthrown. Floods, earthquakes,
hurricanes and conflagrations may all be regarded as examples of one
particular element overstepping its normal bounds and encroaching on
the territory of others. A sense of shocked amazement at things getting
out of hand in this way is registered through the poets' use of contradictory imagery in which there is a corresponding semantic encroach-
ment. Thus Gabriel Bocángel, for instance, in a short *romance* describing
an earthquake, sees the catastrophe in terms of a storm at sea:

Ondas padece la tierra,
O se nauega, ò lo finge,
Enjutos naufragios truecan
Las cumbres con las raízes.

. . . .

Repitese la discordia
Del Chaos?[18]

(The land submits to waves;
things sail, or so it seems;
dry shipwrecks switch the place
of treetops and tree roots.

. . . .

Have we returned once more
to Chaos's discord?)

The trans-elemental image 'enjutos naufragios' heightens the expression
of confusion with its suggestion that the impossible has come true. And
this feeling of impossibility is expressed at the end of the poem when
Bocángel wonders what will become of the love-poets' favourite *argumentum ab impossibile* if the impossible can really come to pass.[19]
Nevertheless, despite the confusion, there is at the same time a hint of
method in nature's madness. The overthrowing of the old order of
things has led to the establishment of a new pattern, a new relationship
between land and sea. The earth-tremor produces waves on the land

[18] Bocangel *Obras*, I, 95–6.
[19] Como, los montes se mueuen?/ A donde podràn (dezidme/ Ioue excelso)
los amantes/ Vincular sus impossibles?

comparable to waves at sea, and, just as strong waves may capsize a ship (a seafaring tree), so the waves of the earthquake may overturn trees on land. Hence the metaphor has revealed a new correspondence in nature, a new, if tortuous, link between earth and water.

The legend of Phaeton, to which both Villamediana and Soto de Rojas devoted full-scale poems, provided another example of a catastrophe which invited dramatic description, particularly that part of the story in which Phaeton loses control of the chariot of the sun and the earth is scorched. Villamediana describes the conflagration as 'el adusto diluvio' ('the dry flood'), thus reminding us of the similarity between flood and conflagration. And Soto de Rojas, too, boldly mixes the elements in his imagery:

Ondas las crines son, que en mar de fuego
Alçan borrasca en los celestes giros:
Naue pues sin timon, piloto ciego,
Discurren por los campos de safiros,
Ya de Topacios, que centellas llueuen
Vientos quatro fortissimos los mueuen.

(*Obras*, p. 351)

(The tails are waves that in a sea of fire
whip up a tempest in the heavenly spheres.
Without a rudder, then, the helmsman blind,
the ship is driven through the sapphire fields,
or those of topaz, which rain showers of sparks,
propelled along by four most powerful winds.)

De fuego, copos nieua el firmamento,
Y las nuues centellas a porfia,
Granizo dan; y el humedo elemento
A Libia en lo arenoso desafia.

(*Obras*, p. 361)

(The firmament snows flakes of fire,
the clouds in rivalry hail sparks;
and the once humid element
now rivals Libya for sand.)

Here, the image 'nevar copos de fuego' is rather more striking than 'mar de fuego' and 'centellas llueven' in that it is more sharply contradictory, combining as it does extremes of heat and cold. But all these images, including that in which the chariot is seen as a ship, involve a degree of tension caused by the association of one element with another.

In the foregoing examples we see the poets using disturbed imagery to describe a disturbed situation in nature. But another context in which trans-elemental imagery was used is in the description of situations in which an innocent onlooker because of an optical illusion might be deceived into thinking that he is faced with an anomaly, although in reality there is no disturbance or confusion in nature. The poet's imagery expresses wonder at the apparently magical transformation brought about by such a trick of the senses. The following lines from the first *Soledad* are a case in point:

No bien pues de su luz los horizontes
—que hacían desigual confusamente
montes de agua, y piélagos de montes—
desdorados los siente. . .

(lines 42–5)

(Scarce had he sensed the sun's horizon's light,
which in a muddled and uneven way
made hills of water, and gulfs of the hills,
lose its golden tinge. . .)

Here Góngora describes the illusion confronting the shipwrecked stranger as dusk falls and prevents the eye from clearly distinguishing between land and sea. But in conceiving of the possibility of such a deception, Góngora is not simply producing a negative image whose sole function is to show how the normally reliable process of observation has been upset. He is also inviting in the reader a positive appreciation of one of nature's patterns—the similarity between waves on the sea and hills on dry land. Unless there were some physical similarity there could be no confusion, since the one could not then be mistaken for the other.

Góngora's interest in the confusing effects of distance on the eye is seen a little later in the first *Soledad*, where a magnificent panorama stretches out like a map before the stranger:

Si mucho poco mapa les despliega,
mucho es más lo que, nieblas desatando,
confunde el sol, y la distancia niega.

(*Soledades*, I, 194–6)

(If on this little map much is revealed,
there is much more which, by unleashing mists,
the sun obliterates, and distance hides.)

One may compare this with Gabriel Bocángel's sonnet beginning:

Ya falta el Sol; que quieto el mar, y el cielo,
niegan vnidos la distante arena.[20]

(The sun is gone; the tranquil sea and sky
in union negate the distant sand.)

[20] Bocangel, *Obras*, p. 271.

Here, the view is from a ship at sea. The distant land lies beyond the horizon. All that can be seen is the continuous expanse of calm sea and sky, a featureless union which denies the observer the sight of land, in that if the land were visible, it would be interposed between the two.

Another writer who was particularly fascinated by seascapes is Francisco de Trillo y Figueroa, who took as the starting point of a number of his images the illusion created by the reflection of sunlight on water. It is a theme extensively treated in his 'Pintura de la noche'. The following is an extract from a passage on this theme:

Tan otro el Occeano
Era en ardiente pira,
Que no mar, si no incendio
Embuelto en cristal mudo parecia
Assi en la vndosa llama
Las ondas sumergidas,
Tal vez desmienten rayos,
Y tal neuado incendio se acreditan.
Neuado incendio, adonde
Aun mal se determina,
Se las ondas se apagan,
O si es ceniza el sol donde se abrigan.

(Obras, pp. 226–7)

(The Ocean was so changed
into a burning pyre
that rather than a sea it seemed to be
a conflagration in mute crystal trapped.
Thus in the wavy flame
the waves, being submerged,
now contradict the rays,
and now pass for a snowy holocaust,
a snowy conflagration within which
one cannot surely say
if the waves are snuffed
or if the sun, their refuge, is but ash.)

The shining waters seem mysteriously to combine the qualities of fire and water, and the whole passage is packed with trans-elemental imagery. But, of course, Trillo is not suggesting through such images that natural law has broken down, but merely that it gives the illusion of having done so, as the use of such expressions as 'parecer' and 'aun mal se determina' suggests.

Trillo was obviously much impressed by the poetic possibilities of the contradictory linking of fire and water in such images as 'la undosa llama', since he used the same basic formula many times in the course of his works.[21] Again it is the idea of the reflection of light upon water which gives rise to the trans-elemental imagery of the following passage from Book Five of Trillo's *Neapolisea*:

Ya en las ondas la llama fluctuaua,
Y el mar en los reflexos, cuyas sumas
Prozelosas Deydades, alteradas,
Huyen al mar, del mar arrebatadas.
Del Ancho golfo Tetis diuidia
Las mal texidas obas presurosa,
Y al Iupiter marino se oponia
Con rayos de cristal, a llama vndosa;
Penetra de las ondas la porfin,
Y apagando del Sol la llama hermosa,
Corriendo al dia el cristalino velo,
Dos vezes en las ondas se vió el Cielo.

(*Obras*, p. 508)

(In the waves the flame now fluctuated,
in the reflected light, the sea, whose high
and stormy deities in shocked alarm,
torn from the sea, flee to the sea.
Across the broad straits Tethys cleaved her way
making a speedy path through the loose weed,
and to the marine Jove she stood opposed
with crystal rays against the wavy flame.
And when she reached the limits of the waves,
extinguishing the sun's beautiful flame,
drawing the crystal curtains of the day,
the heavens were seen twice within the waves.)

Trillo sees the sunset as a dramatic conflict in which the Ocean, invaded by flame, tries to defend itself and wins when the Ocean goddess Tethys manages to extinguish the sun. As the sun sinks the sky is seen twice in the waves because firstly, the sun on the horizon literally seems to be entering the water, and secondly, because the reflection of the light in the water makes it appear to emanate from the sea itself.

The Italian poet Marino, too, had given expression to the magic of seeing the sky reflected in water in a sonnet from his anthology *La Lira* (1614):

Ve como van per queste piagge e quelle
con scintille scherzando ardenti e chiare,

---

[21] e.g. 'Húmedas centellas' (*Obras*, pp. 289, 388, 453), an expression borrowed from Góngora's *Polifemo*; 'húmedas cenizas' (p. 233), though wet ashes are at least a physical possibility; 'ardientes espumas' (p. 290); 'fogoso cristal' (p. 466).

volte in pesci le stelle, i pesci in stelle.
Si puro el vago fondo a noi traspare,
che fra tanti dirai lampi e facelle:
—Ecco il ciel cristallin cangiato in mare![22]

(See how along this shore and along that
playing with bright and fiery sparks there go
the stars changed into fish, the fish to stars.
The depths show through so clear and beautiful
that mid such lamps and torches you will cry
'Behold, the crystal heaven's become a sea!')

The exclamatory conclusion to this sonnet expresses the sense of wonder stimulated by the illusion.

In the two main kinds of trans-elemental image so far discussed—those describing natural catastrophes, and those describing optical illusions—it would be fair to say that the poet is describing phenomena which by their very nature excite wonder. Most people with normal human responses are likely to be impressed by earthquakes, mirages, or perfect reflections. But trans-elemental images were also used by the baroque poets to add a sense of excitement to situations and phenomena which on the surface appear more ordinary. They draw attention to some of nature's subtle patterns which cut across the anticipated divisions and contrasts between the four elements.

A good example of a very simple metaphor painting to such a pattern in Góngora's description of the stormy sea from which his shipwrecked stranger emerges in the first *Soledad* as 'una Libia de ondas' ('a Libya of waves'). The image is surprising because it describes that which is extremely watery—the ocean—in terms of that which is extremely dry—the desert. But once the reader has recovered from the shock of seeing the Ocean denied its dominant trait, he may go on to appreciate the aptness of the metaphor in pointing out a correspondence in nature between ocean and desert. Both are, after all, vast waste expanses in the middle of which it is inconvenient to be stranded. And pursuing the comparison one may note that the desert has its sand-storms which correspond to the storms at sea, and its dunes which correspond to ocean waves.

The source of many of the metaphors of this type is the pursuit of analogies between the characteristic inhabitants or phenomena of different elements. If in their images poets could convert land into sea, they could also remove creatures from their proper element, plunging birds into the sea, and so on. For example, the comparison between air and water in terms of their expansiveness and similarity of colour is given added point when Góngora invites us to consider the

---

[22] *Opere Scelte*, pp. 219–20.

flight of birds through the air in aquatic terms in his well-known comparison between a group of peasant girls and a flight of cranes:

Cual en los equinocios surcar vemos
los piélagos del aire libre algunas
volantes no galeras,
sino grullas veleras,

(*Soledades*, I, 603–6)

(Just as at the equinox we witness
cleaving the ocean of the open sky
not flying galleys, rather, cranes with sails.)

The same basic idea is admirably exploited in Polo de Medina's remarkable *Ocios de la soledad*, in which the poet seeks to persuade a friend to come and share the pleasures of life in the country:

El baharí britano. . .
las veredas del aire va cruzando
hasta una garza, que la vió nadando
(con un ruïdo lento)
en el golfo del viento,
donde si no era espuma
viviente escollo es, isla de pluma.[23]

(The British Sparrowhawk. . .
crosses the pathways of the air
after a heron it saw swimming there
(with a leisurely sound)
in the gulf of the wind
where, if it was not foam,
it is a living rock, a feathered isle.)

In true Gongoristic fashion Polo offers a number of alternative ways of looking at the object of his description whilst shunning the most obvious. The bird's colouring against the blue of the sky suggests the foam of the sea against its blue background. Alternatively, the bird is like a rock because it gets in the path of the hawk as a rock might get in the path of a ship. At the same time, in its solitariness the bird resembles an island.

Polo then goes on to explore another analogy in which fish and birds are related:

Y en este estanque (mapa cristalino
del árbol y del monte convecino)
prenderás con las redes a las aves
que en vientos de cristal vuelan suaves.

---

[23] *Obras completas*, ed. A. Valbuena Prat, (Murcia, 1948), p. 172.

(And in this fishing-pond, a crystal map
of the tree and the mountain close at hand,
with your nets you will intercept the birds
who wing their streamlined flight through crystal winds)

One interesting feature of this passage is that to feel its full force the reader should ideally be already familiar with Góngora's poetic vocabulary. The term *vientos de cristal* is less sharply contradictory than *vientos de agua*. But because *cristal* is a word so commonly used by Góngora and his followers to refer to water, to those familiar with the tradition it is tantamount to *agua*, and the image retains its sharpness as a trans-elemental metaphor. Another subtle aspect of Polo's image is the hint that optical illusion plays a part in the sequence of thought which leads one to expect to see birds in the water. In the water is reflected a nearby tree, so that casting a net into the water may be thought of as tantamount of placing it on the tree where it might be expected to ensnare birds.

But at the basis of Polo's image lies the perception of a natural correspondence between fish and birds. It was an observation which was not entirely new in the seventeenth century. Indeed, it is one which had earlier excited Fray Luis de León's admiration, as the following dialogue from the introduction to Book Three of his *Nombres de Cristo* illustrates:

'I was just heading for the river until I saw you.'

'You must have business with the fish,' said Julian.

'But yesterday I said I was a bird,' said Sabino.

'Well, birds and fish are of the same family,' replied Julian, 'so that fits.'

'How do you mean, the same family?' asked Sabino.

'Because', answered Julian, 'Moses says that on the fifth day God created the birds and fish from the water.'

'Quite so,' said Sabino, 'but they succeed in hiding the family likeness, judging by how little they resemble each other.'

'On the contrary,' Julian then replied, 'they resemble each other very closely, for swimming is like flying; and just as flying cuts through the air, so swimming cleaves the water; and for the most part both birds and fish are born from eggs. And when you come to look at it, the scales on fish are like the feathers on birds; and the fish too have their wings, and steer themselves with these and their tail when they swim, just as the birds do when they fly.'

Sabino laughed, 'But birds generally sing and chatter, whilst the fish are all dumb.'[24]

Here, Sabino expresses the traditional expectation that creatures inhabiting different elements can have little in common. But his companion

---

[24] Luis de León, *Obras completas castellanas*, ed. F. García (Madrid, 1959), pp. 660–1.

wittily demonstrates the plausibility of the opposite view. What the baroque poets offer in their trans-elemental imagery is a more concentrated presentation of the same kind of perception. In their poetry the juxtaposition of ideas which one finds in simile is replaced by the superimposition of ideas which is the unique feature of metaphor. Often the reader may have to supply the reasons for the correspondence himself. Sometimes the basis of comparison may simply be some physical similarity. At other times the link may be slightly more abstract, as when, for example, Soto de Rojas describes falconry as 'la pesca mas plumosa' ('more feathery fishing') and fishing as 'la caza de las ondas más mojada' ('a wetter kind of hunting in the waves'),[25] images akin to Góngora's description of the seal-hunting of the girls in the second *Soledad* as 'nauticas venatorias maravillas' ('marvels of nautical venery') as they go into action against the 'toro marino' ('marine bull').[26]

In other cases, the poet may spell out in detail the basis of his surprising idea. A good illustration of the variety of approach is provided by instances of another very common trans-elemental theme—the correspondence between the stars in the sky and the flowers on earth.[27] The bright flowers scattered haphazardly against the green background of the grass are compared with the bright stars scattered in similar fashion against the blue background of the sky. The traditional concept of Elysian Fields, and of Paradise as a garden further help the comparison. The analogy is cometimes stated quite simply, as when Soto de Rojas says of the flowers in his garden 'trasladan a las estrellas'[28] ('they transfer the stars'), or when Villamediana describes flowers as 'emulación fragrante a las estrellas'[29] ('a fragrant emulation of the stars'), images which are arguably not even metaphorical. Again, we have a very simple metaphor when an anonymous *Romance a las estrellas* describes the stars as 'flores al celeste campo' ('flowers in the celestial field').[30] By contrast, Matías Ginovés in his *Selva al verano*, a poem which as we saw in the previous chapter adopts a highly original approach to enumerative description, takes delight in tracing out in detail links between earth and heaven. Detailed resemblances are found between individual flowers and particular heavenly bodies. And he concludes with a delightfully witty comparison between the shape of the flower buds and the orbital path of the planets, and between the perfume

[25] Soto, *Obras*, p. 406.
[26] *Soledades*, II, 421. See also lines 419—20, 'Cazar a Tetis veo/ y pescar a Diana'.
[27] See E.M. Wilson, art.cit. 38—9.
[28] Soto, *Obras*, p. 386.
[29] Juan de Tassis (Conde de Villamediana), *Obras* (Zaragoza, 1629), p. 272.
[30] Blecua, *Cancionero de 1628*, p. 437, line 5.

emitted by the flowers and the light emitted by the stars.

> Con este alegre confusión de flores,
> cubierto el fértil suelo
> pretende haçer emulación al cielo;
> si ya no vn fiel traslado
> de todo aquesse exército estrellado;
> soles son los claueles,
> lunas las açuçenas,
> el aurora, la rosa, que alegría
> der[r]ama al despuntar de claro día,
> correspondiendo a las demás estrellas
> toda la plebe de las flores bellas,
> que sobre el epiçiclo
> del capullito tierno y delicado
> fragrantes raios dan al verde prado.[31]

> (Covered with this joyous mass of flowers,
> the fertile soil aspires
> to offer competition to the sky,
> or exactly copy
> that entire host of stars.
> Suns are the carnations;
> moons the lily flowers;
> the dawn, the rose, which spreads
> her joyousness at the clear break of day;
> and to the other stars there correspond
> the populace of all the lovely flowers
> who send out from above
> the epicycle of their tender buds
> fragrant rays to grace the verdant meadow.)

Few of the images examined so far in this chapter express the idea of the disruption of nature. And we have seen how even in those which describe natural catastrophes, the destruction of normal patterns goes hand in hand with the construction of new ones. Is this balance between positive and negative still preserved when the poets move from describing natural phenomena to consider what might be regarded as the unnatural activities of man venturing into alien elements? Or is it the poets' intention in using trans-elemental imagery to describe ships, for example, to be purely negative and to imply criticism of man for breaking the natural order of things? Is this a case where the wonder which is so characteristic of other trans-elemental images is totally lacking? These are the issues I shall consider in the following paragraphs.

---

[31] Blecua, *Cancionero de 1628*, p. 202, lines 186–99.

Understandably enough, the great bulk of trans-elemental metaphors describing man's interaction with nature concern seafaring activities. Had the aeroplane been invented in time, doubtless the baroque poets would have found in it a most fruitful source of imagery. As it was, they had to be content with the legends of Icarus and Phaeton for examples of adventurers who took to the skies, although one does sometimes find horseriding described as a kind of venture into the air.[32] The climbing of mountains, which might have offered further opportunities for this kind of theme does not seem to have been fully exploited, although Quevedo criticized the scaling of

Los montes invencibles
que la Naturaleza
eminentes crió para sí sola.[33]

(The invincible, and lofty mountains,
which Nature created just for herself.)

The best known nautical metaphors are to be found in Góngora's first *Soledad*, in the embittered speech of the old man who has lost a son at sea. Here, the world's first mariner—described as 'el que surcó, labrador fiero/el campo undoso en mal nacido pino' ('he who, as a ruthless ploughman, furrowed/the wavy field upon an ill-starred pine')— appears very much as a creature of the land venturing into a foreign element. And his ship is described in equally incongruous terms as 'vaga Clicie del viento' ('wandering Clitie of the wind'), a sunflower which turns to the wind instead of to the sun. Again, the oddity of ships, born of the land, crossing the ocean is heightened by Góngora's vision of fleets of ships as 'selvas inconstantes' (unstable forests'), by which he extends the classical description of a ship as a tree.

It has been suggested that Góngora's imagery here has a symbolic value:

[Góngora] is reminding the reader of the natural order of the physical universe as he conceived it. He describes it in terms of the four elements, each one a domain for some creature. Only man breaks the natural order by venturing on the sea, and does so only to suffer for his folly. Góngora accordingly takes the physical universe to parallel a moral one, and, in this work, in describing the one describes the other ... It seems increasingly probable that Góngora is using the four elements that lie behind his cosmology to symbolize also a moral order inherent in nature, so that in breaking the physical order man is also breaking the other.[34]

But plausible though this account of these metaphors is, one needs to

[32] See Polo de Medina, 'Aprenderás de ave en un caballo' ('on horseback you will learn to be a bird'), *Obras*, p. 173.

[33] Sermón estoico de censura moral' (*Obras completas*, Vol. 1, p. 135).

[34] R.O. Jones, 'The poetic unity of the *Soledades* of Góngora', pp. 193, 194.

beware of generalizing too freely about Góngora's views on the basis of this passage, or about the function of baroque metaphors describing ships. For example, we can find many instances in which trans-elemental imagery is used when far from censuring sailing as an activity, the poet actually seems to be praising it. What, then, is the function of these images if not to suggest confusion? Is it a case of imitators aping Góngora's mannerisms without fully understanding the deeper purpose of his metaphors? We need first to look a little more closely at the moral issues involved.

For Góngora and his contemporaries there could have been nothing intrinsically wrong in man sailing the seas. To put to sea with the greed for gold as one's motivation was morally reprehensible. On the other hand, to set sail with a view to converting the heathen in other lands to Christianity was regarded as wholly praiseworthy, as can be seen from a poem much influenced by Góngora, entitled 'A las grandes navegaciones del Santo Padre Javier', and attributed by its editor tentatively (and highly improbably) to King Philip IV, where the religious purpose of the saint is alluded to in imagery which describes the crossing in heavenly terms:

Apostándole al sol igual camino
si pompa no de favorable Juno,
zodiaco a tu nave cristalino,
sulcaste el cielo undoso de Neptuno.[35]

(Competing with the sun in length of course,
if not in splendour of a kindly Juno,
you clove the wavy heaven of Neptune,
a zodiac of crystal for your ship.)

In itself, seafaring is an ethically neutral activity. Hence there is nothing morally lax in the favourable attitude towards it shown, for example, by Francisco de Trillo, one of Góngora's most assiduous admirers and imitators, in the following passages from some of his heroic poems, since he attributes nothing but noble motives to the shipowners:

O bien sea oprimiendo el Occeano
con las nadantes selvas,
que en los prolijos campos de Neptuno
plantarán tus baxeles vno a vno. . .

(Obras, p. 340)

(Or dominating totally the sea
with the swimming forests
which in the vastnesses of Neptune's fields
your vessels will have planted one by one. . .)

[35] Poetas líricos de los siglos xvi y xvii, ed. A. de Castro, BAE, Vol. 32, (Madrid, 1950), p. 152. These lines are heavily influenced by Góngora, Soledad I, 466–9.

Nadantes selvas de breados Pinos
Buelan el Mar, con las texidas alas,
Cuyas plumas del vno al otro margen
El Orbe escriuen, en copioso Mapa.

(Obras, p. 406)

(Let swimming forests of pines tarred with pitch
now fly across the sea with woven wings
whose quills between one margin and the next
trace out the globe in an extensive map.)

Vió el Trace arar los campos de Neptuno
Largamente a las proras Españolas,
Sin que de tantos defiendese alguno
La mies fecunda de sus rubias olas.

(Obras, p. 523)

(Thrace witnessed how the Spanish prows at length
furrowed their way through the fields of Neptune,
none of which attempted to defend
the fertile harvest of their golden waves.)

But are we to regard Trillo's use of trans-elemental images in this kind of positive context as rhetorically pointless, and as a hollow imitation of Góngora's techniques? The originality with which Trillo follows his images through suggests that they were something more than perfunctory acknowledgements of a poetical tradition. Moreover, the interesting annotations which he provides to a number of his works reveals one who was a thoughtful and meticulous scholar,[36] seriously concerned with the real meaning of what he read and not with the mere surface trappings of scholarship, as his satirical remarks in the following passage show:

I am amazed at the arrogance with which these writers display a couple of scholarly quotations, so smug at having found them, selling them as something exquisite, as if they were not in print, and nobody anywhere else owned books: but I am much more amazed at the naïveté with which they write, skimming over those very passages which they cite as quickly as if they were running away from them. Doubtless it is from the truth that they are fleeing.[37]

[36] He is refreshingly precise in his references, witness his complaint against Quevedo in the following passage: 'Yo tengo el texto Greco Latino de Simplicio, y Geronimo Vvolfio, de Colonia 1596. y el capitulo Griego es 73. como yo le cito, sin acordarse de nombrar a Aristoteles, con quien (como en todo) deuia de estar mal Queuedo en aquella ocasion.' *(Obras*, pp. 429–30).

[37] 'Admirame mucho la arrogancia con que estos Escritores obstentan dos lugarcitos de erudición muy pagados de auerlos hallado, vendiendolos por muy

In fact, we can find a clear precedent for Trillo's use of trans-elemental imagery to express a favourable attitude towards seafaring in the poetry of Góngora himself. True, as far as the *Soledades* is concerned, Góngora does seem to reserve his trans-elemental images about seafaring for cases of undesirable activity. The vessels of the fishermen in the second *Soledad* are normally described simply as *barquillas* or *bajeles*, although the word *leño* is also used. There is not the same attempt to see them as misplaced inhabitants of another element as with the treasure ships. But the reason for this different treatment is not necessarily Góngora's concern with the moral issue. The small rowing boats of the fishermen are not nearly as impressive as the huge sailing ships going to the Indies, hence they were less likely to evoke stunning metaphors. Góngora's ode *Al toma de Larache* is revealing in this respect, in that we have there the same contrast between sailing and fishing vessels, but this time the moral point is in sharp contrast to that we find expressed in the *Soledades*. Góngora describes how the Spanish naval victory permits the fishermen to go about their activities unmolested by pirates:

Leño frágil de hoy más al mar sereno
copos fíe de cañamo anudado,
seguro ya sus remos de pirata.[38]

(Now let the fragile timber to the sea,
now calm, entrust its strands of knotted hemp,
its oars once more secure from plunderers.)

He then goes on to contrast the previous greed of sailors with the humbler fishing activities after the battle:

Piloto el interés sus cables ata,
cuando ya en el puerto
del soplo occidental, de el golfo incierto
pescadora la industria, flacas redes,
que dió a la playa desde su barquilla,
graves revoca a la espaciosa orilla.

(lines 58–63)

(The steersman, greed, now makes his cables fast,
when, safely in the port,
free from the uncertain gulf, and the west wind,
the industry of fishermen draws in

---

esquisitos, como si no estuuieran impressos, y no huuiera en otra parte quien tuuiese libros: pero admirame mucho mas la candidez con que escriuen, dexando passar la vista por los mismos lugares que citan, tan apriesa, como si fuessen huyendo, y es sin duda que huyen de la verdad.' (*Obras*, p. 438).

[38] Góngora, Millé, No. 396, lines 55–7.

the thin nets cast from its boat by the shore,
heavily bulging on the spacious beach.)
Thus far, there would seem to be little difference between this poem
and the *Soledades* in the treatment of the theme. However, it seems
that we are to identify the greed mentioned here with the exploits of
the marauding pirates rather than with those of the men sailing in
search of precious metals, for Góngora a few lines earlier has noted
with approval the way that the treasure ships like the fishing boats
may also sail peacefully now that the sea is adequately policed:

Al viento más opuesto abeto alado,
sus vagas plumas crea, rico el seno
de cuanta Potosí tributa hoy plata.

                              (lines 52–4)

(Braving the wind, now let the wingèd fir
trust in its shifting plumes, its bosom rich
with all the silver sent by Potosí.)
Thus we see Góngora himself using trans-elemental imagery, in this
case comparing the ship with a bird, when no moral criticism is intended.
There is a similar example in his ode of 1588 in honour of the Spanish
Armada, which naturally enough is enthusiastic about the Spanish
fleet, but which nevertheless describes it in terms appropriate to the
land:

Tú que con celo pío y noble saña
el seno undoso al húmido Neptuno
de selvas inquïetas has poblado. . .[39]

(You who with pious zeal and noble wrath
have occupied with ever-moving woods
humid Neptune's undulating hollow.)
It is plain from such examples that we must look for something
more than a concern with moral issues in the characteristic baroque
metaphors describing ships. The key concept which links them all is
not so much that of confusion, whether moral or physical, but that of
amazingness. They are no less concerned with wonder than the other
trans-elemental images. They invite us to consider what a remarkable
invention the ship is. Just as some natural phenomena, such as sunsets
at sea, have an ambiguous status, and seem to ignore the expected
boundaries separating one element from another, so man's invention
the ship, seems miraculously to contravene natural law, although,
of course, neither it nor any other human invention is capable of doing
that. But it is not obvious that wood will float, for one might well

[39] Góngora, Millé, No. 385.

expect the tree, a creature of the land, to share the properties of earth, the grossest element, and sink like a stone. The baroque metaphors express a child-like wonder at this monster, this 'winged tree', which though of the land, seems to swim like a creature of the sea, and with its sails fly through the air like a bird. Whether this prodigy is seen as desirable and praiseworthy or as an unmitigated catastrophe will depend upon the context in which the image appears. For the old man of the first *Soledad*, whose view is coloured by the fact that he has lost a son at sea, the amazement is that of outrage, or so it seems. Yet even he cannot restrain a sneaking admiration for the bold adventurers. For example, it is difficult to detect any negative tone in the passage referring to the triumphant ship Victoria, whose exploits he is content to celebrate:

Esta pues nave, ahora,
en el húmido templo de Neptuno
varada pende a la inmortal memoria
con nombre de Victoria.

(*Soledades*, I, 477–80)

(And so this ship today,
in Neptune's temple damp
hangs, worthy of immortal memory,
by name Victoria.)

Strong support for the view that wonder is a vital ingredient in all trans-elemental images, including those concerned with ships, is provided by the Italian theorist Emmanuele Tesauro, whose treatise on wit, *Il Cannocchiale Aristotelico*, first appeared in 1654. For Tesauro, one of the most highly prized metaphors of all is that which he terms 'Il Mirabile'—the marvellous. He introduces it thus:

But here I would like to reveal to you the most recondite and secret, yet the most miraculous and fertile product of human wit, not yet named by the rhetoricians, but well-known to our author in his *Poetics*, where it has its real origin: which product, derived from this figure, generates many others of the finest you could wish either in prose or verse. These we may call in Greek, *thauma*, that is, *the marvellous*, which consists in the representation of two conceits which are virtually contradictory and therefore ultra-wonderful: as, for example, in the conceit about Xerxes, so highly praised by our author: 'He sailed through lands, he walked across the seas'.[40]

---

[40] 'Ma voglio io quà palesarti il più astruso & segreto: ma il più miracoloso & fecondo Parto dell'humano Ingegno; finquí per le Retoriche Scuole innominato, ma dal nostro Autore ben conosciuto nelle Poetiche. dove hà la propia seggia: che, generato da questa Figura, molti altri ne genera de'più belli che volino per le prose, ò per le rime. Questi è quegli, che grecamente chiamar possiamo THAUMA, cioè IL MIRABILE, il qual consiste in vna *Rappresentation* di *due Concetti*,

So this is a type of metaphor which is not classified by the classical rhetoricians. And despite Tesauro's assertion, there is no convincing evidence that the author he alludes to, Aristotle, was ever aware of it as a category of metaphor.[41] Both from Tesauro's description of it as arousing wonder by achieving the seemingly impossible through linking together contradictory ideas, and from the examples he gives, which contain a high proportion of trans-elemental images, it is clear that the metaphors we have been discussing in this chapter are all examples of Tesauro's *Mirabile*.

Tesauro divides conceits of this type into four groups according to the particular source from which he regards them as deriving. The first group of these paradoxical conceits is of *mirabili per natura*—those things which are by nature marvellous. Tesauro includes examples of monsters which appear to be half one thing and half another, such as the sea lion, which appears to inhabit the wrong element. But any aspect of nature which can be shown to be curious is an appropriate source of these conceits. The Phoenix and the magnet predictably take their place in his list of examples, as does Mount Etna, which at its snow-capped summit miraculously freezes and burns at the same time.

Under his second heading, the *mirabili per arte*, Tesauro includes those paradoxical conceits describing man's inventions rather than natural objects. And it is here that he directs our attention to the ship as an object of wonder: 'It darts like a fish, yet is not a fish, it flies like a bird, yet is not a bird; born on earth, it goes on the sea.'[42]

The third group of metaphors, the *mirabili per opinione* comprises conceits derived from illusion, where the senses are tricked by deceptive appearances, as in the case of a straight stick which, because of the refraction of light, appears to be bent when dipped in water, so that one could say that it is both bent and straight. We have already seen how the Spanish baroque poets used illusion as the basis for some of their trans-elemental images. In fact the whole of our analysis of trans-elemental imagery so far confirms the usefulness of Tesauro's classification. It remains for us to consider Tesauro's fourth group, and to see how far this is applicable to the trans-elemental imagery

quasi'ncompatibili & perciò oltremirabili: come quel di Serse, tanto celebrato dal nostro Autore: *Per terras nauigauit: per maria pedibus incessit.' Il Cannocchiale Aristotelico* (Torino, 1670), p. 446.

[41] Aristotle's remarks about the marvellous in the *Poetics* are only vague: 'Now the marvellous should certainly be portrayed in tragedy, but epic affords greater scope for the inexplicable (which is the chief element in what is marvellous), because we do not actually see the persons of the story)', 1460a, as translated by W. Hamilton Fyfe, (London, 1960).

[42] 'Guizza come pesce, & non è pesce: vola come vcello, & non è vcello: nata in terra, camina il mare,' *Il Cannocchiale Aristotelico*, p. 449.

of the Spanish poets.

Tesauro's final group, that of the *mirabili per fingimento*, comprises those conceits which rely more on the inventive imagination of the poet than on any immediate source in the physical world. Some would claim that the poet's inventiveness is paramount in all conceits, though whether this is a view which would have been accepted by the seventeenth century is a different matter, and is something which I shall consider in the final chapter. But ignoring at this stage the question of seventeenth-century attitudes, we can nevertheless distinguish between paradoxical metaphors which, like those so far examined, are based on some fairly direct analogy of physical appearance or behaviour, and those which, by contrast, are less immediately rooted in the physical situation which the poet is describing. Metaphors of this latter type may, for example, be based on a knowledge of mythology, as when Góngora describes the water-nymph Galatea in these terms:

Galatea es su nombre, y dulce en ella
el terno Venus de sus Gracias suma.
Son una y otra luminosa estrella
lucientes ojos de su blanca pluma:
si roca de cristal no es de Neptuno,
pavón de Venus es, visne de Juno.[43]

(Galatea is her name, whose Graces
sweetly capture those of threefold Venus.
the scintillating eyes of her white down
together form a pair of radiant stars.
She must be a crystal rock of Neptune,
or else Venus's peacock, Juno's swan.)

The two contradictory conceits in the final line of this passage may be regarded as examples of Tesauro's *mirabile per fingimento* (and perhaps also as trans-elemental, in so far as an aquatic and non-aquatic bird are interchanged). The interchange is a sophisticated one which, although it grows out of the preceding images of physical description, cannot be understood in purely physical terms, since it depends upon the arbitrary classical association between a particular goddess and a particular bird. To a reader unfamiliar with this link, it would make no difference if the line read 'Cisne de Venus es, pavón de Juno'. But the effect Góngora achieves by this switch is to show that neither phrase can be an adequate description of the remarkable Galatea, who combines the qualities of both swan and peacock. Like the swan, she is soft, white and aquatic, yet her eyes have the brightness of the feather markings of a peacock, whilst in her general beauty she is akin to Venus.

[43] *Polifemo*, lines 99–104.

A simpler illustration of the same kind of metaphor is the image describing the fisherman's two adventurous daughters in the second *Soledad*:

Cazar a Tetis veo
y pescar a Diana en dos barquillas.

(lines 419–20)

(In two small boats I see
Tethys hunting and Diana fishing.)

Here the interchange of the two goddesses expresses the idea that seal-hunting is an ambiguous activity, lying somewhere between hunting on land and fishing at sea. At the same time the images imply that the two girls described as goddesses are both exceptionally skilled and exceptionally beautiful. Elsewhere, all six of the fisherman's daughters are described as

Seis deidades bellas,
del cielo espumas y del mar estrellas.

(lines 214–5)

(Six lovely goddesses,
spume of the heavens, or stars of the sea.)

As with most trans-elemental metaphors, if we read the passage literally we are presented with a physical impossibility—stars in the sea, and foam in the sky. But these metaphors, unlike those classifiable under Tesauro's other headings, are not based on analogies drawn from nature, from illusion, or from man-made artefacts. The girls are described as 'del cielo espumas' not because Góngora is attempting a physical comparison of sea and sky, but because he has in mind the abstract religious sense of the word *cielo*. The girls are *del cielo* because of their heavenly beauty which leads the poet to describe them as goddesses. Similarly, the metaphor 'estrellas del mar', although it has links with the Petrarchan tradition of describing the bright eyes or the luminous beauty of a woman, also has more abstract overtones, implying that the girls' beauty is comparable with that of Venus herself, the 'star of the sea'.[44] By a *tour de force* Góngora has contrived to make a trans-elemental metaphor out of a common phrase 'estrella del mar' whose paradoxical possibilities might otherwise have passed unnoticed.

The ambiguity of the word *cielo* was again exploited by Soto de Rojas in his *Paraíso cerrado*, in a complex image which describes a wall covered in flowers as:

[44] The Virgin Mary is more often identified as the 'star of the sea', but here, as Pellicer's commentary suggests, the allusion is probably to Venus, the goddess who is a star, and who rose from the sea. For a wide range of interpretations of the symbol 'star of the sea', see H. Bayley, *The Lost Language of Symbolism* (London, 1912), Vol. I, pp. 232–66.

Vn murallon, que de jazmin vestido,
De perlas matutinas coronado,
Si balate, de noche no estrellado,
Cielo es a todas horas florecido.[45]

(A garden wall in jasmine all arrayed,
and with a crown of early-morning pearls,
which, though a terrace without stars at night,
at all times is a flowering paradise.)

One of the subtleties of this conceit is the way in which the poet gives
a new twist to the by now familiar correspondence between flowers
and stars. A reader familiar with the poetic tradition when faced with
Soto's two antithetical metaphors—'balate estrellado' and 'cielo florecido'—naturally expects that the poet intends to describe the terrace
by using the metaphorical adjective *estrellado* to refer to the flowers,
and will describe the night sky as *florecido*, again using a metaphorical
adjective, this time to refer to the stars. But Soto does neither of these
things. His 'cielo florecido' refers not to the skies, but to the garden,
and it is the noun, not the adjective, which is used metaphorically
here. The display of flowers is a *cielo*, a metaphor in keeping with the
title of Soto's poem, and with the original meaning of Paradise as a
garden. The expression 'balate estrellado' also refers to the garden, but
in an unexpected way. And the beauty of the conceit is that each of
these metaphors contrasts as well as compares the garden with the
heavens in a way which apparently contradicts the other. The 'cielo
florecido' of the sky is only *florecido* at night when the stars appear:
but the garden, by contrast, is a 'cielo a todas floras florecido', since
the flowers are there all the time. On the other hand, whereas the sky
is 'estrellado de noche', the terrace is not—it is a 'balate de noche no
estrellado'. Its 'stars' appear at a different time of day. In the early
morning, dew forms on the wall ('de perlas matutinas coronado'), each
drop sparkling like a star, and this is the basis of the poet's image. We
may note as a final complexity the use of the subsidiary metaphors 'de
jazmín vestido' and 'de perlas coronado', where the crown of pearls
is a fitting complement to the garment of jasmine.

As a final example of the activity of the creative imagination in the
construction of trans-elemental conceits we may turn to Góngora's
description of swift-footed athletes:

Su vago pie de pluma
surcar pudiera mieses, pisar ondas,
sin inclinar espiga,
sin vïolar espuma.
                    (*Soledades*, I, 1031–4)

---

[45] *Obras*, p. 389.

(Their fleeting feathered feet
could sail 'cross fields of corn or tread the waves
leaving each ear unbent,
leaving the foam unscathed.)

In this context we are obviously expected to regard the word *surcar* as appropriate to the seas, although it was derived initially from the idea of ploughing the land. Thus we have in the second line two balancing trans-elemental images following on the metaphor in the first line, 'pie de pluma', which in so far as it suggests that normally land-based feet are flying through the air also, literally, suggests an over-stepping of natural bounds. This image of the flying foot could perhaps be regarded as an example of the exploitation of optical illusion, but those which follow it do not derive so immediately from the physical situation the poet is describing. Góngora amplifies the idea of the athletes miraculously defying gravity by going on to consider the hypothetical situation of them crossing the sea or a field of corn. It is only this imaginative detour which enables Góngora to express wonder at the runners' speed by means of images which interchange land and sea.

This final example of the kind of image which Tesauro would have classified as *mirabile per fingimento* provides a useful focus for considering the novelty of the whole metaphorical technique illustrated in this chapter, and the originality of Góngora in particular, who must have a reasonable claim to be the first European poet to exploit it. In the remainder of this chapter I shall be considering the originality of Góngora's description of the athletes in the light of the evidence provided by seventeenth-century theorists and commentators.

A rhetorician's view is provided by Bartolomé Jiménez Patón, who singles out Góngora's description of the runners as the first example he has found in Spanish literature of the rhetorical trope *hypallage*, which he classifies as a type of metonymy:

The fifth type [of metonymy] is made up of those mentioned above, particularly the second and fourth, and it is when there are two epithets, and one attribute is taken for the other. For there are some adjectives which are placed with a pair of nouns in such a way that they do not properly belong there unless they are interchanged, as is the case with Virgil's line 'Dark they went in the lonely night', which should read, 'Alone they went in the dark night'. And this is rightly called *hypallage*, which means a switch of names. I confess that I had not found an example of this amongst the Spaniards until recently when I saw one in the *Soledades* of don Luis de Góngora: *surcar pudiesse mieses, pisar ondas*. Here one has to understand *pisar mieses*, and *surcar ondas*, because although furrowing is associated with sowing seed, when the wheat has reached that stage, one would not say 'ploughing corn', but rather 'treading corn'. And *surcar ondas* is an established Spanish idiom, from the metaphor of the ship cleaving its way like a plough.[46]

There are two senses in which Góngora's idea involves a word-switch. Firstly, taken individually, the expressions *surcar mieses* and *pisar ondas* each involve a switch in so far as they describe movement through one of the four elements by means of a verb normally more appropriate to another. Secondly, taken together, the two expressions function as a pair between which there appears to have been a mutual interchange of terms. As it is this second aspect which mainly concerns Jiménez Patón, his remarks testify not so much to the originality of trans-elemental imagery as such, but to the novelty of Góngora's characteristic use of counterbalanced images. Nevertheless, it is significant that here we have a theorist searching for earlier Spanish examples of Góngora's technique and finding none.

But how new was the technique really if there already existed a technical term to describe it in classical rhetoric, and if Virgil could offer a precedent? Was Góngora really the first in Spain, bearing in mind that Garcilaso in one of his Eclogues had described Hades as 'El triste reino de la escura gente'[47] (The sad kingdom of the sombre people); a not dissimilar example from that of Virgil's cited by Jiménez Patón?

These objections can be met by a closer look at rhetorical theory. For whereas the examples from Garcilaso and Virgil fit comfortably enough into Jiménez Patón's classification, Góngora's is far less easy to reconcile with orthodox views of what constitutes *hypallage*.

Hypallage and *metonymy* were terms which could be used interchangeably. Quintilian indicates that hypallage was merely a rhetorician's term

---

[46] 'El quinto modo [de metonimia] se compone de los de arriba particularmente del segundo, y quarto, y es quando vienen dos epitetos, y se toma vn adiunto por otro, porque ai algunas adietiuos de tal suerte puestos con dos sustantiuos, que estan impropriamente sino los trastruecan, tal es aquello de Virgilio *Iban escuros en la sola noche* Auiendo de decir *Iban solos en la escura noche* y se llama propriamente Hypalage que quiere dezir. Trastrueque de nombres. Confieso que no auia hallado en los Españoles exemplo hasta aora, que le vi en las Soledades de don Luis de Góngora. *surcar pudiesse miesses* [*sic*], *pisar ondas* Donde se deue entender pisar misses [*sic*] y surcar ondas, porque aunque el surco es del sembrar, quando los panes estan en aquel estado, no se dira surcar miesses, sino con mas propriedad pisar. Y surcar ondas, es frasi Española recibida; por la metafora del romper la naue como el arado.' *Mercurius Trimegistus, sive de triplici eloquentia sacra, española, romana.* (Baeza, 1621), fo. 75. The recency of his discovery is confirmed by the fact that the earlier version of his treatise makes no mention of this fifth type of metonymy. See his *Elocuencia española en arte* (Toledo, 1604), Ch. 6.

[47] *Eclogue 3*, line 139. Interestingly, Herrera, who might otherwise have been expected to identify this trope, misreads the text as 'la perdida gente' in his commentary, though his edition of the text gives the correct reading. *Garcilaso de la Vega y sus comentaristas*, ed. A. Gallego Morell (Granda, 1966), p. 564.

for what the grammarians called metonymy.[48] But Jiménez Patón uses
it in the more restricted sense it was sometimes given, to mean not
metonymy in general, but only that particular type of metonymy
which involves an interchange of terms between two expressions.
However, it does not follow that any and every interchange of terms
between pairs of expressions constitutes hypallage. The new expressions
resulting from the interchange must themselves be metonymic, as
Jiménez Patón in effect concedes when he says that hypallage derives
from the four types of metonymy he has previously been describing.
The requirement is that we should be left with two figurative expressions
in which the relationship between the figurative terms used and the
proper terms which they replace falls within the narrow range of
relationships which arbitrarily define metonymy. The relationship
between cause and effect is one of these, and that between containing
and being contained is another. Hence we can see how the example
from Virgil quoted by Jiménez Patón—'dark they went in the lonely
night'—[49] fits these requirements, for in referring to the men as 'dark',
the poet describes the effect (their inability to see) in terms of the cause
(the darkness). And in referring to the night as 'lonely', he describes it
in terms of what it contained or what it caused (lonely men).

If we try to analyse Góngora's description of the athletes in the
same way we run into difficulties. The first unusual feature is that
Góngora's interchange involves two expressions—*pisar ondas* and
surcar mieses—which combine verb and noun instead of the expected
adjective and noun.[50] Secondly, the result of the interchange is not
two metonymic expressions. As a description of running, the verb
surcar is metaphorical rather than metonymic, whilst *pisar* is not only
not a metonym, it is not even a trope, for it describes quite literally
the steps taken by the runners. Indeed, even if we switch the words
back to their 'proper' order (*pisar mieses* and *surcar ondas*) there is no
change in the status of these words: *surcar* remains metaphorical, and
pisar remains a literal term.

This last consideration highlights one of the weaknesses of classical
rhetorical theory, which by encouraging one to think of figurative
language as a modification of literal language, may lead one to assume
that in cases of interchange one can arrive at the poet's meaning by
reconstituting the 'proper' order.[51]

[48] *Institutio oratoria*, 8, vi, 23–7.

[49] *Aeneid*, VI, 268: 'Ibant obscuri sola sub nocte'.

[50] Jiménez Patón refers to the interchange of adjectives as characteristic of
hypallage. See also H. Lausberg, *Manual de retórica literaria*, trans. by J. Pérez
Riesco (Madrid, 1966), Vol. II, pp. 144–5.

[51] Jiménez Patón seems to have assumed this when he says of Góngora's
image 'se deue entender pisar misses [*sic*] y surcar ondas.'

Yet this plainly does not work either in this or any other of Góngora's characteristic images of interchange. When he describes Galatea, for example, as 'o púrpura nevada o nieve roja', he can hardly mean 'nieve nevada o púrpura roja'. And one meets the same problem not only in Góngora's metaphors but also in genuine instances of hypallage, as Lausberg has recognized.[52] Were it otherwise, hypallage would be no more than a particular kind of hyperbaton, a mere formal change of word-order. Where Tesauro's analysis of *Il mirabile* has the advantage over classical theory is in its recognition that it is the function of these images to suggest that the impossible has come true. In other words, although speaking figuratively, the poet may mean much of what he says, even if what he says seems impossible.

Góngora's originality, then, is in no way affected by the classical rhetoricians' familiarity with hypallage, since his typical images of interchange are not genuine examples of this trope. How much more audacious his metaphors must have seemed to any who shared the view of one of his critics, Fernando de Córdoba, who even wondered whether a relatively innocuous example of metonymy in the *Soledades* was not over-adventurous.[53]

Tesauro, who like Jiménez Patón was always keen to illustrate his treatise with practical examples, provides further evidence of Góngora's originality. Despite Tesauro's readiness to cite classical precedents for everything, all his trans-elemental illustrations of *Il mirabile* remain unattributed. His very first example, already quoted, is of particular interest because it bears a close resemblance to Góngora's description of the athletes:

Per terras navigavit, per maria pedibus incessit.

The reference here is to Xerxes' exploits in taking his fleet across the

[52] 'En todos casos el adjetivo, mediante el desplazamiento de relación sintáctica, experimenta un desplazamiento semántico y un enriquecimiento (precisamente la metonomia), que gracias a su carácter de construcción extraña mueve la fantasía del público, de suerte que la retraducción a la dependencia sintáctica normal (por ejemplo *alta moenia Romae*) produce el efecto de algo pedestre y chabacano.' Lausberg, loc.cit.

[53] He writes of Góngora's description of rabbits destined for the wedding feast—'Trofeo ya su número es a un hombro/ si carga no y asombro'—'el assombro no se' como pueda dezirse, porque el assombro se causa en el coraçon o la imaginativa; el pie, la mano, y el ombro, no son capaces dél en modo alguno, de carga sí; y Vm. lo junta todo. Si fuera esse Poema latino salváramos el tal atributo con nombre de Hypallage, que así llaman los Rhetóricos (según Circerón alegado por Quintiliano) al tropo que los Grammaticos Metonymia. . .En nuestra vulgar no sé si puede usarse, creo que a poder no fuera tan ridículo: "La nueva es más peregrina/ que a llegado a tus narizes".' See E. Orozco Díaz, *En torno a las Soledades de Góngora* (Granada, 1969), p. 143. The substitution of the nose for the ears in the concluding quotation is not strictly speaking metonymic, though Góngora's use of *assombro* is, since it substitutes the effect for the cause.

Athos peninsula by means of a specially constructed canal (hence 'sailing through the land'), and in crossing the Hellespont by means of a pontoon bridge (hence 'walking across the sea').[54] Tesauro is in fact quoting from Aristotle's *Rhetoric* (III, ix, 7), which in turn takes its unattributed quotation from Isocrates' *Panegyricus* (89). But what Tesauro chooses to conceal from the reader is that Aristotle is not citing this as an example of metaphor at all, but as one of a list of illustrations of the opposition of clauses in the periodic style. Aristotle expresses no enthusiasm for this or any other of the examples. Moreover, when quoted in its entirety the passage is less enigmatic than in Tesauro, since the allusion to Xerxes' activities is clearly explained. What initially might look like a metaphor is in fact not a metaphor at all, but a literal though striking description of two remarkable feats, although when handled by Parmenion in an epigram, the same conceit could be said to become metaphorical.[55] But in the one Latin poet in whom I have been able to find any reference to Xerxes' exploits, Claudian, the very poet one would expect to derive the maximum wit from his theme, there is no trans-elemental metaphor:

. . .cum classibus iret
per scopulos tectumque pedes contemneret aequor.[56]

(Went with his fleet through promontories,
and disdainfully crossed on foot the covered sea)

There is no evidence to suggest, then, that the Ancients were particularly familiar with the metaphorical technique we have been examining in this chapter. Whatever sporadic examples there may have been,[57] they do not seem to have attracted the attention of Tesauro, who was so keen to find examples in early literature that he was prepared to twist the evidence, as we have seen, to suit his purpose. We

[54] See A.R. Burn, *Persia and the Greeks. The Defence of the West c. 546–478 B.C.* (London, 1962), pp. 318–20.

[55] 'The man who was sailor on land, foot-marcher at sea, on the changed paths of earth and ocean, him the valour of Sparta held off with three hundred spears. Shame upon you, mountains and seas!', *The Greek Anthology. Garland of Philip and some contemporary Epigrams*, edited and translated by A.S.F. Gow and D.L. Page (Cambridge, 1968), Vol. 1, pp. 294–5. Dámaso Alonso draws attention to the similarity between this conceit and some of Góngora's characteristic images of interchange in 'Antecedentes griegos y latinos de la poesía correlativa moderna', in *Estudios dedicados a Menéndez Pidal*, Vol 4, pp. 3–25.

[56] *In Rufinum*, II, 122–3. For further illustration of Claudian's approach to poetry, see my final chapter.

[57] The only one I have so far discovered is Claudian's description of the serpents drawing Ceres' chariot as swimming through the air: 'Nunc spiris Zephyros tranant; nunc arva volatu inferiore secant' ('Now they swim circling through the breezes; now, in lower flight they skim the fields'), *De Raptu Proserpinae*, I, 186–7.

have no reason to believe that the poets of the seventeenth century had discovered what Tesauro failed to find.

As a final illustration of Góngora's independence of thought we may consider the evidence of his commentators, who were always sensitive in their search for possible sources for his images. In their readiness to demonstrate their own erudition and Góngora's they were generally inclined to include as many examples as they could lay hands on. It is significant that neither Pellicer nor Salcedo Coronel find precise precedents for Góngora's trans-elemental technique. For example, Pellicer, with remarkable diligence, lists no less than eight sources for Góngora's description of the athletes, which he claims Góngora has deliberately imitated.[58] Some of these passages are indeed very close to Góngora's, and express fleetness of foot by attributing to the runners the ability to run across both sea and cornfield. For example, Ovid describes the race between Atalanta and Hippomenes thus:

> Signa tubae dederant, cum carcere pronus uterque
> emicat et summam celeri pede libat harenam:
> posse putes illos sicco freta radere passu
> et segetis canae stantes percurrere aristas.[59]

> *(Metamorphoses,* X, 652–5)

Yet neither Ovid nor any of the other forerunners actually uses counterbalanced contradictions. By his original technique, Góngora heightens the sense of the marvellous which is already inherent in his subject-matter.

To conclude, in this chapter I have isolated a type of metaphor very characteristic of Spanish seventeenth-century poetry. Góngora seems to have been the first poet to be aware of its poetic possibilities, and his followers enthusiastically adopted it. Like the theme of *Cornucopia,* its significance is that it epitomizes the sense of wonder which is so important in the descriptive poetry of this age. A convincing demonstration of this is the fact that the Italian theorist Tesauro includes images of interchange between the four elements within his most highly prized category of metaphors, which he admired precisely

[58] See José Pellicer de Salas Ossau y Tovar, *Lecciones solemnes a las obras de don Luis de Góngora y Argote* (Madrid, 1630), col. 118. The precise references, not given by Pellicer, are: Homer, *Iliad,* XX, 226–9; Nonnos, *Dionysiaca,* XXVIII, 284–8; Hesiod, *Catalogues of Women and Eoiae,* 84; Apollonius, *Argonautica,* I, 182–3; Ovid, *Metamorphoses,* X, 652–5; Claudian, *De Tertio Consolatu Honorii,* 197–200; Calpurnius, *Ecloga IV,* 135–6, Virgil, *Aeneid,* VII, 808–11.

[59] 'The trumpets had sounded for the race, when they both, crouching low, flashed forth from their stalls and skimmed the surface of the sandy course with flying feet. You would think that they could graze the sea with unwet feet and pass lightly over the ripened heads of the standing grain', *Metamorphoses,* with an English trans. by F.J. Miller (London and Cambridge, Mass., 1964), Vol. 2, p. 111.)

because it seemed to him to epitomize the marvellous. Alongside such a theory of wit, classical rhetorical theory seems rather inadequate as a tool for analysing baroque images, and it was doubtless partly the shortcomings of traditional theory which led to the development of the new theory of wit in the seventeenth century. Modern accounts of images of interchange between the elements have tended to regard them as images of confusion. I hope to have shown that although a degree of insecurity or confusion at seeing familiar patterns overthrown is an important ingredient in such metaphors, it is not the only one. It is closely linked with a degree of positive delight in seeing a surprising new relationship established. Such is the nature of the *discordia concors* of wit.

VI

MAN AND NATURE

It would be difficult to evaluate the baroque poets' view of nature without taking into consideration their concept of man's relationship to the natural world. There are a number of radically different approaches which they might have adopted. On the one hand, one might have a view of nature and human life being closely integrated, with man seen as one of the animals, perhaps; on the other hand, one might have an antithesis established between man and nature, with man emerging as perhaps superior or inferior. Again, the natural environment could be seen as either hostile or friendly. And so on. Such contrasting views are not necessarily incompatible, in that one could without contradiction take one view of one aspect of the natural world or of human behaviour, and a quite different view of another aspect. Many complications are possible, and in order to avoid too fragmented a discussion I make no attempt in this chapter to examine all the diverse ways in which the baroque poets relate man and nature. Much of the evidence would in any case be irrelevant. We have already seen in Chapter Three how, for example, a panegyrist may use imagery from nature in order to stress his patron's superiority, or how a love poet may stress his isolation from nature in order to give a more dramatic picture of his alienated state. In Renaissance poetry these images were used not because poets had any interest in expounding their views about man's place in nature, but on an *ad hoc* basis as a convenient means of heightening and universalizing other more conventional themes.[1] The fact that such nature imagery is greatly expanded in later descriptive poems in the same genres does, as I have suggested, reveal a new sense of the wonder of nature, but it does not imply that the poet is any more interested than were his Renaissance predecessors in putting across a view about man's place in the world. Indeed, the tendency is for the human interest to get pushed further into the background.

The kind of poem which it seems much more fruitful to examine for attitudes towards man's relationship to nature than, say, love poetry, is that in which we see country life explicitly praised, or in which life in a rural community is depicted. Góngora's *Soledades* is

---

[1] For further argument on this point in connection with Garcilaso's poetry, see my article 'Rhetoric in Garcilaso's first eclogue,' *MLN*, 84 (1969), 143–50.

an obvious example. It has also been suggested that his *Polifemo* fits into this category. Because of the seminal importance of these two poems, their accessibility, and the fact that there has already been some discussion by other critics of Góngora's view in them of man's place in nature, I have chosen to centre my discussion on them. But the arguments I advance will, I hope, be capable of a wider application.

I begin with Góngora's *Polifemo*, the theme of which is identified by C. Colin Smith as 'the world of nature and man's place in it'. Professor Smith argues that in this poem Góngora pictures man living in a close and rather special relationship with nature. His comments can conveniently serve as a basis for discussion.

In Góngora's Sicily there is farming both pastoral and arable, and there is trade in its products; there are wine, music and jewels. This represents a fairly high point on the scale of man's development, and we may take it that Góngora approves of it, poetically at least. But the necessary concomitants of that stage of development are absent: there are no cities, no governments, no persons in positions of authority, no roads, no money, no organized religious cults. Of these, we take it, Góngora poetically disapproves. The anomaly is deliberate and meaningful. Man was happiest when he lived in enjoyment of the things in the first category and had not yet discovered those in the second . . . Góngora shows us man living in the closest possible contact with Nature, having no need of all those apparent benefits which he subsequently procured for himself.[2]

Professor Smith goes on to point out that Acis and Galatea are portrayed as naked figures, which we may take as a sign of man's innocence at this time, and another way of showing the protagonists' closeness to nature. There follows an analysis of a number of specific images linking Galatea with water, and of the description of the death of Acis which unites him with the sea, all cited as further evidence of closeness to nature. But in spite of all these links, he concludes that the world Góngora depicts is one in which there is a lack of divine design, for Góngora shows us the cruel side of nature, and life seems to be a struggle in which only the strongest survives.[3]

If Góngora is deliberately trying to suggest that a particular level of civilization prevails on his island, then this is clearly a matter of some importance. It would perhaps not have been surprising if he had set out

---

[2] C.C. Smith, 'An approach to Góngora's *Polifemo*', 221.

[3] 'Cruel and horrific features are not absent from the poem; we find the large cat still a peril to man (9), the wolf (22d), the serpent (36ab), the eagle as a bird preying on the young of other birds (33fg). Even man's apparently domesticated animals do damage, when the goats attack the vines' (Smith, op.cit.229); 'The situation is Darwinian enough. Polyphemus kills the wild beast, for clothing; the wolf kills the sheep, for food; and Polyphemus kills Acis, his competitor in love. Being preys on being, and the strongest survives' (ibid. 231).

to show man living in a very simple state in some ideal Golden Age, in that there was already an association in people's minds between the Renaissance pastoral and the classical myth of the Golden Age.[4] And in his *Nombres de Cristo* Fray Luis de León had stressed the primitive purity of nature and the moral superiority of a life led in intimate contact with nature.[5] But we should bear in mind that the myths which Ovid relates, as he makes clear in the opening of his *Metamorphoses*, are set not in the Age of Gold, but after the fall of man had ushered in the Age of Iron. The great bulk of the stories he recounts are of misadventure and woe. One is certainly hard put to it to find the happiness to which Professor Smith alludes in Góngora's version of the legend of Poliphemus.

If we pass under review the various characters who appear in the *Polifemo* we note that Poliphemus is unhappy,[6] and that Galatea's other suitors, apart from Acis, have an equally miserable time. In fact, the lives of the young men are totally disrupted, and they abandon their farming activities.[7] Galatea has a far from happy time when we first see her, constantly fleeing from unwanted suitors, and giving vent to her misery when she has a breathing space.[8] Fear and timidity are still present even when she meets Acis, and no special attempt is made to stress the happiness of their love, although she is at one stage described as laughing.[9] The only emotion we see in Acis is his extreme frustration when Galatea staves off his advances.[10] As for the conclusion of the poem, although there is a certain amount of trumpet-blowing on the part of Doris, one doubts whether Galatea and the transformed Acis should be regarded as feeling any the better for their experiences. If these, then, are the delights of a primitive life spent in close contact with nature the reader might be forgiven for taking the poem as an argument in favour of life in the modern city.

But what of the conditions on Góngora's island? Is he really concerned to show the island as having a particular degree of civilization? He is not exactly insistent about the music, wine, and jewels noted by Professor Smith. The only music heard is that of Poliphemus, which is described as quite terrifying. The only jewel on the island mentioned by the poet is Galatea's pearl earring—a product of nature rather than civilization, in that it does not require mining and does not

---

[4] Herrera in his commentary on Garcilaso's first eclogue writes, 'Las costumbres representan al siglo dorado'. See *Garcilaso y sus comentaristas*, ed. A. Gallego Morell, p. 456.

[5] The relevant chapter is entitled 'Pastor'.

[6] Line 465 refers to his inner torment.

[7] See Stanza 21.

[8] 'Dulce se queja', (line 181).

[9] Line 307.

[10] Line 327 refers to the 'infierno' he is suffering.

need to be cut or worked. Indeed, if we are to accept the giant's flattering remarks, pearls sprang up wherever Galatea walked. Even if we regard the golden bow which Poliphemus offers Galatea as a decorative accoutrement rather than an instrument of war, it is significant that it is not a product of the island, but was the gift of a shipwrecked merchant. Grapes are grown on the island, and are referred to in connection with Bacchus, but Góngora seems to be thinking more of the fruit than the wine which might be produced from it.[11] And the reference to the trade in wheat with Europe (143—4), interesting as it is, does not necessarily mean that Góngora has introduced this because it is a sign of civilization. A more likely explanation is that this theme has the rhetorical function of emphasizing the richness of Sicily in natural products. She is so rich in wheat that she can provide for the whole of Europe.

As for the conclusions drawn from the things which Góngora does not mention, these are even more dubious. We are asked to believe that because Góngora does not mention roads or people in authority he has consciously rejected all reference to them, and that, for the purposes of the poem, he disapproves of them. One might as well argue that because there is no reference to clothing in Garcilaso's eclogues that his protagonists are all naked and that he disapproves of clothing. Moreover, the nudity which Professor Smith sees in the *Polifemo* as a sign of innocence is hardly insisted on by Góngora. The only definite reference is the image of Galatea's breasts as 'pomos de nieve' ('apples of snow'). The occasional arm or leg which displays itself elsewhere need not lead one to assume that all modesty has been thrown to the winds. There is no special reason to assume that Acis is stark naked. When Góngora says of him 'la persona ostenta' (line 298), we are not obliged to think of this as a full frontal display. But even if Acis were naked, this could hardly be a sign of innocence, since he is far from innocent, and cunningly feigns sleep in order to win Galatea (line 256). And to regard the reference to the giant's clothing as a sign of diminished innocence is to ignore the rhetorical purpose of the image in its context:

No la Trinacria en sus montañas, fiera
armó de crüeldad, calzó de viento,
que redima feroz, salve ligera,
su piel manchada de colores ciento;
pellico es ya la que en los bosques era
mortal horror al que con paso lento
los bueyes a su albergue reducía,
pisando la dudosa luz del día.[12]

---

[11] See lines 137—40, and line 468.
[12] Stanza 9.

(Never beast within Trinacria's mountains
armed with spite, or shod with the very wind,
could by ferocity or fleetness save
its variegated coat of many colours.
A skin is he who in the woods once was
a mortal terror for slow-footed man
driving his oxen back to his abode,
treading the uncertain twilight of the day.)

This passage does not really concern itself with whether the giant is clothed or not, although one probably assumes that he wears the skins he has acquired. Essentially its purpose is to exaggerate the strength of Poliphemus who could attack and kill savage beasts which more ordinary mortals dreaded.

This last example raises the question of the alleged violence of life on the island, in which, I would claim, Góngora shows no more interest than in the state of dress of his protagonists. The wild beasts mentioned in the stanza quoted are introduced not to show that the island is overrun by savage animals, but to show how strong the giant is in being able to kill them. In fact, the implication is that any wild beast which manages to survive is very lucky. But what of the wolf, who not only survives but even thrives on the poor defenceless sheep of the island? Góngora's powerful description needs again to be referred to its context. Its primary purpose is surely to amplify the disruptive effects of love on the young men of the island, who completely abandon their responsibilities towards their flock. The wolf's attacks are the direct result of the lack of human vigilance. Unattended, the sheep stray into danger, despite nature's own attempts to warn them:

Sin pastor que los silbe, los ganados
los crujidos ignoran resonantes
de las hondas, si en vez del pastor pobre
el Céfiro no silba, o cruje el robre.

(lines 165—6)

(Without the shepherd's whistle, now the flocks
no longer hear the swishing of the slings
resounding, unless in the shepherd's place
the zephyr whistles, or the oak tree creaks.)

Only when love calls a truce will order be restored: 'Revoca, Amor, los silbos!' ('Love, recall the whistles!') exclaims the poet (line 175).

The only other hostile creatures mentioned, the snake and the eagle, are not in fact inhabitants of the island, but terms of comparison used in figures of speech. It is the stillness of Galatea as she silently looks at the apparently sleeping figure of Acis which is compared with the stillness of the eagle hovering over its prey. Unless one pictures Galatea as a kind of vampire about to batten on Acis, her prey, an image which hardly accords with her obvious timidity, the violence of the eagle is totally irrelevant.[13]

We may conclude, then, that Góngora did not select his images on the basis of their relevance to the theme of the island's civilization or lack of it. And if we insist that there is some 'message' in the poem, it is more likely to be that love is a disruptive force, than that man was happier when living under the conditions prevailing on Góngora's island. Even if we find that Góngora's images suggest that his protagonists are living particularly close to nature, we will not necessarily be able to draw any conclusions from this about Góngora's view of man's place in the world, simply because none of the main figures in his story is human. Poliphemus is a giant; Acis is the son of a faun and a nymph; Galatea is a water-nymph. Nevertheless it is interesting to consider the significance of some of the ways in which Góngora links his characters with the natural environment. And it is to this question that I now turn.

In discussing the poetic links between the inhabitants of a particular environment and that environment we need to bear in mind the difference between examples of interaction between the two on the one hand, and of mere correspondence between the two on the other. For example, a poet may, like Adrián de Prado, describe ants almost as if they were human beings, or, like Góngora in his *Polifemo*, describe human beings in terms of ants.[14] But although there is an analogy drawn here between man and nature, there is no interaction between the two. In neither case is there any contact between man and ant: both pursue their independent way of life. This lack of contact makes it inappropriate for us to conclude that in images of correspondence like this the poet is trying to show us man living in close harmony with nature. A more promising source of material for studying the poet's view of the relationship between man and nature is imagery in which the two actually interact.

This distinction between interaction and mere correspondence was recognized by Matteo Peregrini, the Italian theorist of wit, who in his *Fonti dell'ingegno*, saw in the relationship between man and nature a rich source of conceits:

The material Universe is designed with such marvellous artifice, that all things have close mutual correspondences with each other. And this is even more the case in respect of man, who forms an outstandingly important part of the Universe, and is not just one thing, but rather a world of things. Hence, the comparison, or rather the intercourse

[13] See lines 261–4.
[14] See Blecua, *Cancionero de 1628*, p. 211; Góngora, *Polifemo*, lines 143–4.

between things and man provide a very copious source of material for wit.[15]

He goes on to explain the distinction between those sources of wit which are dependent on the idea of some kind of interaction, and those which are simply based on analogies in which there is no interaction between man and nature. He refers to this latter type as 'idle correspondences'.[16]

Góngora's description of the fruits in Poliphemus' bag in anthropomorphic terms is on such example of 'idle correspondence'.[17] There is no general view about man's place in the natural world to be gleaned here. Nor do Góngora's images describing Poliphemus and Galatea in terms of nature take us a great deal further, although they are not 'idle' in the sense of having no useful poetic function to fulfil in the context of the poem as a whole.

Poliphemus himself is described by the poet as a great mountain, down whose slopes there runs the torrent of his straggling beard:

Un torrente es su barba impetuoso
que—adusto hijo de este Pirineo—
su pecho inunda—o tarde o mal o en vano—
surcada aún de los dedos de su mano.

(lines 61—4)

(His beard is an impetuous mountain stream
which, the dry offspring of this Pyrenee,
floods his chest, and is late, ill, or in vain,
still parted by the fingers of his hand.)

Comparisons between giants and mountains were not, of course, unprecedented, and followed naturally from the fact that mountains are the tallest objects known to man in the normal physical world. But perhaps one of Góngora's purposes in dramatizing his description with a bold metaphor is to remind the reader of an association already suggested by classical legend. The defeated giants who had once manipulated mountains in their attempts to storm the heavens themselves became mountains, in effect, when they were crushed beneath great land masses. The crushing of Tiphoeus under Mount Etna is alluded

---

[15] 'L'Vniversità delle cose stá con tale mirabile artificio concertata, che tutte hanno molte vicendevole corrispondenze l'Vna con l'altra. Questo accade anche molto maggiormente rispetto all'huomo, che nell' Vniverso fà parte segnalatamente principale, e che non è vna sola cosa, ma più tosto è vn mondo di cose. Per questo dunque il Confronto, ò diciamo Commercio, delle cose con l'huomo, riesce per l'Ingegno vn Fonte di materia molto copioso,' *I fonti dell' ingegno ridotti ad arte* (Bologna, 1650), pp. 84—5.

[16] 'Questo chiamo corrispondenze otiose, perche secondo esse, ne dall' Huomo verso le cose, ne dalle cose verso l 'Huomo, si opera cosa veruna' (ibid. 98).

[17] See above, p. 89.

to by Góngora at the start of his narrative.[18] But in any event, Góngora integrates his images with the poem as a whole, since the description of the giant's beard flows naturally from the immediately preceding description of his black hair as 'imitador undoso/de las obscuras aguas de el Leteo' ('an undulous imitator/of the river Lethe's obscure waters'), an image which in turn is highly appropriate in its associations of death and extreme blackness in view of the destructive role played by Poliphemus in the poem and the blackness of his cave which the poet has already described.

As for the descriptions of Galatea, the metaphors of 'snow' and 'crystal' used to describe her white limbs do seem to have a significance which goes beyond their traditional function of praising or exaggerating feminine beauty. Some could even be construed as indicating not just a correspondence, but also some interaction between Galatea and nature. But in so far as they do this, their function seems to be to create a poetic link between the water nymph and her native element rather than to lead us to any general conclusions as to the closeness between terrestrial man and water. For example, as Salcedo Coronel perceptively notes, the flight of Galatea towards the sea at the end of the poem is described in terms of melting snow, an image which with beautiful economy suggests that she is seeking security in her own element. Góngora's passage reads:

Viendo el fiero jayán, con paso mudo
correr al mar la fugitiva nieve. . .[19]

(The fearsome brute, seeing the fleeing snow
running her silent course towards the sea. . .)

Galatea only abandons the sea in the first place to escape some of her importunate suitors. One of them, Palemo, is apparently unable to leave the water, and his frustrated pursuit is described by the poet with a characteristic awareness of the symmetries between different elements:

Tantas flores pisó como él espumas.
(line 128)

(She skimmed as many flowers as he did waves)

Oh, cuánto yerra
delfín que sigue en agua corza en tierra!
(lines 135–6)

[18] See lines 28–30,
[19] Lines 481–82. Salcedo comments: 'llamó *nieve* a Galatea por su blancura y lo helado de su condición, y habiendo dicho *fugitiva*, dijo que corría al mar. tocando la propiedad de la nieve desatada, que corre como los demás ríos a su centro, y la naturaleza de Galatea, pues, siendo ninfa del mar, pretendía asegurarse en sus ondas.' As quoted by A. Vilanova, *Fuentes y temas del 'Polifemo'*, I, 224.

(Oh, how deluded is the dolphin
who chases on the sea a deer on land!)

But having taken to the land, Galatea naturally gravitates towards the spring beside which she rests, her reflection in the water being described as a gift of snow to the water (line 180).[20] Another image compares her with the stream in a way which suggests that both partake of the same substance:

Acis su boca dio, y sus ojos cuanto pudo
al sonoro cristal al cristal mudo.

(lines 191-2)

(He gave his mouth and eyes as best he could
to the sonorous crystal and the mute.)

It is the juxtaposition of the two metaphors rather than the isolated expression *cristal mudo* which achieves this effect. In fact, this second metaphor is dependent upon the first, in that crystal is usually silent, hence the adjective *mudo* would seem enigmatic if the image were taken out of its context. Perhaps Góngora is reminding us that just as snow is a form of water, so was crystal for his contemporaries, as is clear from Salcedo Coronel's commentary: 'Crystal is a white, transparent stone, which originates from solidified water or snow, hardened over a long period of years, and petrified by age.'[21]

There is much to be admired, then, in the imagery describing Góngora's characters. But the value of these images seems to consist more in their poetic contribution to this individual poem than in any contribution towards the philosophy of man's relationship to the natural world. To say this is not, of course, to jeopardize Góngora's reputation in any way. He had the intelligence to avoid themes which, however interesting they might be philosophically, are poetically sterile. For example, despite Góngora's constant preoccupation with the four elements in his poetry, we do not find him capitalizing on a well-known and universally accepted theory of his time which traced man's relationship to the elemental structure of the universe, namely, the theory of the temperaments or humours.[22] But although such a theory might make a satisfying addition to somebody's so-called world picture, it is hard to see how it could have benefited baroque descriptive poetry, since description must take the visible as its starting point, and the alleged elemental composition of man was not something apparent

[20]   Professor Smith (op.cit. 224) sees this as another example of melting snow.

[21]   'El cristal es una piedra cándida, y transparente, que se engendra de agua, o nieve congelada, endurecida por largo espacio de años, y convertido por la vejez en piedra.' As quoted by Vilanova, op.cit. II, 27. Herrera gives a lengthier account of the various theories about the origins of crystal in his *Anotaciones* to Garcilaso. See A. Gallego Morell, *Garcilaso y sus comentaristas*, p. 419.

[22]   For an account of the theory, see E.M.W. Tillyard, op.cit. 87.

to the eye. If the theory of humours was poetically useful, it was likely
to be of most use in love poetry, where one could talk of the invisible
fire of passion, or of the water of tears.[23]

So far we have examined instances of the description of Góngora's
characters in terms of the natural world. It remains for us to look at
some cases where aspects of the natural world are described in terms
of human civilization, singling out those examples which imply some
view as to the relationship between Góngora's characters and their
environment, or between man and nature. One example is the description of the rock which seals Poliphemus' cave as a gag, an image
which perhaps is intended to do more than merely draw a physical
analogy between gags in mouths and rocks in caves. The overtone of
violence is an important one, and the implication is that Poliphemus,
who is the destructive force in this poem, is doing violence to the
natural environment.

There are a number of other examples where we see the intervention
of nature in the courtship of Acis and Galatea. Nature, whose fertility
has already been described by Góngora, provides the two lovers with
all the amenities they could wish. There is the bed on which Galatea
sleeps:

Vagas cortinas de volantes vanos
corrió Favonio lisonjeramente
a la (de viento cuando no sea) cama
de frescas sombras, de menuda grama.

(lines 213—16)

(Favonius considerately drew
ever shifting drapes with flimsy flounces
around the bed which, if not of the breeze,
consisted of cool shadows and fine sward.)

A canopy offers shade, whilst ivy provides blinds to preserve privacy:

Lo cóncavo hacía de una peña
a un fresco sitïal dosel umbroso,
y verdes celosías unas hiedras,
trepando troncos y abrazando piedras.

(309—12)

(There was provided by a hollow rock
a shady canopy for a cool seat,
while ivy, too, provided verdant blinds
climbing up tree-trunks and embracing rocks.)

---

[23] One poem which exploits the theory of the elements in man is the anonymous 'Vientos del sol soberano' (*Cancionero de 1628*, pp. 369—70), addressed to
a lady fanning herself, of whom the poet says 'En vos el mundo breue/de elementos se compone'.

Sobre una alfombra, que imitara en vano
el tirio sus matices, si bien era
de cuantas sedas ya hiló, gusano,
y, artífice, tejió la Primavera. . .

(313–16)

(On a carpet whose hues no Tyrian dye
could hope to imitate, since it was made
from as many silks as ever silk-worm span,
and Spring, the craftsman, ever interwove. . .)

One of Góngora's purposes in showing this kind of direct intervention of nature into the story, may be to suggest the virtual inevitability of the events involving the two lovers. Every detail is just right, as if it had all been planned in advance. Nature's complicity is further shown in the billing and cooing of doves which acts as a spur to Acis, and in the showering of flowers upon the spot where the lovers will mate. The idea of an external force coercing Acis and Galatea is further conveyed by a number of references to the intentions of Cupid and of Love. These recur with a frequency which suggests that this is more than a trivial personification. It is Cupid who is described as painting the picture in Galatea's fancy of the suitor who might have left her the gifts which she awakes to find. It is Cupid who is seen as responsible for the timing of the love-making of the doves which acts as a signal to Acis. It is Love which has precisely selected the spot where the love of Acis and Galatea is to be consummated.[24]

It is interesting, though, that Góngora should describe the perfection of his natural setting in terms appropriate to civilized life—carpets, canopies, blinds, and four-poster beds. Presumably we can construe this as a favourable attitude towards civilization. His metaphor describing the vegetation as a carpet woven by the Spring assumes that human craftsmanship, although it may be outstripped by the creative skill of nature, merits praise, and that rich carpets are worthy of our admiration. Góngora sees the beauty of nature here as a kind of artifice, which means that he cannot be said to be seeking to establish an antithesis between the untamed natural world on the one hand, and the creations of artifice on the other. It is to the *Soledades* which we must now turn to see whether Góngora's view of rustic life there advances matters any further.

It has been argued that in his *Soledades* Góngora takes a hostile attitude to artifice, showing it to be vain, transient, and sterile, by contrast with the permanence and fertility of nature, who destroys

---

[24] The following lines contain these and other references to Cupid or to the personification of love: 175, 193, 237, 271, 286, 295, 329, 335.

artifice and punishes presumption.[25] If we equate artifice with deceit
and other moral imperfections, and equate nature, or natural values,
with innocence and simple goodness; if by 'opposing nature' we mean
no more than 'rejecting innocence and simple goodness'; if by 'permanent' we mean 'of lasting moral worth' rather than 'physically
durable', then we can accept without difficulty that Góngora stood
for nature rather than artifice, as, indeed, any moralist would have
done. His contrast between rustic sincerity and mendacity at the court
makes this quite clear,[26] as does the vehement attack on avarice by the
village elder. But Góngora's poem is not merely concerned with artifice and nature in an abstract moral sense, for he shows us a community living in a physical setting with which they physically interact.
Does Góngora through his portrayal of this community express disapproval of man's use of artifice to oppose nature physically, to
exploit his environment, to adapt nature to his own purposes, and to
forcefully control the world about him rather than letting himself be
controlled by it? In the following paragraphs I shall be examining
some objections to such a view.

Firstly, as in his *Polifemo*, Góngora describes some of the beauties
of nature in terms of human artefacts. For example, he describes girls
resting in a shady spot thus:

Ellas en tanto en bóvedas de sombras,
pintadas siempre al fresco,
cubren las que sidón telar turquesco
no ha sabido imitar verdes alfombras

$$(I, 612-5)$$

(Meanwhile, 'neath shady vaults of permanent
alfresco artistry,
the girls cover the green carpets which
the looms of oriental Sidon cannot match.)

Here the poet starts with an architectural image for the branches of the
trees, whose colours he goes on to describe in terms of mural painting,
punning on the expression *al fresco* which refers here to cool air
instead of to fresh plaster. His final image shows us nature outdoing
the best of man-made carpets. But it would be wrong to conclude from
this last example that he is suggesting that human art is a waste of time
merely because on occasions nature's creations outshine man's. Not
only does Góngora state in terms that art commands our admiration,[27]

[25] See the important article of R.O. Jones, 'The poetic unity of the *Soledades*'
189–204. Professor Jones reiterates his views in the introduction to his *Poems
of Góngora*.
[26] See *Soledades*, I, 104, 120, 140, 129.
[27] II, 706 refers to 'la admiración que al arte se le debe'.

he also hints at a positive attitude to human craftsmanship in all his images which describe aspects of nature in terms of jewels and precious metals. One has to bear in mind here that it is only when stones and metals are mined and cut or refined by human artifice that they assume their characteristic brilliance. No poet who, like Góngora, uses the metaphor 'gold' to express, for example, the beauty of a field of corn can consistently expect his readers to accept at the same time that gold is worthless and unattractive. In the very selection of his metaphor he has tacitly conceded that man is capable of creating beauty through artifice. Nor could a poet successfully persuade us that the kind of artifice which goes into the making of works of art is worthless without condemning his own poetry. However, it would be open to him to praise the beauty of human artefacts whilst at the same time criticizing the uses to which they are put. The love poet who praises his lady's beauty whilst bemoaning her cruelty is, after all, in a not dissimilar position.

We may accept, then, that Góngora had no wish to deny that man is a creator of beauty. But this does not tell us how he saw the value of man's skills in a social context. Hence we need to examine the way of life of the characters in the *Soledades* before we can draw any over-all conclusion. Before doing so, it is worth noting in passing that the question of permanence or impermanence has little bearing on the relative aesthetic values of human and natural objects. Buildings do not become artistically worthless because some of them eventually go to ruin, any more than snow is ugly because it melts.

The enthusiasm with which rustic life is described in the *Soledades* leaves the clear impression that Góngora regards the way of life of his peasants as wholly admirable. But if we were expecting to see as the object of this enthusiasm a primitive community which sets no store by arts and crafts, accepting their natural environment without striving to modify it, free from the trappings of civilization, then we are in for some surprises. What we are in fact shown in a community which with vigour and confidence completely dominates the natural world. It is not merely that the peasants engage in organized agriculture, and have under their control such animals as sheep, goats, dogs, and chickens. Góngora seems to go out of his way to stress how adept the peasants are at overcoming natural obstacles, and how helpless even the more aggressive creatures are, and how useless their defences when they are faced with *homo sapiens*.

One indication of the aggressiveness of the peasants' attitude to nature is to be found in the wedding-song which wishes the bride and groom healthy offspring:

Ven, Himeneo, y nuestra agricultura
de copia tal a estrellas deba amigas

progenie tan robusta, que su mano
toros dome, y de un rubio mar de espigas
inunde liberal la tierra dura.

(i, 819–23)

(Come, Hymen, let our husbandry now owe
to favourable stars children galore
who, born of this sturdy stock, may by their toil
subjugate bulls, and may the stubborn soil
be flooded with a sea of golden corn.)

Here successful farming is seen not as the passive acceptance of nature's
gifts, but as the wresting of an advantage from a resistant source.
Admittedly, brawn emerges as no less important than brain in this
context, and the value of sheer physical strength is again heightened
in the peasants' wrestling and other athletic contests. But brute strength
without artifice is of very limited help in the breaking in of wild animals.
The success of artifice rather than toughness emerges clearly enough
from the description of the exploits of the fisherman's two daughters
one of whom takes on an aquatic bull—a bull-seal—and the other of
which successfully harpoons a horrifying sea monster. (II, 418–511).
Their achievements are described as 'nauticas venatorias maravillas'
('wonders of nautical hunting'), and the feeling that they are in complete
control of the situation is stengthened by the comparison between one
of the daughters and the Parcae, on the basis that on the line attached
to her harpoon hung the fate of seals, just as the threads of the Parcae
controlled the fate of men. (II, 435–440). The vulnerability of the seals
is stressed by the statement that the sea-God Proteus was unable to
save these hapless members of his flock. (II, 425–6). As for Efire's
attack on the monster, this is another demonstration of personal skill
which is enjoyed for its own sake rather than dictated by necessity.
It is significant that her father, who attempts in vain to persuade her
not to go, has so much confidence in her ability to tackle dangerous
creatures that he is more worried by the possible threat to her virginity
constituted by the sea-gods, than he is of the threat to her life by sharks
and swordfish, these last being a familiar danger to him. (II, 453–464).

Many more animals are killed by man in the course of the *Soledades*,
and Góngora constantly refers to the inadequacy of their natural
protection when they are faced with the artifice of man. The he-goat
whose aggression stood him in good stead against his rivals, and who by
eating the vines was bold enough to take on the God Bacchus himself,
is reduced by man to strands of dried meat. Other humbler creatures
succumb to the wholesale slaughter for the wedding feast. It is useless
for the peacock to try to contort its features in a display of aggression,
for it is destined to be killed for the feast. The little rabbit's attempt

to protect itself in the peace of its burrow is of no avail:

No el sitio, no, fragoso,
no el torcido taladro de la tierra,
privilegió en la sierra
la paz del conejuelo temeroso;
trofeo ya su número es a un hombro
si carga no y asombro.
                                        (I, 303–8)

(Neither the rough terrain,
nor yet the twisting burrow in the ground
protected in the hills
the peace of the timid little rabbit;
now in weighty numbers on men's shoulders,
a source of popular astonishment.)

This passage is paralleled by another in the second *Soledad*, where
after the endearing description of the rabbits' behaviour it is hard
not to feel pity at their being shot by man against whom their natural
caution is no protection:

A pocos pasos le admiró no menos
montecillo, las sienes laureado,
traviesos despidiendo moradores
de sus confusos senos,
conejuelos, que—el viento consultado—
salieron retozando a pisar flores:
el más tímido, al fin, más ignorante
del plomo fulminante.   •
                                        (II, 275–82)

(Nearby, he was no less amazed to see
a little hill, with laurel round its brows,
expelling mischievous inhabitants
from its complex hollows,
small rabbits, who, consulting first the breeze,
came out to gambol on the flower-strewn ground.
Yet the most timorous suspected least
the thunderbolt of lead.)

As for the fish in the estuary, they are easy prey, and we are told that
the oyster's tough shell was an ineffective defence against the fishermen.[28]

Finally, an example in which the feeling that man is doing violence
to animate nature is very strong is the passage describing the hacking

[28]   II, 83–6.

down of trees and greenery for use in the wedding celebrations:

> Vence la noche al fin, y triunfa mudo
> el silencio, aunque breve, del rüido:
> sólo gime ofendido
> el sagrado laurel del hierro agudo;
> deja de su esplendor, deja desnudo
> de su frondosa pompa al verde aliso
> el golpe no remiso
> del villano membrudo;
> el que resistir pudo
> al animoso Austro, al Euro ronco,
> chopo gallardo—cuyo liso tronco
> papel fue de pastores, aunque rudo—
> a revelar secretos va a la aldea,
> que impide Amor que aun otro chopo lea
>
> (I, 686–700)

> (At length night won the day, and silence dumb
> triumphed, however briefly, over noise.
> Alone was heard the moan
> of the sacred laurel, wounded by sharp steel.
> The relentless axe blows
> of the strong-armed peasant
> stripped the glory from the verdant alder,
> stripped the tree naked of its leafy pomp;
> the tree that once withstood
> the lively south wind and the harsh east wind,
> the handsome poplar-tree, whose smooth trunk served
> as a crude writing-paper for the swains
> soon in the village secrets will disclose
> which Love forbids its fellow trees to read.)

In a passage like this, far from emphasizing that his peasants are living in harmony with nature, Góngora shows them humiliating the natural world in the interests of artifice. The natural peace of the evening is disturbed by the cries of pain resulting from the sacrilegious attack on the laurel. A note of pathos is introduced into the description of the stripping of the alder with the repetition of the verb *dejar*. And the use of the word *pompa* further suggests that vanity and the transience not of artifice but of natural beauty. The felling of the poplar tree is again characteristically described in a way which shows how its robustness which defended against buffetings from the winds cannot protect it from man. Finally, to add insult to injury, the trees are set up in the village to form a mock forest:

> Estos árboles, pues, ve la mañana
> mentir florestas, y emular viales

cuantos muró de líquidos cristales
agricultura urbana.

(I, 701–4)

(And so when morning came it saw these trees,
faking forests, and copying their paths,
all immured in liquid crystals, thanks to
urban agriculture.)

The verb *mentir* and the contradictory expression *agricultura urbana*
stress the artificiality of the result. Yet Góngora seems to still approve
of the peasants' actions. The light-hearted reference to rustic inscriptions dispel any real sense of tragedy, and Góngora goes on to show
how the wanderer admired these decorations, described—again in
terms of artifice—as tapestries, despite being familiar with sumptuous
draperies at the court. (I, 714–21).

The image *agricultura urbana* is an interesting one, as it suggests
that far from drawing a crude contrast between town and country
in the *Soledades* Góngora is showing us a number of instances where
the two meet. He is praising the peasants' way of life not merely on
the basis that it is lived in beautiful surroundings, but also because
it shows a level of intelligence and civilization which are admirable,
and which belie the facile assumption that the countryside is inhabited
by nothing but bumpkins. Although the peasants do not stand on
ceremony, they are none the less hospitable and courteous. Góngora
specifically uses the adjectives *cortés* and *urbano* to describe the manner
in which the fishermen receive the stranger (II, 56–9; II, 216).

As for the peasants' domination of all creatures great and small,
this again seems to be in no way alien to the courtly ethic. Some
critics have suggested that the episode at the end of the second *Soledad*
in which a noble party go hunting with their hawks in a courtly episode
which contradicts the fundamental theme of the poem, and conclude
that the poet is beginning to run out of inspiration. But if one considers how important a part hunting plays in the life of the peasants
this scene is perfectly in keeping with the rest of the poem, as indeed
is the opening dedication of the poem to the Duke of Béjar, who is
also pictured as a triumphant huntsman. It would have been difficult,
of course, for Góngora to attack an activity which his noble patron
enjoyed as an example of cruelty and a violation of natural harmony.
But throughout the *Soledades* all the indications are that Góngora
positively approved of hunting as one of the proofs of man's resource-
fulness. His attitude is one likely to have been shared by the bulk of
his contemporaries. It is significant that despite the popularity of
Ovid's *Metamorphoses* at this time as a source for poetic ideas, no
poet seem to have been attracted towards imitating the argument of

the extensive and eloquent speech against the slaughter of animals in Book XV,[29] despite the fact that the story of the Phoenix recounted in the course of the speech was often extracted from this very source.

The one voice raised in protest against hunting seems to be that of Luis de Ulloa, who not only takes a contrary position to most poets in arguing that country life is distasteful because it is rough and uncivilized, but also hints that hunting is a barbaric activity. He tells Bocángel: 'Hunting is a laudable activity. . .but by disposition I utterly hate it, and so will continue in my insistence that huntsmen abolish it, and for myself, whenever it is proposed I shall condemn what I regard as its bad taste.'[30] And in a passage from his poem attacking life in the country, he again makes a respectful protest:

Que gustoso dixera de la caza,
Quanto de vicio su virtud encierra,
Sino temiera el freno, ò la mordaza.
O nunca fuera imagen de la guerra
Con que vsurpò Imperiales votos,
Y nuestros labios respetiuos cierra.[31]

(How gladly would I point out how the hunt
contains within its virtue so much vice
if I did not fear gagging or restraint.
Would that it had never been war's symbol,
thus gaining for itself Imperial votes,
bringing respectful silence to our lips.)

Ulloa refers here to the traditional argument that hunting was a noble activity because it resembled warfare, and because warfare gave men the opportunity to display their virtue in the shape of valour. This classical concept of virtue had a strong tradition in Spanish Renaissance poetry, and Góngora does not seem to be seeking to overthrow this in the way he depicts peasant life. The goatherd who shows the wanderer some castle ruins apparently hankers after the days when he was a soldier

Cuando el que ves sayal fue limpio acero.

(I, 217)

(When burnished steel replaced the cloth I wear)

Certainly there is no suggestion of his repenting of his warlike outlook, since he gives immediate vent to his frustrated military inclinations

---

[29] Lines 60–478.

[30] 'La caza es un exercicio loable . . . pero yo la aborrezco mortalmente por ynclinacion, y así quedará esta instancia para que la borren los cazadores, y yo, siempre que se ofreciere, condenaré su mal gusto en mi opinion.' As quoted by J.G. Araez, op.cit. p. 70.

[31] Ullos, Prosas y versos, p. 80.

when a wolf-hunt passes by, breaking off his conversation to join the chase with a ferocity which the stranger is obviously bemused to find in a goatherd, and which makes the peasant the very incarnation of war:

Bajaba entre sí el joven admirando,
armado a Pan o semicapro a Marte.

(I, 233–4)

(The young man wandered down, surprised to see
Pan bearing arms, or Mars become half goat.)

There is no suggestion of any division between court and country here. Indeed, Jammes goes so far as to conclude that the goatherd and the two old men in the *Soledades* seem so courtly that we perhaps should see them as noblemen who have retired to the country.[32] But such an interpretation seems to me to take too much of a liberty with text.

We have so far examined mainly the peasants' prowess in dominating animate nature, but there are other indications of their degree of culture and civilization. Their skill at singing, dancing, and playing musical instruments shows admirable artifice, as does their manufacture of many of the items required to meet their domestic needs. It is significant that Góngora never takes these artefacts for granted but constantly reminds us of the human skill which has gone into their making. All these suggests that far from censuring artifice Góngora is praising it. For example, the rustic meals which the poet describes invite admiration for a number of artefacts. He seems to delight in drawing our attention to the actual process of manufacture in describing the table-cloths, for example, and the tables on which they rest:

Nieve hilada, y por sus mano bellas
caseramente a telas reducida,
manteles blancos fueron.
Sentados, pues, sin ceremonias, ellas
en torneado fresno la comida
con silencio sirvieron.

(II, 343–48)

(The table-cloths were of
spun snow, which by their lovely hands had been
transformed into material at home.
And so, having sat down without ado,
upon an ash tree that the lathe had turned
they quietly served the meal)

The same admiration underlies another description from the first *Soledad*:

[32]   Jammes, op.cit. 618.

Limpio sayal, en vez de blanco lino,
cubrió el cuadrado pino;
y en boj, aunque rebelde, a quien el torno
forma elegante dió sin culto adorno,
leche que exprimir vió la Alba aquel día,
mientras perdían con ella
los blancos lilios de su frente bella,
gruesa le dan y fría,
impenetrable casi a la cuchara,
del viejo Alcimedón invención rara.

(I, 143–52)

(Clean homespun cloth instead of linen white
covered the square pine tree;
and in resistant boxwood, which the lathe
gave graceful shape but not fine ornament,
they gave him cream which Dawn saw squeezed that day,
while she thereby gave up
the snow-white lilies of her lovely brow.
Cool and thick, it was,
almost impenetrable to the spoon,
old Alcimedón's renowned invention.)

Here, the image *cuadrado pino* stresses even more strongly than the
torneado fresno of the first passage that tables are creations resulting
from the modification of nature by human artifice. We are acutely
aware that pine trees are not naturally square, and the element of
contradiction in this image places it within the category of Tesauro's
mirabile per arte, the wonder being directed at the inventiveness of
human craftsmanship. The peasants' table is every bit as artificial as
the sailing ships which the poet describes in similar terms as modified
trees. The concluding reference to the spoon is characteristic of Góngora's approach. Few people will have given this familiar utensil a
second thought, but Góngora reminds us that although we take it for
granted it is a remarkable product of human invention. The description
of the wooden bowl again invites us to consider the process of manufacture. Its creation represents another natural obstacle overcome,
for the boxwood does not willingly submit to the lathe. The end-
product is not crude but elegant, although the bowl lacks refined
trimmings. The distinction between *forma elegante* and *culto adorno*
is an important one which lies at the heart of the distinction which
Góngora makes between court and country life. We may now go on to
examine the nature of this antithesis.

As I have already argued, far from being critical of artifice, Góngora
actually praises it in the peasant community, and does so with remarkable

insistence. For him the court has no monopoly of artistry or civilization. It is the materialism of the court and its ostentation rather than its artifice which provokes Góngora's criticism. The pursuit of wealth and excessive luxury with a view to impressing others is a constant target. The wooden bowl with its elegance yet lack of adornment marks the dividing line between true art and vulgar ostentation.

It is interesting to see Góngora working out these ideas in his descriptions of buildings. The peasants' dwellings are always described as poor, and the huts on the fishermen's island are even ill-constructed:

Dos son las chozas, pobre su artificio
más aún que caduca su materia.

(II, 200−1)

(There are two huts, yet poorer in design
than they are flimsy in materials.)

In the first *Soledad* the poverty of the rustic cabin is contrasted with ambitious edifices:

No moderno artificio
borró designios, bosquejó modelos,
al cóncavo ajustando de los cielos
el sublime edificio;
retamas sobre robre
tu fábrica son pobre.

(I, 97−102)

(No modern artifice
erased designs or sketched out models here,
scaling the lofty edifice to fill
the very vault of heaven.
Broom stretched upon oak-wood
is all you are made of.)

On the face of it, these passages might be thought to be critical of artifice. The references to castle ruins and to the Pyramids have been regarded as further evidence in support of such a view, as signs of the vanity of the constructions of human artifice. But there are many objections to such a view which make another interpretation more plausible.

One objection is that Góngora's poem would be contradictory if he were to oppose architecture whilst approving of other forms of human artifice. Another is that to argue that architecture is worthless because it is sterile and impermanent is contrary to common sense. Far from being sterile, artifice is creative. There is nothing very fertile about rocks in their natural state, yet from this sterile source man can create buildings which are both practical and beautiful. And if a building goes to ruin it can only do so because of a lack rather than an excess of artifice. We may blame inadequate construction or poor maintenance, or, in the case of the castle ruins described in the first *Soledad*, perhaps an enemy cannon ball is the most likely culprit.[33] But the poorer the artifice, the less permanent the building. Góngora can hardly argue that the flimsy peasant dwellings last longer because they are more natural. The material from which they are built is actually described as perishable—*caduca*. Moreover, the existence of ruins is not a very cogent argument against building. Most buildings outlast those who build them. Life passes: the inanimate remains. True, man's constructions do not last for ever, and a moral point may well be made where a person arrogantly believes that he can construct an everlasting monument to himself. But what we would be criticizing here would be his mistaken belief in his own greatness rather than the triumph of nature over artifice. Natural rocks are not immune from erosion either.

Perhaps it is the vanity of erecting monuments for posterity which only serve to emphasize the transience of the lives of those who build them which Góngora had in mind when referring in passing to the Pyramids in the course of an image describing the bride as a Phoenix:

> . . . . . .Seguida
> la novia sale de villanas ciento
> a la verde florida palizada,
> cual nueva fénix en flamantes plumas
> matutinos del sol rayos vestida,
> de cuanta surca el aire acompañada
> monarquía canora;
> y, vadeando nubes, las espumas
> del rey corona de los otros ríos:
> en cuya orilla el viento hereda ahora
> pequeños no vacíos
> de funerales bárbaros trofeos
> que el Egipto erigió a sus Ptolomeos.
>
> (I, 945–57)

> (. . . . . .The bride
> with a hundred lasses in train, sets out
> towards the verdant, flower-strewn palisade
> like a new-born Phoenix in plumes brand-new,
> clothed in the radiance of the morning sun,
> attended by as many singing queens
> as populate the air;
> and, flying onwards across clouds to crown

---

[33] See I, 212–21. Note how sympathetic nature is to man's plight in these lines.

the waters of the river, king of all,
upon whose bank the wind inherits now
the hollows, far from small,
of barbarian, funebral trophies
which Egypt set up for her Ptolemies.)

It perhaps seems more plausible to read *vacíos* as referring to the emptiness of the tombs through which the wind now whistles rather than to their non-existence as Dámaso Alonso suggests in his prose paraphrase of this passage. The Pyramids remain to mock the kings who have long since passed away. But whatever our reading, the chances that Góngora is making a pointed contrast between the young bride and the Pyramids and their makers is diminished by the fact that the relevant aspects of the Phoenix with which the bride is compared here are not its longevity or its fertility, for neither is the bride immortal, nor is the Phoenix fertile—it could not be less fertile without its species becoming extinct. Rather the basis of the comparison is the outstanding beauty of the Phoenix, which sets it apart from the other birds which, as Claudian recounts in his version of the legend,[34] all follow behind the new-born bird in respectful homage, just as in Góngora's poem the village girls excitedly follow in the wake of the bride who outshines them all.

How, then, are we to read the contrast made between humble peasant dwellings and lofty palaces? Humility is the first feature which Góngora singles out in the case of the fisherman's island cottages.[35] Pride in personal wealth is the implied target of attack rather than architectural expertise. Thus although in the first *Soledad* the peasants' homes are simple, their temple is constructed on sufficiently grand a scale to have a tower. The other side of the coin when we are considering noble palaces is that it is not so much the creation of architectural beauty on a certain scale which provokes criticism as ostentation in building where things have got out of all proportion. There is a significant distinction between the palace which he admires in the second *Soledad* and those which he contrasts with the peasant hovels. The admired building is described thus:

Antiguo descubrieron blanco muro,
por sus piedras no menos
que por su edad majestuosa cano;
mármol, al fin, tan por lo pario puro,
que al peregrino sus ocultos senos
negar pudiera en vano.
Cuantas del Ocëano
el sol trenzas desata

[34] Claudian, ed.cit. II, 228–9.   [35] II, 198.

contaba en los rayados capiteles,
que—espejos, aunque esféricos, fïeles—
bruñidos eran óvalos de plata.
La admiración que al arte se le debe,
áncora del batel fué, perdonando
poco a lo fuerte, y a lo bello nada
del edificio . . .

(II, 695–709)

(They spied an ancient wall, whose whiteness owed
as much to stone as venerable age,
marble from Paros of such purity
that from the wanderer
it could not hide from view its secret depths.
The sun registered on the capitals,
which, although spherical, true mirrors made,
of oval form, burnished and argentine,
each lock of hair which he
unfastened from the sea.
The admiration which is owed to art
was the boat's anchor, overlooking none
of the beauty, and little of the strength
of the edifice. . .)

This noble building is not the product of the *moderno artificio* attacked
by Góngora in an earlier passage (I, 97), but of a former age whose
palaces were grandiose enough to sport columns yet were not lacking in
simplicity. The beauty of the stonework lies not in its surface decoration
but in its purity which is such that Góngora describes it as transparent.
The perfection of symmetry is suggested by the spheres which form
the capitals. The purity of their surface is such that they act as perfect
mirrors. The proportional word *cuantas* which relates sunbeams to
mirrors again subtly suggests symmetry.[36] Despite its age the building
remains strong. Perhaps we are to imply that it owes some of its strength
to simplicity of construction as well as to the fineness of its materials.

The passage criticizing modern artifice shows its interest in sheer
size rather than in fine proportions, and hints at a lack of simplicity
and of any clear direction when it refers to the rough models and the
erased sketches as the dissatisfied architect conceives bigger and bigger
buildings. Another important passage which just precedes the description of the ancient palace again contrasts rustic huts and the palaces
which the wanderer has left behind him:

[36] Pellicer explains the apparent inconsistency between spheres and ovals
by suggesting that the spheres are marked off in divisions, each of which is an
oval mirror. *Lecciones solemnes*, 589.

Al peregrino por tu causa vemos
alcázares dejar, donde, excedida
de la sublimidad la vista, apela
para su hermosura;
en que la arquitectura
a la gëometría se rebela,
jaspes calzada y pórfidos vestida. . .

                                        (II, 665–671)

(For your sake, Love, we see the wanderer
leave palaces behind in which the eye
defeated by sheer height, is left to grope
for beauty manifest
in architecture which,
in jasper shod, and clad in porphyry,
defies geometry.)

Here the whole idea of appreciating beauty of form and proportion is defeated by the huge scale of a building which the eye simply cannot take in all at once. All that is left is the showy beauty of exotic stones which, unlike the pure simplicity of the ancient palace, works against the appreciation of perfect geometrical forms ('a la geometría se rebela'). There is thus a close analogy between the peasants' wooden bowl with its elegance of shape and its lack of sophisticated ornament and the ancient palace which shares a kindred elegance whilst shunning some of the decorative extravagances of vulgar, ostentatious architecture.

Two further signs that it is the flaunting of personal wealth rather than the worthlessness of artifice which preoccupies Góngora are firstly, the warning expressed in one of the wedding songs that moderate prosperity is more desirable than great wealth which may cause jealousy, even where that wealth is in natural rather than artificial products;[37] secondly, the reference to the fact that the peasants drink from glasses rather than from golden goblets, which is clearly a distinction comparing different standards of wealth or luxury rather than different standards of artifice.[38] Glasses require no less artifice than goblets in their manufacture.

This last example serves as a reminder that Góngora's peasant community is not totally independent of the outside world, despite its thriving cottage arts. The glasses from which the peasants drink, the guns with which they hunt, the fireworks with which they celebrate the wedding,[39] their tree-felling implements, their harpoons of steel,

---

[37] I, 926–33.
[38] I, 867–71.
[39] I, 648–51. The adverb *artificiosamente* again shows Góngora's enthusiasm for artifice.

are all examples of products which one envisages being supplied from outside. This would seem to suggest that Góngora is not hostile to the idea of commerce as such.[40] Although he draws attention to the fact that none of the fish consumed during a lengthy rustic meal were bought, despite the rarity of some of them,[41] this is not really an argument on the other side, for it is precisely those with the most commercial outlook who would be the most likely to approve of the idea of partaking of delicacies for which they have not been obliged to pay.

The fact that the fishermen do not buy fish does not, of course, mean that they do not sell them. The reference to the fact that some of the fish they catch are of species which grace the tables of monarchs and consuls (II, 98−101), may be intended to suggest not only that the peasants eat richly but that they supply the nobility.

Finally, and briefly, the question of seafaring in the *Soledades* offers yet further confirmation of the reasoning behind Góngora's contrast between peasants and courtiers. If the artifice of seafaring itself were Góngora's target, then logically the fishermen, who spend so much time in boats, ought to be under attack. One might perhaps regard their rowing boats as less sophisticated than the sailing vessels bound further afield. But the disasters suffered by the treasure ships are not the result of excessive artifice. Looked at from the shipbuilder's point of view, the moral to be learned from a shipwreck is that more skill needs to be put into the construction and navigation of ships. Looked at from the point of view of the old man in the first *Soledad*, the lesson is concerned not with artifice but with the distorted values of those avaricious men who seem to value wealth more than human life. Purely in the interest of accumulating riches, lives are quite unnecessarily put at risk on the high seas, and on foreign shores where the natives are engaged in battle.

Góngora's *Soledades*, then, unlike his *Polifemo*, gives us a remarkably detailed picture of man interacting with his natural environment. The poet leaves us in no doubt as to his admiration for the whole life-style of the peasant community which although it lives close to nature is far from subservient to it. Here we see the triumph of artifice as man uses his skill and ingenuity to provide himself with an abundance of food and with both practical utensils and artefacts and recreational amenities. The moral superiority of rural life resides for Góngora not in its freedom from artifice, for his peasants are far from primitive, but in its freedom from the typical vices of court life such as greed, avarice, and false pride.

Góngora explores man's relationship with the natural world more

---

[40] R.O. Jones has suggested that the *Soledades* are an example of anti-commercial pastoral.

[41] 'Raros muchos y todos no comprados' (II, 247).

fully than his contemporaries in that no other poet explores rural life
in such detail. But the point of view which he illustrates in his *Soledades*
does not seem to differ in principle from that of most other writers.
This is doubtless because his enthusiasm for the way in which the
peasants overcome natural obstacles is based entirely on commonsense
and is far less likely to lead to inconsistencies and contradictions
than arguments directed against artifice. It is not simply that to write
poetry at all presupposes that one accepts an advanced level of civilization, but that cogent general arguments against human artifice are
very hard to find. As soon as one accepts that it is desirable that man-
kind survive as a species one is committed to the view that it is right
that he should protect himself from adverse climatic conditions with
clothing and shelter. Already the idea of overcoming natural obstacles
by the use of ingenuity has to be accepted. Moreover, the argument
that there is a natural scheme of things which is laid down and which
man perverts as soon as he artificially modifies his natural environment
has little force since it is easily countered by the argument that man is
himself a part of the scheme of things, and that he would be going
against his own nature if he failed to utilize the superior intelligence
which distinguishes him from other species.

Some of the difficulties of sustaining a consistent argument against
man's physical interference with nature are illustrated by the poetry of
Quevedo, who perhaps more than most was attracted towards portraying moral degradation in terms of man's perversion of the natural
world. His *Sermón estoico de censura moral*, for example constantly
links human vice with the ravaging of the natural world. The iced
drinks in lavishly decorated glasses enjoyed by the wealthy are described in terms of a perversion of nature.[42] The exploitation of the
earth's mineral resources, associated with a greed which leads man to go
far afield to distant shores and inaccessible mountains, is seen in particularly violent terms. Of greedy man, he writes:

> Por saber los secretos
> de la primera madre
> que nos sustenta y cría,
> de ella hizo miserable anatomía.
> Despedazóla el pecho,
> rompióle las entrañas,
> desangróle las venas

[42]   Y a la naturaleza, pervertida
         con las del tiempo intrépidas mudanzas,
         transfiriendo al licor en el estío
         prisión de invierno frío. . .
                                        (lines 146–9)
         Obras Completas, I, p. 134.

que de estimado horror es⁺aban llenas;
los claustros de la muerte
duro solicitó con hierro fuerte.
Y espantará que tiemble algunas veces,
siendo madre y robada
del parto a cuanto vive preferido?
No des la culpa al viento detenido,
ni al mar por proceloso:
de ti tiembla tu madre, codicioso.[43]

(lines 108–22)

(Probing secrets of
our first mother of all
who rears and nurtures us,
he left her wretchedly dissected.
He ripped her breast apart;
he tore open her bowels;
her veins, which once inspired respectful awe,
he drained of all their blood;
with tough iron, ruthlessly
death's cloisters he sought out.
Small wonder that she sometimes trembles, then
being a mother, robbed
of that offspring, prized above all that lives!
Heap not the blame upon the lingering wind,
nor on the stormy sea:
your mother, man of greed, quakes, thanks to you.)

There is the suggestion also that in sailing to remote lands in pursuit
of minerals man is committing sacrilege. Quevedo talks of the first
sailor bringing together extreme climes and breaking the earth's sacred
boundaries.[44] Similarly, as we have seen (p. 129 above), he regarded the
onslaught on mountains as an interference in a part of the world
never intended for man. As in Góngora, birds, beasts and fish are seen
as defenceless against man the hunter, but here hunting is associated
with gluttony, and with an insatiability which could lead to the destruction of all life. The same kind of criticism of hunting is implied
in another poem in which Quevedo comments on how once the birds

---

[43]   Ibid. 133.
[44]   'Unió climas extremos;
        y, rotos de la tierra
        los sagrados confines,
        nos enseño, con máquinas tan fieras,
        a juntar las riberas.'
                  (lines 67–71).

and beasts died naturally of old age.[45]

If we regard all these examples as a warning to man that he should not interfere with nature, then Quevedo will emerge as a rather inconsistent thinker, since there are other poems in which he views the same basic activities in a quite different light. For example, the shooting of game birds is enthusiastically viewed in his poem describing the country home of Gonzalo Chacón,[46] as is the shooting of a hog by the Infanta Doña María.[47] Nor is it merely in such courtly poems that Quevedo apparently changes his ground. There are others in which he sets out to praise human artifice. His poem addressed to the paint brush sees art as a competitor to nature and goes out of its way to stress the marvel of painting as a means of overcoming limitations of time and space.[48] His poem in praise of the chiming clock expresses wonder at the way human daring and ingenuity brings inanimate metal to life, despite the fact that elsewhere he is critical of the very mining of metals let alone their fashioning into ingenious artefacts. Quevedo's *silva* addressed to the inventor of the gun introduces yet further contradictions. Here man's boldness in attempting to control the element of fire comes under attack. But in making his point Quevedo looks favourably on man's attempts to dominate the other three elements.[49] This contradicts his structures against seafaring and the probing of the earth's farthest recesses which one finds in other poems.

What all these variations suggest is that in fact for Quevedo the

---

[45] 'Caducaban las aves en los vientos,/y espiraba decrépito el venado/grande vejez duró en los elementos.' *Epistola satírica y censoria contra las costumbres presentes de los castellanos*, lines 85–7. *Obras completas*, p. 143.

[46] *Obras completas*, I, 235, lines 60–76.

[47] *Obras completas*, I, 242–5.

[48] *Obras completas*, I, 249–253.

[49]   Ve al alto mar furioso,
    enséñale a sufrir selvas enteras;
    su paciencia ejercita con galeras;
    y en las horas ardientes,
    den venganza del sol, bebe las fuentes;
    y el pueblo de los ríos
    imita en resbalar sus campos fríos;
    y por sendas extrañas,
    obediente a tu vida,
    por más grato reparto a tus entrañas,
    la parte más remota y escondida,
    visite, nuevo alivio, al calor lento,
    con sucesiva diligencia el viento.
    Estos corteses elementos trata,
    blando aire, tierra humilde, mar de plata;
    las soberbias del fuego reverencia,
    y teme su inclemencia.

                (Ibid. 128).

physical interference with nature was morally neutral. Where it is motivated by any of the seven deadly sins Quevedo attacks it: otherwise he admires it. If sometimes he suggests that the action of opposing nature is in itself wrong then it seems most sensible to regard this as an example of poetic exaggeration, and as a use of *ad hoc* imagery designed to have a particular emotional impact within the context of a particular poem. Most readers are perhaps emotionally prone to accept that to oppose nature is somehow wrong, but would if asked to define more closely what they understood by 'opposing nature' probably find that they were not in principle against the exploitation of natural resources. Quevedo's attack on sin relies on this initial emotional response rather than on closer intellectual analysis. His poems praising painting and clock-making show that he saw human ingenuity when correctly motivated as a source of wonder.

Quevedo and Góngora's enthusiasm for properly motivated artifice is not entirely unexpected if we take into account the approach to descriptive poetry which I have outlined in previous chapters. It is not simply that their attitude enables them to avoid the nonsensical philosophy to which the contrary view leads. It also offers a positive confirmation of the view that the baroque descriptive poets were particularly sensitive to wonder. We have seen in earlier chapters how these poets portrayed the wonder of the natural world. But to say that nature is wonderful is not to say that man is despicable. Both may legitimately claim our admiration. Poets were ready to acclaim the marvellous from whatever source it might derive. Tesauro's theory of wit is a reminder of this, for in admitting both the *mirabile per arte* and the *mirabile per natura* he confirms that his contemporaries saw a positive creative role for man in the world.

VII

AN AGE OF WONDERMENT

In the course of this book I have tried to show how an attitude of wonder towards the natural world and towards human achievement is characteristic of descriptive poetry in the age of Góngora largely through an analysis of poetic texts of the period. But these texts are not the only evidence of the taste of the time available to us, and it is the aim of this final chapter to take a broader view and to seek from other sources both confirmation that within the sphere of poetry the marvellous was indeed an important preoccupation and some indication of whether these developments in poetry have any significance in the context of the broader world of letters, or whether they remain narrowly poetic.

Useful clues to the poetic taste of the time may be derived from a knowledge of which authors, if any, were singled out for special admiration by the baroque poets. Like their predecessors, seventeenth-century poets continued the practice of consciously imitating the classical poets. The desire to appear erudite exerted an important influence, and tended to result in a wider range of authors being imitated, so that Francisco de Trillo, for example, can proudly claim of his *Neapolisea*

Eight times I have written it in eight years, letter by letter, in my own hand, comparing even its most minute clauses with the best poets in the world. I particularly singled out Virgil, Statius, Lucan, and Claudian, and Ovid, without omitting a single letter, and also the best of the poets in the vulgar tongue, and of the Greeks the poet without equal, sparing no effort, expense, or midnight oil in order to imitate their greatness, erudition, descriptions, rites, and ideas, in so far as my own discourse, extensive experience, and inspiration permitted.[1]

But such eclecticism was not incompatible with a preference for particular authors, and if any one Latin poet enjoyed a special place in the affections of Góngora and his followers it was surely Claudian. Trillo

---

[1] 'Ocho vezes le he escrito en ocho años, letra por letra, por mi mano, confiriendo aun sus mas minimas clausulas, con los mayores Poetas del orbe, particularmente elegia Virgilio, Stacio Pap. Lucano, y Claudiano, y Ouidio, sin omitirles letra. De los vulgares ta[m]bien los mejores; de los Griegos el sin igual, no perdonando fatiga, espensa, ò desvelo, para imitar su grandeza, erudicion, pinturas, ritos, y conceptos, en quanto el discurso, la esperiencia continuada, y el aflato permitian.' *Obras*, 430–1.

himself, for example, who in his commentaries on his own poems cites Claudian time and time again as a source, admits to the Marques de Montalbán his particular fondness for this poet, 'whose tendencies you will recognize piecemeal in my poem before even starting to read it, an author truly without equal, and whom, as you must know, I imitated in a not inconsiderable number of places.'[2]

Anastasio Pantaleón de Ribera, another self-confessed Gongorist,[3] seems to have been equally enthusiastic about Claudian, as was Góngora's commentator, Pellicer, who writes in his prologue to Pantaleón's works: 'Anastasio had sound judgement, for among the Poets he used Virgil and Claudian alone.'[4] As for Góngora, Salcedo Coronel notes his predilection for Claudian in commenting on one of the sonnets, 'No poet was imitated by Don Luis as much as our Claudian.'[5] Here, Salcedo's reference to the Latin poet as 'our' Claudian is a sure sign that he agrees with Góngora's choice, and is a further pointer to the remarkable esteem in which Claudian was held.

In modern times, Eunice Gates has drawn attention to a number of Góngora's borrowings from Claudian.[6] But we can, I think, go further than her study takes us, not merely because there are examples which she overlooks (including both debts acknowledged by Góngora's early commentators and those which no critics seem to have noticed yet), but, more importantly, because she leaves us with no real impression of the character of Claudian's poetry, or the significance of Góngora's imitation of him.

A brief survey of Claudian's output reveals a number of cogent reasons for the baroque poets' interest in him. Firstly, there is his preoccupation with nature, which is revealed not only in the choice of subjects from the natural world for the great bulk of his fifty or so shorter poems, but also in the way he handles the imagery in his full-scale poems which, with the notable exception of his *De Raptu Proserpinae*, concentrate on panegyric and invective. For example, Claudian's panegyric on the consuls Probinus and Olybrius offers a good illustration of his penchant for natural description.[7] This poem of 279 lines takes

---

[2] 'Cuyas direcciones reconocerá V.m. desmembradas del Poema antes de auerle empeçado. Autor verdaderamente sin igual, y a quien (como V.m. conocerá) imité en partes no pocas.' *Obras*, 362.

[3] 'Poeta soi Gongorino', *Obras*, ed. R. de Balbín Lucas (Madrid, 1944), Vol. II, p. 129.

[4] 'Tenía *Anastasio* la eleccion acertada, porque de los Poetas se seruia de Virgilio no mas, i Claudiano.' *Obras*, I, 31.

[5] 'A ningun poeta imitó más don Luis que a nuestro Claudiano'. *Obras de don Luis de Góngora comentadas*, Vol. 2 (Madrid, 1644), fo. 32.

[6] 'Góngora's indebtedness to Claudian', *Romanic Review*, 28 (1937) 19–31.

[7] For this and other texts see *Claudian, with an English translation by Maurice Platnauer*, 2 vols. (London, 1922), Loeb Classical Library.

as its central idea Rome, here personified as a goddess, hastening to beg the Emperor to grant the consulship to the two sons of Probus in recognition of the heroic deeds of their father. We have a vigorous description of Rome, and of her chariot and its journey through the inhospitable Alps to meet the Emperor, pictured as resting from the toils of battle on the green-sward (*caespite graminaeo*)[8]–a passage whose closeness to the opening dedication of Góngora's *Soledades* where the Duke of Béjar is similarly pictured as reclining 'sobre el de grama césped no desnudo' seems to have escaped the notice of Góngora's commentators. Another character depicted by the poet is that of the river-god Tiber, who emerges from his cave upon hearing the thundering of Jupiter which greets the new consular appointment. He is described in remarkable detail in a passage which may well have influenced Góngora's description of the giant Polifemus, whose shaggy locks are described as a stream flooding his chest, and inadequately groomed by his fingers.[9]

When not describing the characters and their actions, Claudian exploits natural imagery as a means of amplifying his theme of praise. For example, the extent of Probus' reputation is described by considering the various parts of the world in which his name is renowned (lines 34–7); his family is said to outshine others as the moon outshines the stars (22–7); his generosity is compared with that of rivers rich in minerals (48–54); the Emperor's loyalty to Rome is described in terms of his willingness to bear the discomfort of extreme climates for her sake (131–4); the impossibility of ever forgetting the feats of Probus is expressed in a series of natural *impossibilia* (169–73); the river-god, Tiber, expresses his delight by inviting all the Naiads and all the rivers in the land to celebrate.

Another major poem exploiting natural description to the full is his unfinished *De raptu Proserpinae*, which provided the seventeenth century with a model for the *fábula mitológica*, showing how the tales which Ovid has strung together in his *Metamorphoses* could be isolated and greatly expanded.[10] And among the shortest poems we even have examples of natural description providing the sole *raison d'être* of the poem, as in the two vignettes depicting a harbour.[11]

---

[8]   Ibid. 10, line 114.

[9]   *Polifemo*, lines 61–4. Compare Claudian, lines 222–3: 'Distillant per pectus aquae; frons hispida manat/ imbribus; in liquidos fontes se barba repectit'. A. Vilanova's study of Góngora's sources, *Las fuentes y los temas del 'Polifemo' de Góngora*, makes no mention of this passage.

[10]   Both Herrera and Lope de Vega are reputed to have translated Claudian's poem into Spanish, though unfortunately neither manuscript has survived. See O. Macrí, *Fernando de Herrera* (Madrid, 1959), p. 51; T.S. Beardsley, Jr., *Hispano-Classical Translations printed between 1482 and 1699* (Pittsburch, 1970), p. 69.

[11]   Claudian, op.cit.II, 174, 178.

But what is particularly significant about Claudian's poetry is not simply its richness in natural description, but the quite unmistakable sense of wonder that emerges from it. For example, there is a remarkable passage in his *De raptu Proserpinae* where, having described the physical setting of Mount Etna in terms which Góngora clearly had in mind when opening his *Polifemo*, he goes on to depict in very vigorous terms the tremendous power of the volcano, muses on the paradox that despite its great heat, its summit remains snow-capped—a feature which led Tesauro to include this conceit among his examples of *mirabili per natura*—and goes on to wonder at the cause of volcanic eruptions.[12] Time and time again Claudian is attracted towards the inexplicable and the curious in nature. His poem on the magnet, for example, which concludes with a conceit about Cupid's power causing attraction even between iron and the lodestone, expresses the idea that this ordinary looking stone has marvellous properties which baffle human comprehension, as do all the great phenomena of nature.[13] Other poems are inspired by the river Nile, which mysteriously floods in Summer instead of in the rainy season (XXVIII), the hot springs of Aponus (XXVI), and the legendary Phoenix with its unique properties (XXVII). And, like the baroque poets, Claudian has a keen eye for the marvels of nature on the small scale. Poems devoted to individual creatures include those on the procupine, whose natural defence is marvelled at as unequalled by man (IX), and the sting-ray with its natural protection (XLIX). But human skill is also marvelled at in a poem in praise of Archimedes' sphere (LI), and another in honour of a beautiful statue (VII). An excellent example of Claudian's fascination with nature's anomalies, however, humble, is the series of no less than seven epigrams on a droplet of water enclosed in a piece of crystal. How, he asks, can this miraculous stone be both hard and soft at the same time?—[14] a paradoxical reflection which again could have served as a perfect example of Tesauro's *mirabile per natura*.

From the fact that Góngora and his followers gave pride of place to Claudian, thus immersing themselves in a literature in which the sense of the wonder of natural phenomena is so transparent, we can conclude that they too are likely to have given the marvellous a prominent place in their thinking. Further confirmation that this is likely to have been a conscious preoccupation is provided by the frequent recurrence of the idea of the marvellous in literary theory from the end of the sixteenth century. In Italy, Marino's often-quoted

---

[12] Claudian, op.cit. I, lines 141–79.
[13] Claudian, op.cit., *Shorter poems*, no. XXIX.
[14] 'Qua frigoris arte/torpuit et maduit prodigiosa silex?', Ibid. no. XXXIV, lines 3–4.

'E del poeta il fin la maraviglia' is by no means the first example of an awareness of the importance of this poetic aim. Not only are earlier references to the marvellous impressive by their sheer number,[15] but some theorists accorded wonder a central place. For example, Denores (1588) regards *maraviglia* as the basic cause of all pleasure in poetry.[16] Sperone Speroni (1596) describes the marvellous as the distinguishing feature of poetry,[17] as does Patrizi (1587), who sees it as poetry's fundamental characteristic, and devotes a whole ten books of his treatise on poetry to this very subject.[18]

Despite the fact that one can trace the origins of some of these ideas back to Aristotle's *Poetics* and *Rhetoric* it is clear that they now had a momentum of their own. It is significant that Giovanni Talentoni thought wonder of sufficient independent importance to devote his address to a Milan Academy in 1597 to a systematic philosophical examination of the subject.[19]

Spanish poetic theory also recognized the importance of wonder, as E.C. Riley has shown.[20] López Pinciano (1596), for example, took the view that unless it aroused wonder, no poem was capable of being moving.[21] Francisco Cascales, too, insists on the importance of wonder as the source of pleasure in all types of poetry.[22]

There is ample evidence, then, that by the seventeenth century the pursuit of wonder was a very familiar poetic objective, which is not to say that there would have been universal agreement over the best methods of obtaining this objective. Blinkered by Aristotle's *Poetics*, what most of the sixteenth-century theorists have in mind is drama and epic poetry—poetry of action, narrating marvellous events, rather than lyrical poetry describing the natural world. They showed little interest in one of the most important sources of the marvellous for the poets of the following century—the attempt to depict the infinite variety of nature and, through poetic wit, to reveal nature's unexpected patterns. Yet it was this source which links the

[15] See Bernard Weinberg, *A History of Literary Criticism in the Italian Renaissance*, 2 Vols., (Chicago, 1961), who indexes relevant references under the heading *marvelous*.

[16] Ibid. 786-7.

[17] Ibid. 688.

[18] Ibid. 771-5.

[19] Ibid. 238-9.

[20] 'Aspectos del concepto de *Admiratio* en la teoría literaria del siglo de oro,' in *Studia Philologica. Homenaje ofrecido a Dámaso Alonso*, 3, 173-83.

[21] 'Ha de ser admirable, porque los poemas que no traen admiración no mueuen cosa alguna, y son como sueños fríos algunas vezes'. As quoted by Riley, loc.cit.175.

[22] 'La admiración es una cosa importantisima en qualquier especie de Poesía: pero mucho mas en la heroica. Si el Poeta no es maravilloso, poca delectacion puede engendrar en los corazones'. Riley, loc.cit.

baroque poets with other contemporary thinkers who, like them, were fascinated by the complexities of nature, and approached their subject not in a coldly scientific way, but with a heightened sense of the marvellous. It was left to the new theories of wit of the seventeenth century to begin to explore the relationship between poetry and science or natural philosophy, as we shall see later.

Who were these thinkers who were sentitive to the wonder of nature? Not surprisingly, they included those with a religious message to impart, for the wonder and mystery of the universe was a perennial topic for the Christian apologist. But what we see in a writer like Fray Luis de Granada, the first book of whose *Introducción del símbolo de la fe* (1582) is devoted to the creation, is how the traditional religious arguments could become revitalized. Fray Luis not only cites Patristic accounts of the nature of the universe, such as the *Hexamera* of Saint Ambrose and Saint Basil, and Saint Augustine's *De Genesi ad litteram*, which were extended commentaries on the account of the creation given in the book of Genesis, but also cites *in extenso* part of Cicero's *De natura deorum.*[23] This is significant, because Cicero, who, says Fray Luis, puts many Christians to shame, actually refers to one of the arguments for the operation of a divine providence in the world as the argument from wonder,[24] and in expounding it, begins to reflect on the psychology of wonder. He speculates on how miraculous the sunrise would appear to men deprived of the sight of the sun: 'But daily recurrence and habit familiarize our minds with the sight, and we feel no surprise or curiosity as to the reasons of the things we see always; just as if it were the novelty and not the importance of phenomena that ought to arouse us to inquire into their causes.'[25]

But what we see in Fray Luis is not merely a more philosophical approach to his subject brought about by the inclusion of classical material,[26] but an approach in which the whole argument is brought alive by the incorporation of material derived from the author's own observation of the world of nature. Just as the baroque poets examined even nature's humblest products in unprecedented detail, so Fray Luis not only echoes Saint Augustine's view that small creatures are even more marvellous than great ones, but devotes individual sections of his treatise to spiders, bees, silkworms, and tiny mites. He tells us how

---

[23] *Introducción del símbolo de la fe*, I, iii, 4. See Fray Luis de Granada, *Obras*, ed. J. Joaquín de Mora, Biblioteca de Autores Españoles, Vol. 6, (Madrid, 1914), pp. 189 ff.

[24] *De natura deorum*, II, xxx.

[25] Ibid. II, xxxvi, 96. See Cicero, *De Natura Deorum Academica*, English trans. by H. Rackham (London and New York, 1933), p. 217.

[26] Book I of his *Introduccion del símbolo de la fe* actually appeared in a separate Latin translation by Gaspar Manzio under the title *Philosophia Christiana*.

he has observed an insect on his own thumb-nail sharpen its sting by rubbing it between its own front legs, having failed to penetrate the tough nail.[27] No less charming is the long and highly detailed description in his chapter on plants and fruits of the pomegranate:

Which, since it is so beautifully made, I cannot resist describing here. For first God clothed it outside with a made-to-measure gown which completely surrounds it and protects it from extremes of sunshine or wind, and which on the outside is rather tough and hard, but on the inside is softer, so as not to roughen the fruit enclosed within, which is very tender. But inside, the seeds are distributed and secured in such a way that no space, however small, remains empty or unoccupied. It is all divided up into various segments, and between one segment and another there is a membrane finer than crape, separating them from each other: for as these seeds are so delicate, they keep better divided up by this membrane, than if they were all together. . .[28]

In Gracián's *Criticón* we see the incorporation of the religious argument from wonder into a novel. As one of Gracián's eighteenth-century critics perceptively observed, the whole novel is based upon surprise.[29] But it is the opening of the work which conerns us here, where Andrenio recounts to Critilo his reactions on seeing the world for the first time as a young man after being liberated from the subterranean cavern in which he had been imprisoned since birth. In working imaginatively through Andrenio's experience, the programme for which was doubtless suggested to Gracián by Cicero's *De Natura Deorum*,[30] the author brings alive its emotional impact. And Critilo's comments are the vehicle by which Gracián can probe further into the psychology of wonder. Critilo observes that Andrenio's situation is akin to that of Adam.[31] Here we have one whose faculties are already fully developed when he first sees the world, unlike a new-born child who cannot appreciate the significance of what he sees. Critilo states that wise men have always tried to imagine what it would be like to see the world

[27] *Obras*, 229.

[28] *Obras*, 208.

[29] 'Todo el artificio de esta composición satírico-moral consiste en sorprender.' Antonio de Campmany, *Teatro histórico crítico de la eloquencia española*, Vol. 5 (Madrid, 1794), p. 207, as quoted by M. Romera-Navarro in the introduction to his edition of Gracián's *El Criticón*, (Philadelphia and London, 1938), Vol. I, p. 36.

[30] The probability that he had Cicero directly in mind rather than Luis de Granada's work is increased by the description of Andrenio's reaction on first seeing ships, which corresponds to a passage in Cicero about the Argonauts which is absent from Fray Luis de Granada's account of Cicero's views. See Cicero, op. cit. II, xxxv; *El Criticón* Part I, Crisi IV. See below, p. 198.

[31] 'Privilegio único del primer hombre y tuyo llegar a ver con novedad y con advertencia la grandeza, la hermosura, el concierto, la firmeza y la variedad de esta gran máquina creada.' Gracián, *Obras completas*, ed. Arturo del Hoyo (Madrid. 1960), p. 527.

afresh.[32] As we shall see later, the combination of innocence and mature reflection which such an attitude towards the world entails is further discussed in Tesauro's theory of wit. It is interesting to see how Gracián, a fellow theoretician of wit, here ennobles wonder by seeing it as a hallmark of wisdom.

Another group of writers who are perhaps less well known, but who are no less concerned with the wonder of nature, are the theorists of natural magic.[33] It is interesting to see how this branch of learning acquires a new impetus in Spain in the seventeenth century. The medieval magician tended to be a clandestine operator and an outcast whose practices were condemned by the church, but the Renaissance magus, as Frances Yates has shown, cut a very different figure, for he had on his shoulders the cloak of learning.[34] It was none other than Marsilio Ficino, the great scholar, who put aside urgent work on Plato's texts in order to translate for Cosimo de' Medici the newly discovered Greek manuscript of the *Corpus Hermeticum.*[35] Scholars erroneously believed that these texts, which set forth theories of astrology and sympathetic magic based on the knowledge of occult relationships in nature, were the work of one man, the legendary Hermes Trismegistus, scribe of the gods, and that they originated from Ancient Egypt from before the time of Plato. The excitement of the discovery of a manuscript of such antiquity led many scholars to be more disposed to remember Lactantius' praise of Hermes as a prophet foretelling Christ's coming than Saint Augustine's condemnation of his demonology. Magic was now beginning to develop a new respectability, and there was a blossoming of treatises on the subject in the sixteenth century.

Nevertheless, the Renaissance theorists were by no means free from attack by the Church. Moreover, it seems that it was the Spanish theologians who were the most vigorous in the attack.[36] We must therefore see how in this climate of opinion the interest in natural magic could have spread in Spain, and how it was that in the seventeenth

---

[32] Ibid: 'Los varones sabios se valieron siempre de la reflexión, imaginándose llegar de nuevo al mundo, reparando en sus prodigios, que cada cosa lo es, admirando sus perfecciones, y filosofando artificiosamente'.

[33] Kitty Scoular relates some of the authors discussed below to English poetry of the period in her *Natural Magic* (Oxford, 1965). Her book was not known to me at the time I wrote this chapter.

[34] Frances A. Yates, *Giordano Bruno and the Hermetic Tradition* (London, 1964), p. 17 ff.

[35] Ibid. 13.

[36] The most comprehensive and the best-known critique was M.A. Del Rio's *Disquisitionum magicarum libri sex* (Mainz, 1603) Other works were Pedro García's attack on Pico della Mirandola (See Lynn Thorndike *A History of Magic and Experimental Science* (New York, 1923–58, Vol. 4 (1934), pp. 497–507.), and Benedictus Pererius, *Adversus fallaces et superstitiosas artes* (Ingolstadt, 1591).

century, in Spain as elsewhere, Jesuit writers were some of the keenest exponents of natural magic.

It is hardly surprising that the church should have frowned on discussions of how to draw down celestial influences, albeit beneficial ones, by means of talismans and incantations. Such magic in effect set up a rival religion, or at least had blasphemous implications, in that it claimed to produce extraordinary effects without having recourse to divine aid.[37] But there were aspects of magical theory which were theologically harmless, and quite easily reconcilable with Christianity. Natural, as opposed to celestial or demonic magic, involved studying in nature the occult properties of things, and the occult relationships linking one thing to another. This kind of study of nature is placed in a Christian tradition even by a theorist who is as suspicious of magic as Del Rio. He, like other theorists, talks of Adam's knowledge of the world, which permitted him to name and to understand the things about him, as a kind of natural magic.[38] And the wisdom of Solomon was commonly regarded in the same light.[39]

Some of the phenomena which concerned the theorists of natural magic seem surprisingly ordinary to us today, and it is apparent that natural magic included within its realm what we would tend to call experimental or even domestic science. For example, Giovan' Battista Porta includes books on cooking and cosmetics in his very popular treatise on natural magic.[40] Francis Bacon regarded his *Sylva sylvarum*, which proposes such experiments as the sweetening of sea water and the grafting of fruit trees, as a treatise on natural magic.[41] Pedro García, who has been on the commission of theologians investigating Pico della Mirandola's writings on magic, notes this practical aspect of natural magic with all the snootiness of a pure mathematician contemplating a mechanical engineer:

[37] See R.L. Colie, 'Some paradoxes in the language of things', in *Reason and the Imagination*, ed. J.A. Mazzeo (New York and London, 1962); D.P. Walker, *Spiritual and Demonic Magic from Ficino to Campanella* (London, 1958), p. 83.

[38] 'Naturalem verò legitimamque magicen cum ceteris scientiis Adamo Deus largitus. . .', Del Rio, op.cit. 7. Compare Hernando de Castrillo: 'El nombre Magia, no solo se debe al conocimiento natural, que se le dio a Adan de todas las cosas naturales si no tambien al que tuvo de las diuinas, y sobrenaturales.' *Magia natural* (Trigueros, 1649), fo. 2.

[39] See Benedictus Pererius, op.cit. 21: 'Magiae autem naturales, non humano studio partae, se à DEO vel Angelis bonis acceptae, manifestum est argumentum perfectissima rerum omnia naturalium scientia diuinitatis infusa Salomoni'; Castrillo, op.cit. 38v–41.

[40] *Magia Naturalis* (Naples, 1558).

[41] For this *Writing* of our *Sylva Sylvarum*, is (to speake properly) not a *Naturall History*, but a high kinde of *Naturall Magicke*. For it is not a Description only of Nature, but a Breaking of Nature, into great and strange Workes', as quoted by R.L Colie, op.cit. 100.

To assert that such experimental knowledge is science or a part of natural science is ridiculous, wherefore such magicians are called experimenters rather than scientists. Besides magic, according to those of that opinion, is practical knowledge, whereas natural science in itself and in all its parts is purely speculative knowledge.[42]

Nevertheless, practical though natural magic may have been, it did have an important theoretical side. The combination of the two aspects sometimes results in a fascinating incongruity, as in the case of a work like Gerónimo Cortés' *Physionomia y varios secretos de naturaleza* (Tarragona, 1609), which turns from offering homely advice on how to clean shoes to an explanation of the elemental structure of the universe.[43] In addition to the theory of the elements, which was touched on by most writers in the field, there was the theory that there exist certain occult 'sympathies' and 'antipathies' between natural objects. This convenient way of explaining certain natural wonders, such as magnetism, had a fundamental place in treatises on natural magic. Already Pliny, in his *Natural History*, had explained certain marvellous natural effects in terms of the affinity or repugnance of some objects for others, referring to the Greek origins of these ideas.[44] In the Renaissance one finds whole treatises devoted to the listing of such occult relationships.[45] These were not always particularly edifying, and the whole attempt to explain natural phenomena in this way rather begs the question. Yet the difficulty of replacing such theories at this time, when no scientific method existed, is well illustrated by Fracastoro's treatise on sympathy and antipathy. Here we see an attempt to explain all phenomena in terms of direct physical contact rather than in terms of some vague action at a distance. But in the event, as Thorndike has pointed out,[46] his account of natural forces is hardly less superstitious than the traditional ones, since he virtually spiritualizes physical force by postulating the interaction of bodies by means of their emitting subtle *corpora sensibilia*.

In Spain, interest in occultism was doubtless promoted by the

[42] As quoted by Lynn Thorndike, *A History of Magic and Experimental Science*, 4, p. 501. The very title of Thorndike's work indicates the relationship between the two subjects. Compare D.P. Walker, op.cit. 75–6.

[43] See Cortes op.cit., fo. 40, where the reader is advised to rub his shoes over with tanners dye 'cuya experiencia tengo hecha, renouando los borceguis y çapatos, no vna vez, sino muchas, porque los que tenemos poca renta y mucho gasto, auemos de ahorrar por vna parte, lo que gastamos por otra.'

[44] Pliny, *Natural History*, English trans. by H. Rackham *et al.* (London, 1938), xx, i.

[45] e.g. G. Fracastoro, *De sympathia et antipathia rerum* (Venetiis, 1546); A. Mizaud, *Receuil de Sympathies et Antipathies de plusieurs choses mémorables* (Paris, 1556). See Charles Chesneau, *Le père Yves de Paris et son temps* (Paris, 1946), II, 89.

[46] Op.cit., V, 495–6.

fact that Juan de Herrera, the architect of the Escorial, was an authority on magic who was close the King Philip II, and, it seems, not without influence on him.[47] But the most important developments are in the seventeenth century, when a number of important books on natural magic are published. One of the better organized treatises is Hernando de Castrillo's *Magia natural, o ciencia de filosofía oculta*, the first part of which appeared in 1649.[48] Produced on inferior paper, it was presumably intended for the popular market. Certainly there were already signs of there being a vigorous demand for books in this field, to judge by the popularity of the writings of Juan Eusebio Nieremberg, a fellow Jesuit whom Castrillo constantly cites, referring to him as Eusebio. Nieremberg's *Curiosa filosofía, y tesoro de maravillas de la naturaleza*, first appearing in 1630, enjoyed a remarkable success, and was followed in 1638 by a second part, entitled *Oculta filosofía de la sympatía y antipatía de las cosas.*[49] Part I in particular of this treatise tends to be something of a rag-bag of examples of natural curiosities and anomalies. In his introduction, Nieremberg tells us that he had hoped to produce a full-scale treatise on the subject in Latin, but that the impatience of his friends to see his ideas in print had persuaded him to produce something more modest and in the Spanish tongue. Whatever his real intentions may have been, this seems to be further evidence that there was a very keen interest in the wonders of nature at the time he was writing. And that this interest was often immediate and practical, rather than abstractly academic, is further shown by the existence of collections of natural history specimens which it was fashionable for seventeenth-century noblemen to display in their *cabinets de curiosités.*[50]

The links between natural magic and some other disciplines extend beyond sharing of a general interest in the marvellous in nature to something more precise. In the case of poetry, for example, there are interesting signs of poets and theorists of magic being mutually aware of each other's work. When considering the phenomenon of magnetism,

[47] See René Taylor, 'Architecture and Magic', in *Essays in the History of Architecture Presented to Rudolf Wittkower*, ed. D. Fraser *et al.* (London, 1967), pp. 81–109.

[48] At Trigueros. No further parts were published, but another edition appeared in 1692. There seem to have been considerable delays in getting the first edition out, since the *Licencia* and *Privilegio* are dated 1643. The *Fe de errata* is dated December, 1647.

[49] Palau notes editions of the *Curiosa filosofía* appearing in 1630, 1632, 1634 and 1644. Part two of the work was published in 1638 and re-edited in 1645. Both parts were published together in editions dated 1643 and 1649, and appeared yet again in volumes IX and X of Nieremberg's *Obras filosóficas* (1651).

[50] Alan Soons draws a parallel between such collections of curiosities and Góngora's *Soledades*. See his 'Situación de las *Soledades* de Góngora' in *Ficcion y comedia en el siglo de oro* (Madrid, 1967), pp. 138–43.

for example, Nieremberg actually quotes a passage from Góngora's first *Soledad* as an authoritative statement on the behaviour of magnets, and claims that Góngora had a better knowledge of the subject than all but a selected few, and that Pellicer in commenting on the poet's work had misunderstood the lines in question.[51] And if one might be inclined to doubt whether Góngora is likely to have troubled himself with such technical detail, we have the interesting testimony of another theorist, named by Castrillo in his treatise on magic, Francisco Torreblanca Villalpando, who refers on more than one occasion to his friendship with Góngora, and praises his wide knowledge.[52] There is every likelihood that Góngora would have been aware of the preparation of Torreblanca's book and that they would at some stage have exchanged views on matters pertinent to natural magic.

Torreblanca's reference to the *encyclopaedia* draws our attention to the links between natural magic and the system builders who were attempting to find a key to all the sciences and thereby to provide a method whereby one could encompass the whole of human knowledge. The century saw many attempts, some more fanciful than others, to unite all the sciences under some universal system. These encyclopaedic ambitions were greatly helped by those theories which,

---

[51] 'Otro argumento forçoso niega a la Iman el respeto de los quicios celestes, y es el que se puede forjar del mouimiento que hay de declinacion, ò inclinacion en esta piedra, o la bruxula que hallò Roberto Normano, conocido aun de pocos, si bien alguno quiso sospechar, no le ignorò el Pindaro Español don Luis de Góngora, en lo que desta piedra con comprehension cantò

Nautica industria investigò tal piedra,
Que qual abraça yedra
Escollo, el metal, ella fulminante.
De que Marte se viste, y lisonjera
Solicita el que mas brilla diamante
En la nocturna capa de la Esfera.
Estrella a nuestro Polo mas vezina,
Y con virtud no poca
Distante la revoca
Eleuada la inclina.
. . . .
Sino se desuiara don Ioseph Pellicer a otro sentido, cerca de aquellas palabras: *Eleuada* la inclina, nos diera noticia deste punto, su explicacion es la que cupo sin el conocimienta desta nueua, y por tantos siglos ignorada marauilla de los muy eruditos.' *Curiosa i oculta filosofia* (Madrid, 1643), p. 140.

[52] 'Vt sic merito totius enciclopediae laude vnus nostro aeuo clarissimus conciuis, & amicus noster D. Ludouicus de Góngora sic canit Solit. 1. . .' See Torreblanca, *Daemonologia, sive de magia naturali* (Mainz, 1623), p. 33. This remark is noted by Salazar Mardones in his *Ilustracion y defensa de la Fabula de Piramo y Tisbe* (Madrid, 1636), fo. 88. See also Torreblanca, *Defensa de los libros de Magia* (1618), which prefaces his *Daemonologia*, where he again refers (p. 54) to 'nuestro amigo Don Luis de Góngora', quoting from the ode 'De la toma de Larache'.

like that of sympathies and antipathies, saw some common substructure in nature, some significant ordering beneath the surface. Hence it is not surprising to find a keen interest in natural magic amongst some of these encyclopaedists. Two general methods incorporating magical theory were Yves de Paris' *Digestum Sapientiae*,[53] and Athanasius Kircher's *Ars Magna Sciendi*.[54] Two Spanish writers on universal method were Pedro Sánchez de Lizarazo, with his *Generalis et admirabilis methodus ad omnes scientias facilius et citius addiscendas* (Tarazona, 1619), and Sebastián de Izquierdo, with his *Pharus scientiarum* (Lyons, 1659). All these writers were strongly influenced by Ramón Lull's method,[55] which is significant in that Lull was regarded as an important authority on magic in the Renaissance, and a number of treatises on the subject were wrongly ascribed to him.[56]

Finally, when we read Nieremberg's *Oculta filosofia* we see how natural magic was based on a view of nature which was fundamentally similar not only to that of emblematists,[57] who sought hidden significance in outward manifestations, but, more importantly from the point of view of baroque poetry, with that of the theorists of wit. When Nieremberg remarks on the wonder of nature, he does so in terms which are precisely those of the theorists of wit, stressing nature's artifice, its correspondences, its wit, in fact:

It is certainly true that even the immediate outward appearance of nature is in itself wonderful, for the entire excellence and wonder of art results from it being a copy of nature, and the better it simulates it, the more wonderful it is. But somehow or other the tables are turned, so that the most wonderful part of nature seems to be that which it imitates from art—that is, its artifice and design, and it is what least occupies our thoughts. For if art is simulated nature, nature is natural, or divine art. And so what is most marvellous about the world is not the immensity of these Heavens, nor the number of stars there, nor the sheer bulk of essences, but its wit, its design, its framework, its order, its correspondences. In short its art is the most splendid there is, and the least appreciated.[58]

---

[53] First edition, 1648. For bibliography see C. Chesneau, *Le Père Yves de Paris et son Temps* (Paris, 1946), Vol 2, p. 643.

[54] Amsterdam, 1669.

[55] See Chesneau, op.cit. 2, 45–9, where an extensive list of other Lullists of the time is also given.

[56] See Thorndike, op.cit. 5, 628.

[57] See Mario Praz, *Studies in Seventeenth-Century Imagery* (Rome, 1964), pp. 19–20; Hector Ciocchini, *Góngora y la tradición de los emblemas* (Bahia Blanca, 1960), p. 51.

[58] 'Bien es verdad, que por si es admirable, aun su primer gesto, y corteza, pues toda la excelencia, y admiracion del arte, es por ser remedo suyo, que tanto es mas admirable, quanto mejor la contra haze. Pero no sé como se truecan las manos, que lo mas admirable de la naturaleza parece que lo es lo que imita el arte;

Although Nieremberg's view of nature as expressed in this passage would have received widespread acceptance, his view of art, if it is intended to imply that the artist is concerned only with nature's outward appearance and not with its inner structure would have been disputed by many. For example, Vincencio Carducci, an Italian painter who had lived long enough in Spain to think of himself as a native and adopt the name Carducho,[59] took a radically opposite view in his very thoughtful treatise on painting. Attacking any attempt to see art in crude representational terms, he remains unimpressed by the traditional artistic ideal of copying a subject so faithfully that the eye is deceived into taking the painting for the original. In Carducci's view, painters possessing such prowess may be excellent technicians, but they lack the knowledge which a true artist must have: 'Those who produce such paintings of simple imitation I revere in the same way as empirical physicians who achieve miraculous results without knowing the cause.'[60] Further qualities are required of the 'compleat' artist: 'I would have him be a consummate natural and moral philosopher, so that by contemplating he might arrive at the qualities of things, and according to the particular objects, would be able to demonstrate their affections, changes, and alterations by their causes, explaining the exact physiognomy behind their forms, colours, and actions.'[61]

The theory of Physiognomy to which Carducci refers was not clearly distinguishable from that of natural magic, and could be regarded as an extension of the theory of 'signatures', which figured prominently in many of the treatises dealing with nature's occult sympathies and antipathies, and according to which hidden qualities are manifested by outward signs.[62] Carducci notes that 'These effects caused in the external body, sometimes correspond to and allude to what lies within. . . How can he who is a mere imitator of the exterior in nature and lacking

---

esto es su artificio y traça, y es lo que menos nos ocupa: porque si el arte es naturaleza contrahecha, la naturaleza es arte natural, o diuina; y assi no es lo mas marauilloso del mundo la inmensidad de essos Cielos, ni el numero de sus luces, ni el bulto de sus essencias, sino su ingenio, su traça, su armaçon, su orden, sus correspondencias; al fin su arte es lo mas vistoso que tiene, y a que menos se respeta.' Nieremberg, *Curiosa y oculta filosofia* (Madrid, 1643), p. 300. Cicero refers to 'nature's art' in his *De natura deorum*, II, xxxiii, 83.

[59] See Vincencio Carducho, *Dialogos de la pintura* (Madrid, 1633), fo. 3.

[60] 'A los que hazen las tales pinturas de simple imitacion, los venero como a medicos impiricos, que sin saber la causa hazen obras milagrosas.' Ibid. 56 v.

[61] 'Yo le hiziera consumado Filosofo natural y moral, para que contemplando alcançasse las calidades de las cosas, y por sus causas supiera demostrar los afectos, mudanças, y alteraciones, segun los objetos, explicando la rigurosa fisionomia en las formas, colores y acciones.' Ibid. fo. 71 v.

[62] On signatures see Thorndike, op.cit. 5, 628. Gerónimo Cortés' *Physionomia y varios secretos de naturaleza* (Tarragona, 1609) could equally appropriately have been entitled *Magia natural*.

in these precepts and this knowledge succeed, since he is ignorant of those differences and agreements?'[63] The artist needs to have such knowledge because very often such correspondences are not apparent in nature, and in these cases it is the task of the artist to improve what he sees so that the hidden structure is revealed.

The philosophical basis of Carducci's theory rests upon an important distinction between nature (*la naturaleza*) and the natural (*lo natural*). The artist who is interested merely in external appearances imitates *lo natural* rather than *la naturaleza*. Nature herself is essentially perfect. But when one looks at nature from the point of view of external characteristics, of accidents rather than of essence or final cause, then she is seen as subject to imperfections which are the result of man's original sin. The world of external appearances is *lo natural*: *la naturaleza* is the perfect design which underlies reality and in which the artist should be versed.

From what we have so far seen of Tesauro's *Cannocchiale Aristotelico* in the course of this book it would seem that he, like Carducci, saw it as part of the artist's function to reveal nature's hidden patterns. And it may well be that when it came to poetry, Nieremberg, who had after all regarded Góngora as knowledgeable about some of nature's secrets, would have agreed with him. Nevertheless there still remains one problem concerning the relationship between the arts and the sciences, and the status of wit in poetry which it is very important to clarify, and which will necessitate us delving a little more deeply into the theory of wit.

We have seen in this chapter how widespread was the sensitivity to the marvellous in the seventeenth century. On the one hand it is prominent in poetic theory of the time, and on the other it is reflected in the natural philosophy of the age, which expressed wonder both at nature's variety and her perfection in miniature, and at her surprising anomalies and her occult patterns. All this seems to correspond with the poetic practice of the time as examined particularly in Chapters Four and Five of this book. All this provides ample evidence of a common outlook, but the question still remains as to how far one can pursue the parallel between the poet on the one hand providing examples of surprising relationships in the form of the poetic conceit, and the philosopher or scientist on the other hand investigating nature's hidden secrets. Two radically different viewpoints have emerged from studies on Tesauro's theory of wit, and in the remainder of this chapter I shall attempt to disentangle the issue on which they focus.

[63] 'estos efectos causados en el cuerpo exterior, tienen a vezes correspondencia y alusion a lo interior. . .El que fuere mero imitador de lo natural exterior, desnudo destos preceptos y conocimientos, como ha de arcertar, puesto que no conoce essas diferencias y concordancias?' Carducho, op.cit. 49.

One point of view is put by Joseph Mazzeo, who claims that Tesauro envisages metaphor as a conceptual tool for exploring the universe and exciting wonder in the reader by revealing a series of more or less elaborate correspondences in nature.[64] The wonder is due not merely to the remoteness of the analogies drawn, but also to the fact that the poet has glimpsed universal analogies which are hidden truths of nature. Tesauro implies that the world is a book of witty metaphors to be read and interpreted by the poet. Mazzeo supports much of his case from the section of the *Cannocchiale* devoted to what Tesauro calls 'argutezze della Natura'. One such natural conceit, for example, is the immense variety of flowers in nature which correspond to the stars in the skies— a theme which, as we have seen, is common in Spanish baroque poetry.

However, Eugenio Donato vigorously opposes Mazzeo's view.[65] Donato argues that such a view of the poet's function implies that the universe is already ordered, whereas the poet's aim is precisely to create order, to create his own poetic universe. In doing this the poet imposes concepts on words in a quite arbitrary way. Thus, to take an example from Aristotle which is mentioned by Tesauro, where a cup is metaphorically described as a 'shield of Bacchus', one could by extension refer wittily to wine as 'nectar in the shield of the father of happy dreams'. In Donato's view it is clear that in such a case 'what we have done is to impose a conceptual reality upon the wine through the metaphor, rather than starting with a primary quality of the wine itself'. Moreover, he states, had Tesauro regarded nature as a book, as Mazzeo suggests, a view which tends to relegate the individual creativity of the poet by insisting on his passive, exegetic role, he would not have written what is basically a practical treatise on the invention of metaphor.

Put succinctly, the question at issue here is, are conceits created or discovered? Is it artifice rather than truth which prevails in the conceit? The problem is a complex one, and the opposing points of view are perhaps best tested by taking an example.

If a poet describes the constellation which we know as the Plough as 'tilling Elysian Fields', is this an example of creation or discovery? This conceit takes the well-established association between terrestrial ploughs and terrestrial fields and applies it in an unexpected way to their celestial counterparts, which we are not accustomed to linking

[64] J.A. Mazzeo, 'Metaphysical poetry and the poetic of correspondence', *Journal of the History of Ideas*, 14 (1953), 221–34; 'A seventeenth-century theory of Metaphysical poetry', *Romanic Review*, 42 (1951), 245–55. Both essays are reprinted in Mazzeo's *Renaissance and Seventeenth-Century Studies* (New York and London, 1964).

[65] See his 'Tesauro's poetics: through the looking glass,' *MLN*, 78 (1963), 15–30.

together. But it does rather more than apply a physical image to abstract terms, since part of its basis is the physical resemblance between the configuration of this particular constellation and the shape of a plough, and between the heavens on the one hand, and extensive fields on the other. How, then, should we look at it?

Applying Donato's argument to the case, we would say that what we have here is an example of poetic fiction, and hence of creation rather than discovery. After all, the Plough is not really ploughing. Moreover, in choosing the precise words to put across his poetic fiction the poet has been involved in a creative act. As for the resemblances on which the conceit is based, could we not say that the poet has imposed a relationship on the objects which he describes? Objectively speaking, is it in the nature of the constellation *ursa major* to resemble a plough? Does not the resemblance rely heavily on certain fictions actively supplied by the human mind? Firstly, we need to envisage the seven stars as grouped together, although the astronomical evidence is that they do not function as a group, for two of the stars are moving in a quite different direction from the rest. Then we have to imagine them to be in the same plane, although scientifically we know that they are not. We then imagine a line connecting the points of light in such a way as to resemble the very schematic outline of an old-fashioned plough, although we might equally well have imagined the points to be interconnected in a way which yielded a different pattern. And even the pattern we do imagine is capable of different interpretations, since the Romans were content to regard the outline as resembling that of a bear rather than a plough. Doubtless the Gestalt psychologists would say that there are certain rules which determine the way we are likely to perceive what we see in the sky, but our perceptual manipulation is none the less present whether it be conscious or unconscious. And by the time we have worked our perception into a poetic conceit, is it really plausible to say that we have revealed a pre-existing pattern in the universe?

A major objection to this line of reasoning is that just because one may have to go through a convoluted mental process before being in a position to express a relationship this does not mean that the mind imposes relationships rather than discovers them. After all, if some of the stars are spatially positioned in such a way that when observed by man under certain restricted conditions they bear a resemblance to the outline of a certain kind of plough, then they stand in this relationship quite independently of whether or not anybody as ever been aware of this. It is not in the power of the poet's pen to either bring about such a state of affairs or to prevent it. In this respect he stands in the role of discoverer rather than creator, Nothing happens to the stars when he writes about them.

But, comes the reply, it is not about the real world that the poet is writing, but a world of his imagination. In the real world the Plough is incapable of ploughing. In the real world there are no Elysian Fields. Hence the poet's role differs markedly from that of the scientific investigator or the philosopher.

What this argument fails to take into account, however, is that in conceits fiction is used as a device to explore relationships which are entirely factual. Metaphor, for example, which is so often used, by its very nature exaggerates in order to make its point, and is in that respect fictional. It equates states of affairs which are not identical, but only resemble each other in certain respects. But this does not mean that the resemblance on which the metaphor is based is untrue. Moreover, where the poet says something plausible but manifestly untrue, this may be intended as a comment on the implausibility of the world we know. To appreciate the *discordia concors* of wit the reader must have his feet firmly planted in the real world.

To revert to our example, one can see two ways in which the poet uses fiction to point to facts. At the first level, the conceit draws our attention to the fact that because terrestrial ploughs till terrestrial fields we might expect the celestial Plough to till celestial fields, and yet it does not. In effect this is an invitation for us to reflect on the meaning of names we use, such as 'the Plough' and 'Elysian Fields', often without sparing a thought for their significance, like Parisians who have been walking their native boulevards for years, and strolling along the Champs Elysées to the Place de L'Étoile, as it once was, quite unaware of the significance of their action. At a second, less abstract level, the conceit points out that although the Plough does not behave like a plough in a field it does look like one.

Poets are by no means the only ones to use fiction as a basis for exploring fact. The geometrician, for example, has his fictions—lines without thickness, points without size. Like the poet, he too has to select the words and symbols he uses and the form in which he will set out his proofs, and may handle these with varying degrees of elegance. He can change the rules, adopting now Euclidian, now non-Euclidian axioms, and different results will ensue. Yet we are still inclined to say that he has discovered mathematical truths rather than created a beautiful fiction, despite the arbitrariness of his procedures. Even the empirical sciences have their fictions. The physicist investigating the structure of matter may build models which are simply convenient fictions, and he may assume one moment that light functions like a stream of particles, and the next that light is propagated in waves.

We arrive at a view, then, that in the conceit the creation of beauty through fiction goes hand in hand with the discovery of truth about the world. But how did the seventeenth-century theorists look at the problem? It is interesting to see how the theory develops in the course of the century, until we arrive at Tesauro's treatise which has deeper philosophical roots than the others and seems to offer a more balanced view.

Matteo Peregrini makes a sharp division between scientific discovery on the one hand and the appreciation of witty conceits on the other in his treatise *Delle Acutezze* (1639), the third chapter of which sets out his argument. Having shown that the conceit is not always a purely verbal matter and may consist in a link between objects rather than just words, he goes on to say that the discovery and appreciation of scientific relationships between things involves the operation not of wit, but of the intellect. Wit creates and appreciates artifice: the intellect's function is to discover truth.[66] Peregrini argues that artifice is essential to the conceit because a conceit must arouse wonder, and to do this it must show us something rare or unusual.

Peregrini considers as an example the joining of two things by a tacit link, which he refers to as an 'enthymematical link', by analogy with the argument form of the enthymeme, for whereas a syllogism draws a conclusion from two premises, linking two terms together explicitly by means of a middle term, the less formal enthymeme supresses one of the premisses, and hence the middle term, leaving the link as an implicit one. He writes,

Hence the exceptional nature of the artifice in the enthymematical link which concerns us is revealed not so much in the discovery of a perfect conjunction of the middle term with the extremes, as in the forming of a highly unusual and outstanding reciprocal fit. Where the conjunctive middle term and the things conjoined remain in their natural state, nothing exceptional can be formed. And with artifice totally lacking, the only worthwhile thing that can be hoped for is a good, clear syllogistic connection, thereby greatly satisfying the intellect, but by no means satisfying wit. And so it is necessary that the middle term or the extremes or all three should be full of artifice,

---

[66] 'A proposition of Euclid delights us when we achieve understanding of it, but such a delight is very different from that experienced when we hear a witty epigram of Martial. In short, artifice is present solely, or primarily, not in the discovering of beautiful things, but in their creation; and the object of what concerns us here belongs not to the intellect.'

'Diletta una proposizione d'Euclide quando se ne acquista l'intelligenza, ma simil diletto è molto differente da quello che si provi nell' udir un ingegnoso epigramma di Marziale. In somma, l'artificio ha luogo solamente o principalmente non già nel trovar cose belle, ma nel farle; e l'oggetto del plausibile a nostro proposito non s'appartiene all'intelletto, che solo cerca la verità e scienza delle cose, ma si bene all'ingegno, il quale tanto nell'operare quanto nel compiacersi ha per oggetto non tanto il vero quanto il bello.' See *Trattatisti e narratori del seicento*, ed. E. Raimondi (Milan and Naples, 1960), p. 122.

and, as the rhetorician would say, figurative.[67]

Peregrini seems to imply in this passage that in itself the world is not a particularly surprising place, and that it is for the writer to add the ingredient of wonder. It follows from his view that what the reader admires in a good conceit is not some fact about the world, but the brilliance of the writer who invented the conceit.[68]

Gracián, like Peregrini, places more stress on beauty than on truth in the conceit. But his *Agudeza y arte de ingenio* (1648), the revised version of his *Arte de ingenio* (1642), does show some important differences of approach. Although Gracián states that wit is not satisfied with truth alone, but needs beauty, he regards wit as a part of the intellect, unlike Peregrini.[69] This is important because it means he sees that the faculty of the mind used in the production of conceits is the same as that used to discover the hidden truths of science. Although Gracián is only concerned with the literary conceit in his treatise, he acknowledges that wit covers a wider area than this when drawing distinctions between the different kinds of conceit:

Let us make an initial distinction between the conceit of perspicacity and that of artifice, the latter being the subject of our method. The former tends to bring difficult truths within reach, discovering the most recondite; the latter, being not so concerned with this, aspires to subtle beauty; the former is more useful, the latter more delightful; the former is all the Arts and Sciences in their activities and guises; the latter, through being abstruse and extraordinary, had no fixed abode.[70]

It is significant that in the earlier *Arte de Ingenio* Gracián had stated that the 'conceit of artifice' was not concerned with truth, whereas in the revised version he merely says that it is not as concerned

---

[67] 'Dunque la rarità dell'artificio nel legamento entimematico al nostro fine non si spiega tanto nel trovare una perfetta congiunzione del mezzo con gli estremi, quanto nel formare una vicendevole, molto rara e campeggiante acconcezza. Dove il mezzo congiugnente e le cose congiunte stiano nella natural condizion loro, no si può formar cosa alcuna di raro; e mancando affatto l'artificio, altro di pregio non può sperarsi che una buona e chiara connessione sillogistica: e così all 'intelletto molto sodisfare, ma non già punto all'ingegno. Egli e dunque mestiere che'l mezzo o gli estremi o tutti sieno artificiose e, come direbbe il retore, figurati.' Raimondi, op.cit. 122–3.

[68] 'L'oggetto principale di questa dilettosa maraviglia è la particolar virtú dell' ingegno di chi favella'. Ibid. 125.

[69] 'No se contenta el ingenio con sola la verdad, como el juicio, sino que aspira a la hermosura.' Gracián, *Obras completas*, p. 239. He defines the conceit as an act of the understanding ('un acto del entendimiento') ibid. 240.

[70] 'La primera distinción sea entre la agudeza de perspicacia y la de artificio; y ésta es el asunto de nuestra arte. Aquélla tiende a dar alcance a las dificultosas verdades, descubriendo la más recóndita; ésta, no cuidando tanto deso, afecta la hermosura sutil; aquélla es más útil, ésta, deleitable; aquella es todas la Artes y Ciencias, en sus actos y sus hábitos; ésta, por recóndita y extraordinaria, no tenía casa fija.' Ibid. 241–2.

with truth as the 'conceit of perspicacity'.[71] Indeed, in order to be consistent, Gracián has to concede that truth has some part to play in the
literary conceit, because his actual method for creating conceits involves
examining all the attributes and circumstances of the subject of the
conceit with a view to discovering a relationship between them which is
then expressed in a heightened form.[72] Clearly, in so far as objects in
the real world are concerned all such relationships must of necessity
be true. If the relationships did not apply, then they could not be
discovered.

In 1650, Peregrini returned to the theory of wit with his *I Fonti
dell'Ingegno ridotti ad arte*, and in this treatise which concentrates
more on the method of producing conceits than his previous one, we
find that he now talks of the wonder of the universe, and of its artifice.[73] In thus conceding that artifice is not exclusively a product
of the human mind. he seems to have revised his earlier views, and is
now more closely in line with his contemporaries.

Finally, when we reach Tesauro's *Cannocchiale Aristotelico* (1654),
we have a more comprehensive theory which takes advantage of the
work of previous theorists. That conceits do not tell the literal truth
but have a fictional aspect is recognized by Tesauro in his definition
of the true conceit as an 'urbanely fallacious enthymeme'. Presumably
he took this idea directly from Peregrini's *Delle Acutezze*. On the
other hand, the outward form which the conceit takes does not debar
it from being based on the discovery of some unexpected fact about the
world. And so Tesauro analyses wit as a faculty comprising two aspects,
one investigatory and the other creative:

Natural wit is a marvellous power of the intellect which comprises
two natural talents: perspicacity and versatility. Perspicacity penetrates
the furthest and most minute circumstances surrounding every subject,
such as its substance, matter, form, accidents, properties, causes, effects,
ends, what is similar, opposite, equal, superior, or inferior to it, its
signs, proper names, and double meanings, which all lie crammed into
and hidden in any subject, as we shall show in due course. Versatility
swiftly compares all these circumstances with each other or with the
subject. It joins them or separates them, increases or decreases them,
deduces one from another, indicates one with another, and with

[71] See Ibid. 1168: 'ésta, no cuydando de esso, afecta la hermosura sutil'.
[72] 'Valos (los adjuntos) careando de uno en uno con el sujeto, y unos con
otros, entre sí; y en descubriendo alguna conformidad o conveniencia, que digan,
ya con el principal sujeto, ya unos con otros, exprímela, pondérala, y en esto
está la sutileza.' Op.cit. 246. For a further explanation of the method see my
article 'Gracián, Peregrini, and the theory of Topics', *MLR*, 63 (1968), 854–63.
[73] L'università delle cose sta contale mirabile artificio concertata, che tutte
hanno molte vicendevoli corrispondenze l'una con l' altra.' See Raimondi op.cit.
p. 183. See also p. 188, where Peregrini refers to 'L'armonico gran concerto dell'
universo'.

marvellous dexterity puts one in the place of another, like jugglers with their stones.[74]

Tesauro's approach here is similar to Gracián's, except that whereas Gracián had regarded perspicacity as the characteristic of wit when applied to the sciences, and artifice as the main feature of wit when applied to literature, Tesauro sees both aspects of wit as entering into the literary conceit.

It seems a natural step from the view that wit does show us truths about the world to the kind of philosophical realism which underlies Tesauro's view of the world. If wit initially discovers rather than creates subtle relationships, then presumably these relationships hold good whether or not anybody happens to discover them. We are then tempted to give these relationships some kind of independent onto-logical status. The result is a view of the universe in which even the most distant things are in some strange way interconnected, as if all potential conceits were already there, just waiting to be discovered. Tesauro goes a long way in acknowledging the objective existence of such relationships, and Donato is not on strong ground in saying that Tesauro could not have seen the world as a kind of book. It is a view overtly expressed in his *Panegirici Sacri* (Turin, 1633).[75] In the *Cannocchiale* it underlies his description of what he calls the *argutezze della Natura*, and in his analysis of the *mirabili per natura*.[76] His explanation of the *mirabili per opinione*—conceits derived from illusion —is particularly interesting as an illustration of how far conceits exist objectively. He cites an example from Claudian, in which some children seeing for the first time a man in full armour believe that he is an iron man. A child's remark to this effect can hardly be regarded as a conceit on his part, since he is genuinely deceived. The deception, however, does provide a potential conceit, so that the conceit can be said to exist materially though not formally. Such 'material metaphors',

[74] 'L'Ingegno naturale è vna marauigliosa forza dell'intelletto, che comprende due naturali talenti, PERSPICACIA & VERSABILITA. La *Perspicacia* penetra le più lontane & minute *Circonstanze* de ogni suggetto; come *Sostanza, Materia, Forma, Accidente, Proprietà, Cagioni, Effetti, Fini, Simpatie, il Simile, il Contrario, l'Vguale, il Superiore, l'Inferiore, le Insegne,* i *Nomi Propri & gli Equivochi*: le quali cose giacciono in qualunque suggetto aggomitolate & ascose, come a suo luogo diremo. La VERSABILITA velocemente raffronta tutte queste *Circonstanze* infra loro o col Suggetto: le annoda ò divide, le cresce o minuisce, deduce l'vna dall'altra, accenna l'vna per l'altra, & con maravigliosa destrezza pon l'vna in luogo dell'altra, come i Giocolieri i lor calcoli.' Raimond, op.cit. p. 32.

[75] 'E che altro e questo mondo che un libro grande? Che il sole e le altre sempiterne fiamme del cielo, se non caratteri espressivi de' suoi concetti. . .?' As quoted by E. Raimondi, 'Ingegno e metafora nella poetica del Tessauro', in his *Letteratura Barocca* (Florence, 1961), pp. 21–2 (note).

[76] See Tesauro, *Cannocchiale*, pp. 73–8; 448–50; Raimondi, *Trattatisti e narratori del seicento* pp. 26–31; 92–4.

as Tesauro calls them, become true conceits when we realize that the appearance does not represent the reality, yet at the same time pretend that we have in fact been deceived by what we see.[77] Tesauro sees the maintenance of this same balance between appearance and actuality as the principal cause of delight in painting, where the imagination is at first deceived by the artist's accurate representation of real objects into believing that the painted object is in fact real. The aesthetic pleasure comes when the intellect recognizes the deception, but at the same time is prepared to suspend its disbelief.[78]

One interesting implication of this theory of Tesauro is that if the poet is to recognize the material conceits in the world about him he must have a suitably gullible *imaginativa*. He will need the naïve, innocent eye of the child, and at the same time the intellect of a grown man—precisely the qualities attributed to Adam, whose wisdom was admired both by the theorists of natural magic, and by Gracián in his *Criticón*.

The theorists of wit, and of magic, and the religious thinkers we have examined in this chapter are all united in praising this capacity for wonder. Tesauro's theory shows us how this philosophy has its application to imaginative literature. We have already examined in detail in Chapter Five the applicability of his analysis of *il mirabile* to the Spanish baroque poets. His view that the psychology of wit involves a kind of feigned innocence has also a clear applicability to Spanish literature of the period. For example, as was noted in Chapter Five, in creating some of his characteristic contradictory images of colour, Góngora assumes the attitude of one who is innocent of colours falling outside a certain range, and who is confronted by a new colour for the first time. Similarly, there are a number of examples in other writers of Tesauro's *mirabile per opinione* which show the same approach.[79] In the novel, Gracián can achieve a similar effect by seeing things through the eyes of the innocent Andrenio. Andrenio's reaction to seeing some ships for the first time, which he can only describe in terms of things he already knows, is a good example.[80] And in *Don Quijote*, the innocence is that of the madman who sees giants where

[77] 'I puerili discorsi ch'ei van formando nella lor mente ingannata da quell' obietto, tutte son Metafore Materiale: non ricercate dall'Ingegno viuace ma nate nella Imaginatiua delusa: che diuengano formali & argute: se conoscendo il nostro inganno, pur cosi fauelliamo, come se fossimo ingannati.' Tesauro, *Cannocchiale* (Turin, 1670), p. 452.

[78] Ibid. 24.

[79] See above, pp. 121–4.

[80] Andrenio sees 'Unas montañas que vuelan, cuatro alados monstruos que vuelan, si no son nubes que navegan.' The *metafora materiale* of Andrenio is capped by Critilo: 'no son sino naves, aunque bien dijiste nubes, que llueven oro en España.' *Obras completas*, p. 541. Cf. Góngora, *Obras*, No. 392, 'Nubes son, y no naves'.

there are windmills, and who significantly is called an 'ingenioso caballero' by Cervantes.[81]

Tesauro's psychology of wit, then, helps us to see the underlying unity of thought of a whole range of writers. As for his philosophical realism, I believe that this too must have been shared by others, and helps to explain why people may have been so prone to wonderment in this age. The idea that there exists some kind of connection which is quite independent of the human mind between the most diverse objects in the universe leads to such a complex view of the universe that the mind's inability to grasp it tends to cause bewilderment. The theory of natural magic, with its theories of occult sympathies and antipathies between things obviously depended on some such philosophy, since it postulated occult relationships between things of a mysterious and ill-defined nature. Similarly, religious apologists who invoked the argument from design to demonstrate God's existence must also have depended on a philosophical view which regards relationships as existing *a priori* in the world. Clearly, if relationship is thought of as a product of the human mind, then the argument from design becomes totally ineffective.

Whether the view that wit shows us truths about the world is bound to lead to Tesauro's kind of philosophy is a question which it would be too ambitious to attempt to resolve here. The question of whether relationships are created or discovered is a perennial philosophical problem which emerges in the medieval debate between realism and nominalism, and in more modern resurrections of the same debate.[82]

But whether this question is answered one way or the other does not affect the central purpose behind this chapter which is to show that not only did seventeenth-century thinkers and poets share the same sense of wonder, but that the poets were not isolated from other writers in a world of fiction constructed by themselves, and that they too, like the philosophers, were interested in revealing truths about the real world through the vehicle of their poetic fictions.

In illustrating the poetic techniques and the outlook characteristic of the age throughout this book, my examples have been taken from before the eighteenth century. In conclusion, it is worth looking forward to later poets to see when the poetic era could be roughly said to end.

---

[81] Tesauro regards the fantasies of madmen as an example of wit in his *Cannocchiale*, pp. 93–4.

[82] See W. Quine, *Word and Object* (Cambridge, Mass. 1960), pp. 233 ff. Note also Wittgenstein's remark: 'The great problem round which everything that I write turns is: Is there an order in the world *a priori*, and if so what does it consist in?' *Notebooks*, 53, 11, as quoted by Max Black, *A Companion to Wittgenstein's 'Tractatus'* (Cambridge, 1964), p. 5.

The eighteenth century does offer some continuity in so far as the description of nature continues to play an important role in poetry. But this in itself is not sufficient to place its poets squarely within the tradition I have been examining. For example, Meléndez Valdés, writing late in the century, addresses poems to the seasons, the times of the day, and to other aspects of the creation. But his techniques are not those of the baroque poets. The metaphorical exuberance is lacking, and he expresses his enthusiasm for nature in a quite different way, by means of exclamation ('How beautiful!' 'How colourful!'), or exhortation ('Sing, bird!', 'Flow, stream!' 'Come, Spring!'). He himself saw his poetry as a reaction to the two contrasting trends which preceded him, writing in 1797:

These verses are not wrought in the pompous Gongorine style, which, alas, still has its supporters, nor in that other languid prosaic style into which have fallen all those who, devoid of the necessary talent, sought diction's simple graces, sacrificing to the vain hope of finding them the majesty and beauty of our tongue.[83]

Forner, a contemporary of Meléndez, observes exactly the same division in the poetry of the time, and says of the Gongorists, 'I prefer their sophisms, their impudent metaphors, and their ill-considered flights of fancy, to the chill, semi-barbarous aridity of the majority of those writing verse in Spain today.'[84] His preference is, of course, more an expression of distaste for lifeless poetry than of enthusiasm for poetry in the baroque tradition.

In considering which poets could be said to share the seventeenth-century outlook we can dismiss fairly rapidly those who belong to the prosaic school. By its very nature, uninventive verse with flat diction can hardly be calculated to arouse wonder. Its method is to proceed by bald statement rather than by suggesting rich relationships through metaphor. Thus, despite taking country life as his theme, and despite adopting a basically enumerative technique, Francisco Gregorio de Salas in *El observatorio rústico* seems remarkably distant from his baroque predecessors. In his outline of eighteenth-century poetry, Cueto singles this out as one of the most banal of poems, and the extracts he gives certainly confirm the view that, as the title of the poem suggest, the author seems to be more interested in making an exhaustive inventory

---

[83] 'Estos versos no están trabajados ni con el estilo pomposo y gongorino que por desgracia tiene aún sus patronos, ni con aquel otro lánguido y prosaico en que han caído todos los que, sin el talento necesario, buscaron las sencillas gracias de la dicción, sacrificando la majestad y la belleza del idioma al inútil deseo de encontrarlas.' *Poesías*, ed. Pedro Salinas (Madrid, 1965), p. iii.

[84] 'Prefiero sus sofismas, metáforas insolentes y vuelos inconsiderados, a la sequedad helada y semi-bárbara del mayor número de los que poetizan hoy en España.' As quoted by Nigel Glendinning, 'La fortuna de Góngora en el siglo xviii', *RFE*, 44 (1961), 345.

than in conveying any obvious enthusiasm.[85]

It is among the eighteenth-century Gongorists that one would expect to find the closest links with the poetic outlook of the preceding century. But although there is no shortage of poems which borrow Góngora's turns of phrase, it is much more difficult to find examples of the metaphorical exuberance and the flights of fancy referred to by Forner, as can be seen from an examination of the works of the best known Gongorists of the period, Ioseph de León y Mansilla, José Antonio Porcel, and the Conde de Torrepalma.

Of these three poets, the first, and chronologically the earliest, comes the closest to the baroque tradition. With his Soledad tercera,[86] León y Mansilla sought to provide a continuation to Góngora's Soledades. His poem is of similar length to Góngora's first Soledad, and no less obscure. Its action is concentrated into two hunting episodes, in the first of which (pp. 8–15) is encountered a charging stag, which kills itself by colliding with a rock, and a porcupine whose spines offer a challenge to the pursuers. In the second episode (pp. 37–44) we see a thunderstorm instigated by the wrath of the goddess Ceres at the violation of her territory by the hunt. She is appeased after a little bird gets struck by lightning. Other parts of the poem include descriptions of the natural setting at the start of the poem, and later when the hunting party rest from their labours.There is also a description of a rustic meal. But by far the longest section of the poem (almost 300 lines) is the moralizing speech of the old man who now presides over the hunting community, having arrived as an exiled prince ousted from his throne by a usurper. The rest of the poem tends to be dominated by amatory themes centred around the dominant beauty of this hilltop community, Leusipe.

There is some novelty of situation in the episode of the porcupine, and some of the individual metaphors are within the baroque tradition, as when, for example, a treacherous inlet is described as a *bárbaro cocodrilo* (a barbarous crocodile) (the comparison being between the misleading calm of its waters and the legendary deceptive quality of crocodile tears), or when the love-sick wanderer refers to himself as 'este de ojos volcán, de incendios río' ('This volcano of eyes, this river of fire'). But against this one has to set León y Mansilla's heavy reliance on Góngora not only for many of the situations, but also for individual expressions, many of which lose their lustre because they are poorly integrated into their new context. For example, the use of Góngora's expression 'retrógrado cedió' to describe the reaction of the breeze to

---

[85] Leopoldo Augusto Cueto, 'Bosquejo histórico-critico de la poesía castellana en el siglo xviii', *BAE*, 61, clix.

[86] *Soledad tercera. Siguiendo las que dexo escritas el príncipe de los poetas líricos de España D. Luis de Góngora*, (Córdoba, 1718).

girls' singing is ludicrously inappropriate.[87]

León y Mansilla was not the only poet to imitate the letter rather than the spirit of Góngora's poetry. In his *Adonis*, Porcel, too, uses Góngora's vocabulary, Góngora's turns of phrase, and even borrows whole lines from the *Soledades* and *Polifemo*, altering them in only a minimal way.[88] Yet what little ingenuity there is in the imagery seems to be confined to conceits about love. The descriptions of nature are notably lacking in wit, and, what is more, Porcel acknowledges and perhaps even approves of the more restrained approach to description which one associates with poets before Góngora. None of the four introductory descriptions with which he begins the various sections of his *Adónis* is particularly extensive by baroque standards, yet Porcel seems to have been under the impression that they were rather daring, if one is to judge by the admittedly jocular criticisms of their length and tediousness which he imagines Bartolomé Leonardo de Argensola giving voice to.[89] Despite his enthusiasm for Góngora, Porcel seems to have quite a strong classical streak.[90]

Another interesting example of an eighteenth-century approach to description is Torrepalma's *El juicio final*. The theme of the last judgement was obviously one with splendid descriptive possibilities, and one which seventeenth-century poets might have enjoyed exploiting. Torrepalma rises to the occasion in so far as the vocabulary is concerned, peppering his verse with proparoxytones like *horrisono* and *ignifero*. Yet in other respects his description is far more restrained than one would have expected of a poet in Góngora's tradition. The theme of conflict or confusion amongst the elements, for example, is begun but not fully developed. The following metaphor is perhaps the most daring:

> El mar bramó, y en raudo movimiento
> Subió a la esfera en montes de cristales,
> Descubriendo entre tantos parasismos
> Sus entrañas la tierra y sus abismos.[91]

---

[87] León y Mansilla *Soledad tercera*, p. 6.

[88] Compare the following lines of Porcel with Góngora's *Polifemo*:
'Siendo duda no leve
Si es púrpura nevada,
o nieve purpurada'   (lines 107–8):
See *Poetas líricos del siglo xviii*, ed. Cueto, *BAE*, 61 (Madrid, 1952), p. 145.

[89] 'Empieza la primera egloga con una descripcion de Chipre, pomposa y altisonante, para decir despues que alli vivia Adónis y se entretenia en la caza. A la segunda da principio con otra descripcion de las selvas del mismo Chipre, tan cansada como redundante. A la tercera, con la pintura del rio Luco y sus riberas, tan impertinente como las demas. A la cuarta, finalmente, con la de la noche, que empieza, aunque afectada, más regular, pero despues, queriendo imitar la célebre del gran poeta, se hace fastidioso y vulgar.' Ibid. 138.

[90] See Nigel Glendinning, op.cit. 338.

[91] Cueto, *Poetas líricos del siglo xviii*, p. 133.

(The ocean roared, and with a violent surge,
in crystal mountains climbed to heaven's sphere,
while amid paroxysms were revealed
the chasms and the bowels of the earth)

Even this not particularly startling image seems to be an exception.
On the whole, the poet seems content to impress with grandiose language and with simple metaphor ('el prado y monte gimen') rather than
with the tension characteristic of the conceit, even though his poem
could quite naturally have incorporated a fair amount of trans-elemental
imagery.

From these examples one can see how there was a considerable
weakening in the seventeenth-century tradition even amongst those who
thought of themselves as imitators of Góngora, and whom, therefore,
one might have expected to come the closest to it. One of the rare
examples of a poem using the traditional techniques to convey wonder
is the ode, *La soledad* by José Iglesias de la Casa (1748–91).[92] The
poet develops the theme of nature's artistry in a series of images which
are reminiscent of Pedro Espinosa's *Soledad de Pedro de Jesús.*[93] At
the same time, the description of the view from the hilltop, and of its
capacity to amaze even the most experienced of men, is very much in
keeping with the view described in Góngora's first *Soledad* (lines 182–
211). But Iglesias' other descriptive poems do not seem to have the
same flair. *La Soledad* takes us back only momentarily to a poetic era
which was by now virtually dead. It was on wonder, as we have seen,
that baroque descriptive poetry thrived. But in an age in which fancy
was so often sacrificed to reason, and in which classical restraints
were being reintroduced it became remarkably difficult for wonder
to survive.

Looking back now over the whole poetic age traced in this book in
its various aspects, one is struck by the extraordinary dominance of
Góngora's genius at every stage. It was Góngora who had the originality
to break free from traditional preconceptions about genre, and to
pioneer works in which the description of the natural world took on a
new importance. In his descriptive techniques, particularly in his use
of metaphor, he also broke new ground. Yet it is not merely as an
innovator, or because he attracted so many imitators that he commands
attention. His work succeeds at the same time in perfectly epitomizing
the poetry of wonder. Not only does the *Soledades* constantly and
quite explicitly refer to wonderment as a reaction of people to what they
see, but also some of Góngora's most idiosyncratic images, suggesting

as they do that the impossible has come true, are perfect illustrations of what Tesauro was later to identify as *Il Mirabile* in his theory of wit, and to regard as the kind of metaphor most potently expressive of wonder. Eventually, as Góngora's fortunes declined, so that sense of wonder, at once childlike and sophisticated, was snuffed out by the age of the Enlightenment.

BIBLIOGRAPHY

Foreign and Latin names of places of publication have been anglicized.

MANUSCRIPTS

Bodleian Library, Arch. Seld. A. II. 13.
A volume of miscellaneous works, the second of which is a manuscript copy of Góngora's *Soledades*. Seventeenth-century hands, 28 fos., approx. 15 X 21 cm.

Biblioteca Nacional, Madrid, MS. 3795.
The first of three volumes of miscellaneous poetry, entitled *Poesías manuescritas*. Contains a fragment of Adrián de Prado's *Canción descriptiua*, beginning fol. 7. Seventeenth-century hand, 339 fos. index, approx. 20 X 15 cm.

PRIMARY PRINTED SOURCES

Agrippa, Henricus Cornelius, *De occulta philosophia libri tres* (Cologne, 1533).

Alonso, Dámaso and Ferreres, Rafael (eds.), *Cancionero antequerano, recogido por los años de 1627 y 1628 por Ignacio de Toledo y Godoy* (Madrid, 1950).

Barahona de Soto, Luis, *Primera parte de la Angelica* (Granada, 1586).

Barrios, Miguel de, *Flor de Apolo* (Brussels, 1665).

Berceo, Gonzalo de, *Milagros de Nuestra Señora*, etc., prol. y versión moderna, Amancio Bolaño e Isla (Mexico, 1969).

Blecua, José Manuel (ed.), *Cancionero de 1628. Edición y estudio del Cancionero 250–2 de la Biblioteca Universitaria de Zaragoza* (Madrid, 1945).

Bocángel y Unzueta, Gabriel, *Obras*, ed. Rafael Benítez Claros, 2 vols. (Madrid, 1946).

Boscán, Juan, *Obras poéticas*, edited by Martín de Riquer, Antonio Comas, and Joaquín Molas, Vol. 1 (Barcelona, 1957).

Butrón, Juan de, *Discursos apologeticos, en que se defiende la ingenuidad del arte de la pintura* (Madrid, 1626).

Carballo, Luis Alfonso de, *El cisne de Apolo*, ed. A. Porqueras Mayo, 2 vols. (Madrid, 1958).

Carducho, Vincencio, *Dialogos de la pintura* (Madrid, 1633).

Castrillo, Hernando, *Magia natural, o ciencia de filosofía oculta con nuevas noticias de los mas profundos misterios y secretos del universo visible. Primera parte.* (Trigueros, 1649).

Castro, Adolfo de (ed.), *Poetas líricos de los siglos xvi y xvii*, 2 vols., Biblioteca de Autores Españoles, Vols. 32, 42 (Madrid, 1950, 1951).

Cicero, *De natura deorum academica*, with an English translation by H. Rackham (London/New York, 1933).

Claudian, Claudius, *Claudian*, with an English translation by Maurice Platnauer. Edited by E. Capps *et al.*, 2 vols. (London, 1922).

Colodrero de Villalobos, Miguel, *El Alpheo, y otros assuntos, en verso, exemplares algunos* (Barcelona, 1639).

— — *Varias rimas de Don Miguel Colodrero de Villalobos* (Córdoba, 1629).

Corral, Gabriel de, *La Cinthia d'Araniuez, prosas y versos* (Madrid, 1629).

Cortes, Gerónimo, *Physionomia y varios secretos de naturaleza* (Tarragona, 1609).

Cueto, Leopoldo Augusto de (ed.), *Poetas líricos del siglo xviii*, 3 vols., Biblioteca de Autores Españoles, Vols. 61, 63, 67 (Madrid, 1952).

Del Rio, Martín A., *Disquisitionum magicarum libri sex* (Mainz, 1603).

Encina, Juan del, *Eglogas completas*, ed. H. López Morales (Madrid, 1968).

Espinosa, Pedro, *Obras*, ed. Francisco Rodríguez Marín, 2 vols. (Madrid, 1909).

Ferrero, Giuseppe Guido (ed.), *Marino e i Marinisti* (Milan/Naples, 1954).

Foulché-Delbosc, R. (ed.), *Cancionero castellano del siglo xv*, 2 vols. Nueva Biblioteca de Autores Españoles, Vols. 19, 22 (Madrid, 1912).

Fracastoro, Girolamo, *De sympathia et antipathia rerum liber unus* (Venice, 1546).

Gallardo, Bartolomé José, *Ensayo de una biblioteca española de libros raros y curiosos*, Vol. 1 (Madrid, 1863).

Gallego Morell, Antonio (ed.), *Garcilaso de la Vega y sus comentaristas* (Granada, 1966).

Garau, Francisco, *El Olimpo del sabio. Segunda parte* (Barcelona, 1691).

Garcilaso de la Vega, *Obras completas*, ed. E.L. Rivers (Madrid, 1964).

Gardner, Helen (ed.), *The Metaphysical Poets*, revised ed., Penguin Books, (Harmondsworth, 1966).

Gates, Eunice Joiner (ed.), *Documentos gongorinos. Los 'Discursos Apologéticos' de Díaz de Rivas. El 'Antídoto' de J. de Jáuregui* (Mexico, 1960).

Góngora y Argote, Luis de, *Letrillas*, ed. Robert Jammes (Paris, 1963).

— — *Obras completas*, edited by J. and I. Millé y Giménez, 4th ed. (Madrid, 1956).

— — *Obras en verso del Homero español que recogió Juan López de Vicuña*, facsimile ed. by Dámaso Alonso (Madrid, 1958).

— — *Las soledades*, ed. Dámaso Alonso, 3rd ed. (Madrid, 1956).

Gow, A.S.F. and Page, D.L. (eds.), *The Greek Anthology. Garland of Philip and some Contemporary Epigrams* (Cambridge, 1968).

Gracián, Baltasar, *El Criticón*, ed. M. Romera-Navarro, 3 vols. (Philadelphia/London, 1938).

— — *Obras completas*, ed. Arturo del Hoyo (Madrid, 1960).

Granada, Fray Luis de, *Obras*, ed. J. Joaquín de Mora, Biblioteca de Autores Españoles, Vol. 6 (Madrid, 1914).

Herrera, Fernando de, *Poesías*, ed. Vicente García de Diego (Madrid, 1952).

Holanda, Francisco da, *Da pintura antigua*, ed. J. de Vasconcellos (Oporto, 1918).

Izquierdo, Sebastián, *Pharus scientiarum* (Lyons, 1659).

Jiménez Patón, Bartolomé, *Elocuencia española en arte* (Toledo, 1604).

— — *Mercurius Trimegistus, sive de triplici eloquentia sacra, española, romana* (Baeza, 1621).

Kircher, Athanasius, *Ars Magna Sciendi in xii libros digesta*, 2 vols. (Amersterdam, 1669).

León, Fray Luis de, *Obras completas castellanas*, ed. Felix García (Madrid, 1959).

León y Mansilla, *Soledad tercera. Siguiendo las que dexo escritas el príncipe de los poetas líricos de España D. Luis de Góngora* (Córdoba, 1718).

Leonardo y Argensola, Bartolomé and Lupercio, *Rimas*, ed. J.M. Blecua, 2 vols. (Zaragoza, 1950, 1951).

Marino, Giambattista, *Opere scelte*, ed. G. Getto (Turin, 1962).

— — *Poesie varie*, ed. B. Croce (Bari, 1913).

Martínez, Jusepe, *Discursos practicables del nobilisimo arte de la pintura*, ed. Julián Gallego (Barcelona, 1950).

Meléndez Valdés, Juan, *Poesías*, ed. Pedro Salinas (Madrid, 1965).

Mizaud, A., *Catalogi septem sympathiae et antipathiae, seu concordiae, & discordiae rerum aliquot memorabilium* (Paris, 1554).

Nieremberg, Juan Eusebio, *Curiosa y oculta filosofia. Primera y segunda parte de las maravillas de la naturaleza, examinadas en varias questiones naturales* (Madrid, 1643).

Ovid, *Metamorphoses*, with an English translation by F.J. Miller, ed. T.E. Page *et al.*, 2 vols. (London, 1960).

Pantaleón de Ribera, Anastasio, *Obras*, ed. Rafael de Balbín Lucas, 2 vols. (Madrid, 1944).

Paravicino y Arteaga, Felix Hortensio de, *Obras posthumas, divinas y humanas de DON FELIX DE ARTEAGA* (Madrid, 1641).

Pascal, Blaise, *Pensées*, ed. Louis Lafuma (Paris, 1960).

Pellicer Salas Ossau y Tovar, José de, *El fenix en su historia natural* (Madrid, 1630).

– – *Lecciones solemnes a las obras de don Luis de Góngora y Argote* (Madrid, 1630).

Peregrini, Matteo, *I fonti dell'ingegno ridotti ad arte* (Bologna, 1650).

Pererius, Benedictus, *Adversus fallaces et superstitiosas artes* (Ingolstadt, 1591).

Pérez, Fray Andrés, *Historia de la vida y milagros del glorioso Sant Raymundo de Peñafort* (Salamanca, 1601).

Petrarch, Francesco, *Le rime*, ed. Giacomo Leopardi (Cremona/Rome, 1968).

Piles, Roger de, *Cours de peinture par principes* (Paris, 1708).

Pliny, *Natural History*, with an English translation by H. Rackham, *et al.* (London, 1938).

Poliziano, Angelo, *Stanze*, ed. G. Carducci (Florence, 1863).

Polo de Medina, Salvador Jacinto, *Obras completas*, ed. A. Valbuena Prat (Murcia, 1948).

Porta, Giambattista della, *Magiae naturalis, sive de miraculis rerum naturalium liber iiii* (Naples, 1558).

Pulci, Luigi, *Morgante*, ed. Franco Ageno (Milan/Naples, 1955).

Quevedo y Villegas, Francisco Gómez de, *Obras completas*, ed. F. Buendía, Vol. 1. *Obras en prosa* (Madrid, 1958).

– – *Obras completas*, ed. J.M. Blecua, Vol. 1. *Poesía original* (Barcelona, 1963).

Rabelais, François, *Oeuvres complètes*, ed. J. Boulanger and L. Scheler (Bruges, 1959).

Rodríguez Moñino, Antonio (ed.), *Las estaciones del año* (Valencia, 1949).

Ruiz, Juan, Arcipreste de Hita, *El libro de buen amor*, ed. J. Cejador y Franca (Madrid, 1959), 2 vols.

Saint Amant, Marc Antoine de Gérard, Sieur de, *Oeuvres poétiques*, ed. Léon Vérane (Paris, 1930).

Salazar Mardones, Cristóbal de, *Ilustración y defensa de la fabula de Piramo y Tisbe compuesta por D. Luis de Góngora y Argote* (Madrid, 1736).

Salazar y Torres, Agustín, *Cythara de Apolo* (Madrid, 1681).

Salcedo Coronel, García de, *Obras de don Luis de Góngora comentadas*, 3 vols. (Madrid, 1636, 1644, 1648).

Sánchez de Lizarazo, Pedro Gerónimo, *Generalis et admirabilis methodus ad omnes scientias facilius et citius addiscendas: in qua eximij et pijssimi Doctoris Raimundii Lulij Ars breuis explicatur* (Tarazona, 1613).

Sannazaro, Iacobo, *Opere volgari*, ed. Alfredo Mauro (Bari, 1961).

Scudéry, Georges de, *Poésies diverses* (Paris, 1649).

Soto de Rojas, Pedro, *Obras*, ed. A. Gallego Morell (Madrid, 1950).

Tassis, Juan de, *Obras de Don Juan de Tarsis [sic] Conde de Villamediana. . .recogida por Hipólito de los Valles* (Zaragoza, 1629).

Tesauro, Emmanuele, *Il cannocchiale aristotelico, o sia idea del' arguta et ingegniosa elocutione che serve a tutta l'arte oratoria, lapidaria, et simbolica essaminata co'princtpti del divino Aristotele*. 5th impression (Turin, 1670).

Théophile de Viau, *Oeuvres poétiques*, ed. Jeanne Streicher (Geneva/Lille, 1951).

Torreblanca Villalpando, Francisco, *Daemonologia, sive de magia naturali* (Mainz, 1623).

Trillo y Figueroa, Francisco de, *Obras*, ed. A. Gallego Morell (Madrid, 1951).

Tristan l' Hermite, François, *Poésies*, ed. P.A. Wadsworth (Paris, 1962).

Ulloa y Pereira, Luis de, Obras. *Prosas y versos, añadidas en esta vltima impression recogidas, y dadas a la estampa por D. Iuan Antonio de Vlloa Pereira su hijo* (Madrid, 1674).

Vega Carpio, Lope de, *La Filomena, con otras diversas rimas, prosas, y versos* (Madrid, 1621).

— — *Obras completas*, ed. Joaquín de Entrambasaguas, Vol. 1 (Madrid, 1965).

— — *Poesías líricas*, ed. José F. Montesinos, 2 vols. (Madrid, 1963).

Yves de Paris, *Digestum sapientiae* (Paris, 1659).

SECONDARY SOURCES

Adam, Antoine, 'Le Sentiment de la nature au dix-septième siècle en France', *Cahiers de l'Association Internationale des Études Françaises*, 6 (1954), 1–14.

— — *Théophile de Viau et la libre pensée française en 1620* (Paris, 1935).

Alonso, Dámaso, 'Antecedentes griegos y latinos en la poesía correlativa moderna', in *Estudios dedicados a Menéndez Pidal*, Vol. 4 (Madrid, 1953), pp. 3–25.

— — *Estudios y ensayos gongorinos* (Madrid, 1960).

— — *Góngora y el Polifemo*, 5th ed., 3 vols. (Madrid, 1967).

— — 'Góngora y el toro celeste', in *Litterae hispanae et lusitanae*, ed. Hans Flasche (Munich, 1968), pp. 7–15.

— — *Poesía española. Ensayo de métodos y límites estilísticos* (Madrid, 1957).

Alonso, Martín, *Enciclopedia del idioma*, 3 vols. (Madrid, 1958).

Araez, J.G., *Don Luis de Ulloa y Pereira* (Madrid, 1952).

Azorín, *El Paisaje de España visto por los españoles* (Madrid, 1964).

Bayley, H., *The Lost Language of Symbolism*, 2 vols. (London, 1912).

Beardsley, T.S., Jr., *Hispano-Classical Translations printed between 1482 and 1699* (Pittsburgh, 1970).

Biese, Alfred, *Die Entwicklung des Naturgefühls im Mittelalter und in der Neuzeit* (Leipzig, 1888).

Black, Max, *A Companion to Wittgenstein's 'Tractatus'* (Cambridge, 1964).

Bremond, Henri, *Histoire littéraire du sentiment religieux en France depuis la fin des guerres de religion jusqu'à nos jours*, Vol. 1. (Paris 1916).

Brenan, Gerald, *The Literature of the Spanish People*, Peregrine Books (Harmondsworth, 1963).

Brooke-Rose, Christine, *A Grammar of Metaphor* (London, 1965).

Burn, A.R., *Persia and the Greeks. The Defence of the West c. 546– 478 B.C.* (London, 1962).

Casalduero, Joaquín, 'El sentimiento de la naturaleza en la edad media española', *Clavileño*, No. 22 (1953), 17–23.

Chesneau, Charles, *Le Père Yves de Paris et son temps*, 2 vols. (Paris, 1946).

Ciocchini, Hector, *Góngora y la tradición de los emblemas* (Bahia Blanca, 1960).

Clark, Kenneth, *Landscape into Art*, Penguin Books (London, 1953).

Cohen, Ralph, *The Art of Discrimination*; *Thomson's 'The Seasons' and the Language of Criticism* (London, 1964).

Colie, R.L., 'Some paradoxes in the language of things', in *Reason and the Imagination*, ed. J.A. Mazzeo (New York/London, 1962).

Collard, Andrée, *Nueva poesía. Conceptismo, culteranismo en la crítica española* (Madrid, 1967).

Curtius, Ernst Robert, *European Literature and the Latin Middle Ages*, translated by W.R. Trask (London, 1953).

Dauzat, A., *Le Sentiment de la nature et son expression artistique* (Paris, 1914).

Davies, G.A., 'Luis de León and a passage from Seneca's *Hippolitus*', *Bulletin of Hispanic Studies*, 41 (1964), 10–27.

Donato, Eugenio, 'Tesauro's poetics: through the looking glass', *Modern Language Notes*, 78 (1963), 15–30.

Fairclough, H.R., *Love of Nature amongst the Greeks and Romans* (New York, 1930).

Fucilla, J.G., 'Riflessi dell' *Adone* di G.B. Marino nelle poesie di Quevedo', *Romania* (1962), 279–87.

Gallego Morell, Antonio, *El mito de Faetón en la literatura española* (Madrid, 1961).

García Lorca, Federico, 'La imagen poética de Góngora', in his *Obras completas*, ed. A. Del Hoyo (Madrid, 1964), pp. 62–85.

Gates, Eunice Joiner, 'Góngora's indebtedness to Claudian', *Romanic Review*, 28 (1937), 19–31.

Gilbert, Creighton, 'On subject and non-subject in Italian Renaissance pictures', *Art Bulletin*, Vol. 24, No. 3 (Sept. 1952), 202–16.

Glendinning, Nigel, 'La fortuna de Góngora en el siglo xviii', *Revista de Filología Española*, 44 (1961), 277–80.

Gombrich, E.H., 'Renaissance artistic theory and the development of landscape', *Gazette des Beaux Arts*, 6th ser. 41 (1953), 335–60.

Gregory, R.L., *Eye and Brain* (London, 1966).

Hagstrum, Jean, *The Sister Arts* (Chicago, 1958).

Hulme, T.E., *Speculations*, ed. Herbert Read (London, 1936).

Isaza Calderón, Baltasar, *El retorno a la naturaleza* (Madrid, 1954).

Jammes, Robert, *Études sur l'oeuvre poétique de Don Luis de Góngora y Argote* (Bordeaux, 1967).

Jannaco, Carmine, 'Introduzione ai critici del seicento', *Convivium*, 23 (1953), 160–74.

212   BIBLIOGRAPHY

— — *Il Seicento* (Milan, 1963).

Jansen, O., *Naturempfindung und Naturgefühl bei B.H. Brockes* (Bonn, 1907).

Jones, Royston O., 'Neoplatonism and the *Soledades*', *Bulletin of Hispanic Studies*, 40 (1963), 1—16.

— — 'The poetic unity of the *Soledades* of Góngora', *Bulletin of Hispanic Studies*, 31 (1954), 189—204.

Lausberg, H., *Manual de retórica literaria*, translated by J. Pérez Riesco, 3 vols. (Madrid, 1966).

Lessing, Gotthold Ephraim, *Laocoon*, translated by Sir Robert Philimore (London, 1874).

Lillo Rodelgo, J., *El sentimiento de la naturaleza en la pintura y en la literatura española. Siglos xii al xvi* (Toledo, 1929).

Locke, John, *An Essay concerning Human Understanding*, abridged and edited by A.S. Pringle-Pattison (Oxford, 1960).

Lumsden, Audrey, 'Sentiment and artistry in the work of three Golden-Age poets', in *Spanish Golden-Age Poetry and Drama. Liverpool Studies in Spanish Literature*, ed. E. Allison Peers (Liverpool, 1946).

MacAndrew, R.M., *Naturalism in Spanish Poetry from the Origins* to 1900 (Aberdeen, 1931).

McKellar, Peter, *Experience and Behaviour*, Pelican Books (Harmondsworth, 1968).

Macrí, Oreste, *Fernando de Herrera* (Madrid, 1959).

Mazzeo, J.A., *Renaissance and Seventeenth-Century Studies* (New York/London, 1964).

Miller, G.A., *Psychology; the Science of Mental Life*, Pelican Books (Harmondsworth, 1967).

Mirollo, James V., *The Poet of the Marvelous: Giambattista Marino* (New York/London, 1963).

Molho, M., 'Soledades', *Bulletin Hispanique*, 62 (1960), 249—85.

Mornet, Daniel, *Le Sentiment de la nature en France de J.-J. Rousseau à Bernardin de Saint Pierre* (Paris, 1907).

Mourgues, Odette de, *Metaphysical, Baroque and Précieux Poetry* (Oxford, 1953).

Nicolson, Marjorie Hope, *Mountain Gloom and Mountain Glory; the Development of the Aesthetics of the Infinite* (Ithaca, N.Y. 1959).

Orozco Díaz, Emilio, *En torno a las Soledades de Góngora* (Granada, 1969).

— — *Góngora* (Barcelona, 1953).

– – *Paisaje y sentimiento de la naturaleza en la poesía española* (Madrid, 1968).

– – *Temas del barroco de poesía y pintura* (Granada, 1947).

Pabst, Walter, *La creación gongorina en los poemas 'Polifemo' y 'Soledades'*, Spanish trans. by N. Marín (Madrid, 1966).

Palau y Dulcet, Antonio, *Manual del librero hispano-americano*, 7 vols. (Barcelona, 1923–7).

Parker, A.A., Introduction to Góngora's *Poliphemus*, translated by Gilbert F. Cunningham, privately printed (Alva, Scotland, 1965).

Praz, Mario, *Studies in Seventeenth-Century Imagery*, second ed. (Rome, 1964).

Pring-Mill, Robert D.F., 'Techniques of representation in the *Sueños* and the *Criticón'*, *Bulletin of Hispanic Studies*, 46 (1969), 270–84.

Quine, W.V.O., *Word and Object* (Cambridge, Mass., 1960).

Raimondi, Ezio, 'Ingegno e metafora nella poetica del Tesauro', in his *Letteratura barocca* (Florence, 1961).

– – (ed.), *Trattatisti e narratori del seicento* (Milan/Naples 1960).

Riley, Edward C., 'Aspectos del concepto de *Admiratio* en la teoría literaria del siglo de oro', in *Studia Philologica. Homenaje ofrecido a Dámaso Alonso*, Vol. 3 (Madrid, 1963), pp. 173–83.

Rodríguez Marín, Francisco, *Luis Barahona de Soto* (Madrid, 1903).

Rozas, J.M., *El Conde de Villamediana*. Cuadernos Bibliográficos, No. 11 (Madrid, 1964).

Ruskin, John, *Works*, edited by E.T. Cook and A. Wedderburn, Vol. 2 (London, 1903–12).

Ryle, Gilbert, *The Concept of Mind* (London, 1949).

Salomon, Noël, *Recherches sur le thème paysan dans la 'comedia' au temps de Lope de Vega* (Bordeaux, 1965).

Sánchez de Muniain, J.M., *Estética del paisaje natural* (Madrid, 1945).

Scoular, K., *Natural Magic* (Oxford, 1965).

Segura Covarsi, E., *La canción petrarquista en la lírica española del siglo de oro* (Madrid, 1949).

Shorter, J.M., 'Imagination', *Mind*, 61 (1952), 528–42.

Smith, C. Colin, 'An approach to Góngora's *Polifemo*', *Bulletin of Hispanic Studies*, 42 (1965), 217–38.

Soons, Alan, Situación de las *Soledades* de Góngora', in his *Ficción y comedia en el siglo de oro* (Madrid, 1967).

Taylor, René, 'Architecture and Magic. The idea of the Escorial', in *Essays in the History of Architecture presented to Rudolf Wittkower*, edited by Douglas Fraser *et al.* (London, 1967), pp. 81–109.

Terry, Arthur, 'Pedro Espinosa and the praise of creation', *Bulletin of Hispanic Studies*, 38 (1961), 127–44.

Thomas, Lucien-Paul, *Le Lyrisme et préciosité cultistes en Espagne. Étude historique et analytique* (Halle/Paris, 1909).

Thorndike, Lynn, *A History of Magic and Experimental Science during the first Thirteen Centuries of our Era*, 6 vols. (New York, 1923–58).

Tillyard, E.M.W., *The Elizabethan World Picture*, Peregrine Books (Harmondsworth, 1963).

Turner, A. Richard, *The Vision of Landscape in Renaissance Italy* (Princeton, 1966).

Tuve, Rosemond, *Elizabethan and Metaphysical Imagery; Renaissance Poetic and Twentieth-Century Critics* (Chicago, 1961).

Unamuno, Miguel de, 'El sentimiento de la naturaleza', in his *Por tierras de Portugal y de España*, ed. M. García Blanco (Madrid, 1964).

Valente, José Angel, and Glendinning, Nigel, 'Una copia desconocida de las *Soledades* de Góngora', *Bulletin of Hispanic Studies*, 36 (1959), 1–14.

Van Tieghem, P., *Le Sentiment de la nature dans le préromantisme européen* (Paris, 1960).

Veitch, John, *The Feeling for Nature in Scottish Poetry*, 2 vols. (Edinburgh/London, 1887).

Vilanova, Antonio, *Las fuentes y los temas del 'Polifemo' de Góngora*, 2 vols. (Madrid, 1957).

Walker, D.P., *Spiritual and Demonic Magic from Ficino to Campanella* London, 1958).

Warren, A., and Wellek, R., *Theory of Literature* (London, 1961).

Weinberg, Bernard, *A History of Literary Criticism in the Italian Renaissance*, 2 vols. (Chicago, 1961).

Wilson, D.B., *Descriptive Poetry in France from Blason to Baroque* (Manchester/New York, 1967).

Wilson, E.M., 'The four elements in the imagery of Calderón', *Modern Language Review*, 31 (1936), 34–47.

Wimsatt, W.K., Jr., *The Verbal Icon; Studies in the Meaning of Poetry* (Lexington, Ky., 1954).

Wittgenstein, Ludwig, *Philosophical Investigations*, trans. by G.E.M. Anscombe (Oxford, 1963).

Wölfflin, Heinrich, *Principles of Art History*, translated by M.D. Hottinger (London, 1932).

Woods, M.J., 'Rhetoric in Garcilaso's first eclogue', *Modern Language Notes*, 84 (1969), 143–56.

— — 'Gracián, Peregrini, and the theory of Topics', *Modern Language Review*, 63 (1968), 854–63.

Yates, Frances A., *Giordano Bruno and the Hermetic Tradition* (London, 1964).

INDEX